IMAGES
of America

SCHENECTADY'S STOCKADE

NEW YORK'S FIRST HISTORIC DISTRICT

On the cover: Charles Steinmetz is symbolic of the importance of Schenectady's stockade area. Not only was he one of the most brilliant minds of the 19th and 20th centuries, he represented the spirit and tenacity of Schenectady pioneers who were not afraid to push the limits of exploration. Here he can be seen (lower left) on the porch of his first Schenectady home in 1896 at 53 Washington Avenue along with his sister Clara, his young associate Eskil Berg (lower right), and a friend of Steinmetz's with the name Furdel (in back of him). (Courtesy of the Efner History Center.)

IMAGES
of America

SCHENECTADY'S STOCKADE

NEW YORK'S FIRST HISTORIC DISTRICT

Don Rittner

ARCADIA
PUBLISHING

ISBN 978-0-7385-6312-1

Published by Arcadia Publishing
Charleston, South Carolina

Printed in the United States of America

Library of Congress Catalog Card Number: 2008925857

For all general information contact Arcadia Publishing at:
Telephone 843-853-2070
Fax 843-853-0044
E-mail sales@arcadiapublishing.com
For customer service and orders:
Toll-Free 1-888-313-2665

Visit us on the Internet at www.arcadiapublishing.com

Contents

ACKNOWLEDGMENTS

Special thanks to Chris Hunter, Schenectady Museum; Cynthia Seacord at the Efner History Center; Library of Congress; John Wolcott; Greta Wagle; Marieke Leeverink; Christine M. Beauregard, New York State library, manuscripts and special collections (for Rufus Grider); Kate Weller, Schenectady County Historical Society (for Dutch Church painting); and Rebekah Collinsworh and the staff at Arcadia Publishing.

This book is dedicated to those first true pioneers who left the protected village of Beverwyck to start the western most European village in America: Arendt Van Curler, Bastian De Winter, Philip Hendrickse Brouwer, Sander Leendertse Glen, Symon Volckertse Veeder, Pieter Adriaense Van Wogulum, Tunis Cornelisse Swart, Marten Cornelisse Van Esselsteyn, William Teller, Gerrit Bancke, Arendt Andriesse Bratt (Catalyn De Vos), Pieter Jacobse Borsboom, Pieter Danielse Van Olinda, Jan Barentse Wemple, and Jacques Cornelisse Van Slyck. Special thinks go to Jim Schmitt and Werner Feibes, pioneers in saving the stockade.

INTRODUCTION

On the eastern bank of the Mohawk River, several miles west of where it empties into the Hudson River in upstate New York, lies a four-block area that holds close to three and a half centuries of American history. Schenectady's historic stockade was founded as the western most European settlement in 1661 and since then its inhabitants have contributed more to the development of the American experience than most communities could ever imagine.

In 1661–1662, Arendt Van Curler and 14 other families moved from the protective palisaded village of Beverwyck (present Albany) on the Hudson River and trekked 16 miles to the area that Van Curler wrote was "the most beautiful land on the Mohawk River that eye ever saw."

Almost 30 years later, the residents of this frontier village would pay a dear price with their lives as 114 French and 96 of their Native American allies massacred 60 men, women, and children, burned 60 homes, and took 27 prisoners. The survivors, with a strong will to persevere and prosper, rebuilt their village, and within eight years, more than 100 homes and businesses were again occupying that small tract of land.

After the American Revolution, the stockade prospered, the riverbanks filled with warehouses and businesses, as Schenectady became the gateway to the west for commerce passing through to the inner continent. After battling constant and recurring flooding and a major fire in 1819, businesses and commerce shifted a few blocks east as the new Erie Canal was being built, making it easier to bring people and goods east and west. As Schenectady grew and became a canal town, as well as excelling as a boat building and broom making capital, the stockade area maintained a residential character and attracted many of the city's best people as residents and homeowners.

During the 18th century, Col. John Glenn entertained George Washington in his home at 58 Handlaer's Street in 1775 (present Washington Avenue), while Robert Sanders did the same at his home across the street. Likewise, Daniel Campbell entertained Sir William Johnson at his home at 101 State Street. Gov. Joseph Yates provided refreshments to Marquis de Lafayette in his mansion on Front Street on June 11, 1825, while celebrating the opening of the Erie Canal. During the 19th to 20th centuries, residents included Mohawk Valley architect Samuel Fuller (Guy Park Mansion, Claas Mansion, Johnstown Court House, Schenectady's Episcopal Church and Daniel Campbell's mansion), electrical genius Charles Steinmetz (alternating current, artificial lightening), George Westinghouse Jr. (rotary steam engine, air brake), Katherine Blodgett (invisible glass), and Dr. Elizabeth Gillette (first woman surgeon in Schenectady County and first upstate New York State member of the assembly). Other Stockade firsts include having the first railroad tunnel in America (1831, Saratoga and Schenectady Railroad) pass through it, having the world's first research and development laboratory in Steinmetz's carriage house on Liberty Street (1900), and being the home of the world's first television studio and network—WRGB—on Washington Avenue (1941). Also, name another community that has had a grocery store (Arthur's) in the same location since 1795.

Today you can view architectural styles from Dutch colonial to modern, making it the home of one of the most unique assemblages of American architecture anywhere in the United States. You can feel the history as you walk through the stockade, often on bluestone or slate sidewalks, or get glimpses of the original cobblestone or brick streets. Many of the homes proudly wear a marker giving its age and original owner, many of them 300 years old or older. Some of the buildings are disguised, hiding their former glory. For example, 9 Front Street has recently been discovered to be a 1727 French and Indian War–era military blockhouse. If you look carefully you can find cast iron or wrought iron boot scrapers, hitching posts, and stone carriage steps in front or on the sides of many of the historic homes. Splash blocks from the 19th century and earlier carry rainwater to the street making sure the water does not flood the basement. Look closely, and you can find 17th and 18th century Dutch fleur-de-lis wall ties holding the ancient wooden beams to the brick walls on houses built before 1750.

On May 14, 1962, the City of Schenectady recognized the historical importance of the stockade, after several of its citizens championed the restoration of several of its historic homes, and adopted a historic zoning ordinance making the stockade the first historic district in New York State. Since then, a historic sites commission oversees development, and a citizen-based Stockade Association meets regularly to keep residents up to date on developments affecting the area. Stockade residents are proud to know they live in one of the oldest settlements in America, and they take preservation seriously.

This volume presents the 347-year history of the stockade through photographs of rare maps and many of the surviving buildings, many over three centuries old. You can view the surviving oldest homes in the area, photographs of world renowned Charles Steinmetz on his bike peddling home, images of hundreds enjoying the Mohawk River, or others simply going about their daily business. You will see trolleys and bridges that no longer exist. Unfortunately the same fate fell on several important mansions that can be seen in images published in this book.

The stockade is a unique and rare area that has maintained its sense of place and the original spirit of its founding fathers. We are fortunate to have so many of its residents champion the cause to keep it that way.

—Don Rittner, June 2008

One

Old Schenectady

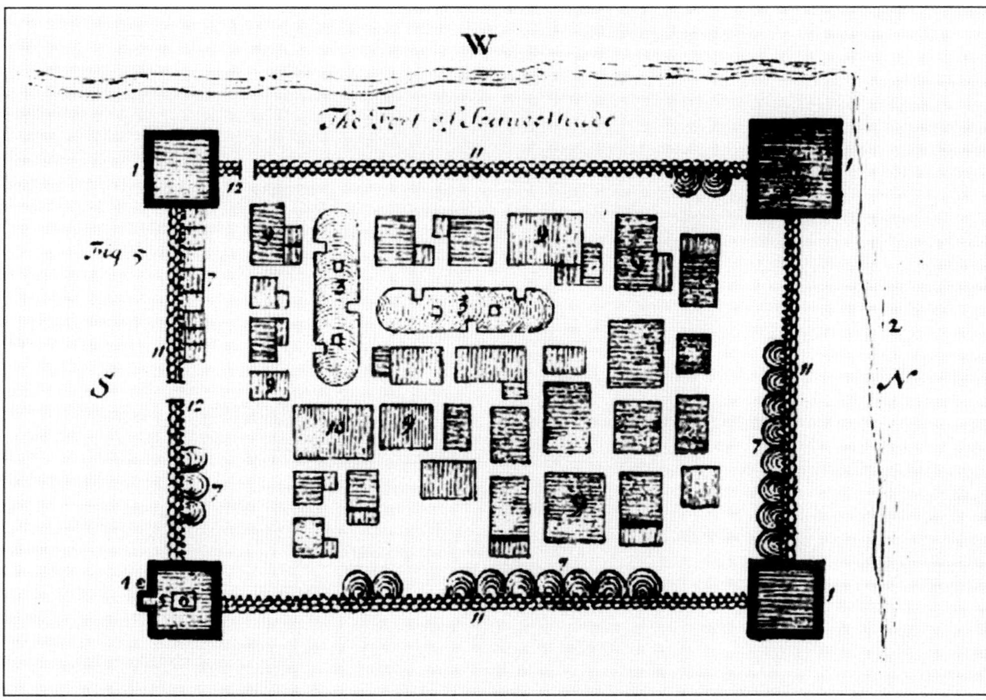

The Miller Map of 1693 is the earliest known map of Schenectady. Unfortunately, Rev. John Miller had the orientation of the fort incorrect on his drawing. Miller was chaplain to the British forces located in New York, and while here, he drew plans of many towns and forts during the King William's War. In 1695, armed with his drawings, he sailed back to England but was captured at sea by French pirates. Alarmed that the French would get important military information contained in his drawings he threw them all overboard. When he finally arrived back in England, he tried to reproduce all his maps by memory. Unfortunately his map of the King's Fort was off by 90 degrees. This is the compound in which the survivors of the 1690 massacre lived while they rebuilt their village.

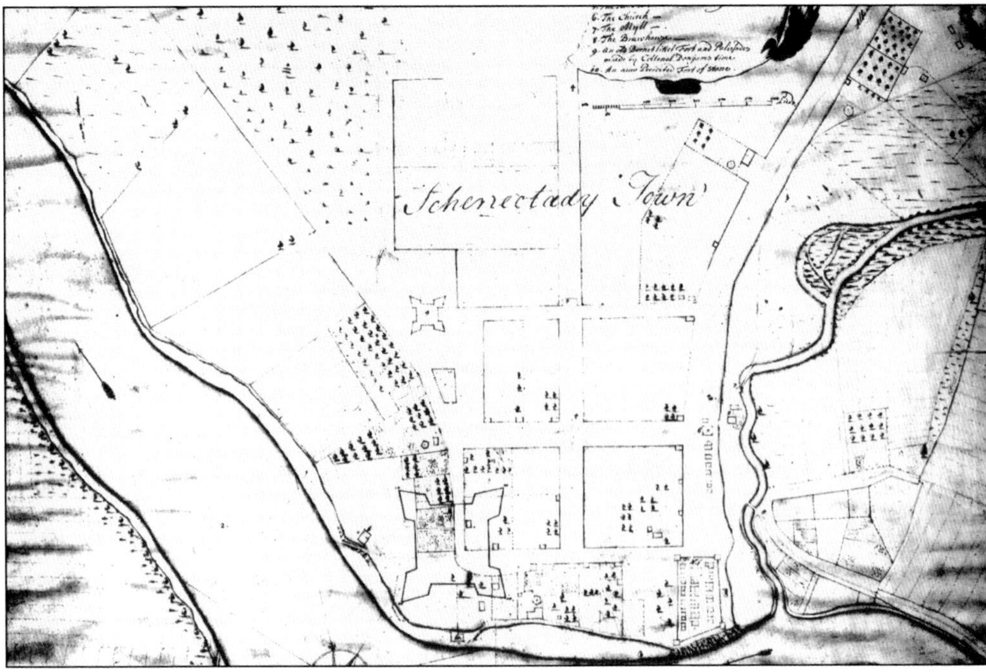

This is a portion of the Wolfgang Romer Map of 1698 and is one of the most detailed maps of colonial Schenectady. It reveals the closest to the original layout of the 1661 settlement. Wolfgang Romer, born of German parents, was a British military engineer engaged in making maps of the colony of New York. His proposed fort (larger of the two depicted) was never built. The King's Fort can be seen in the bottom right corner near Cowhorn Creek.

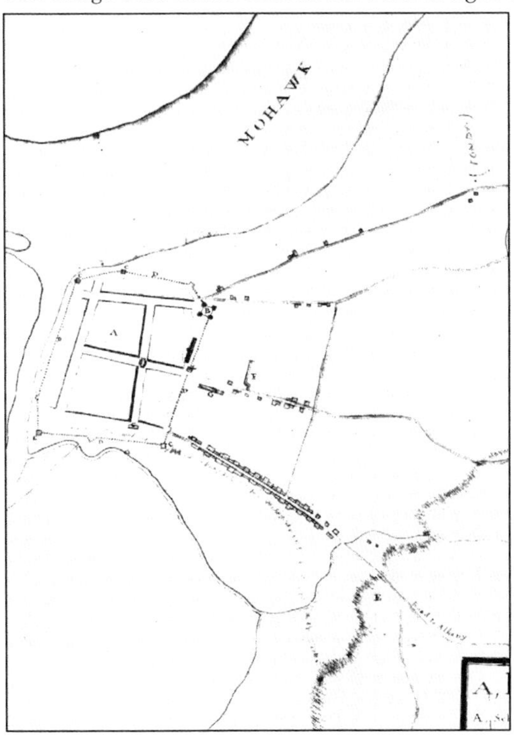

This map from around 1756 has seen many varieties and was part of Mary Ann Roque's collection of maps of royal forts in America. It was apparently drawn from a sketch made by a British officer during the French and Indian War. It reveals the moving of the stockade closer to the river, as well as a larger settlement of homes along the old King's Highway to Albany. Notice that the stockade still maintains its original four blocks as late as 1756.

This 1760s unidentified map shows the King's Highway, originally called the Schenectady Path or Albany Road, that connected the frontier villages of Albany and Schenectady. This road was important up to 1800, when turnpikes became widely used. Several taverns dotted the highway to refresh travelers coming and going. The Palatine Road was cut from this in 1710 as seen just past the *verberg*, Dutch for "far hill."

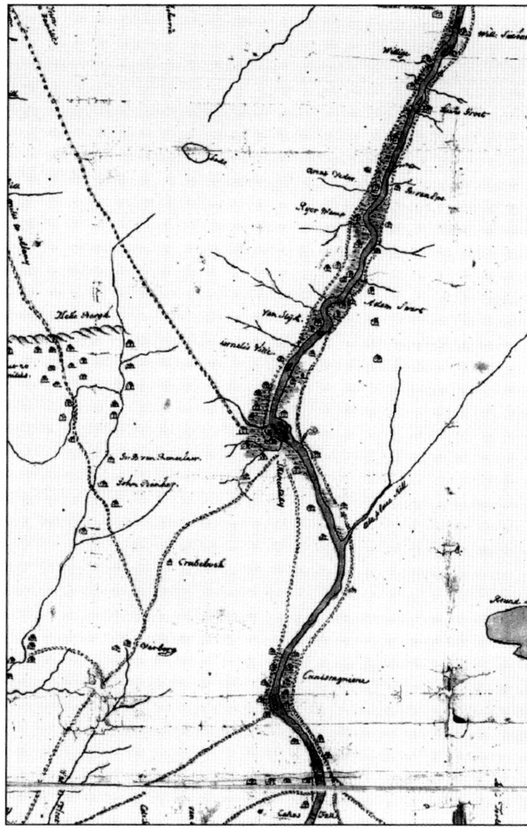

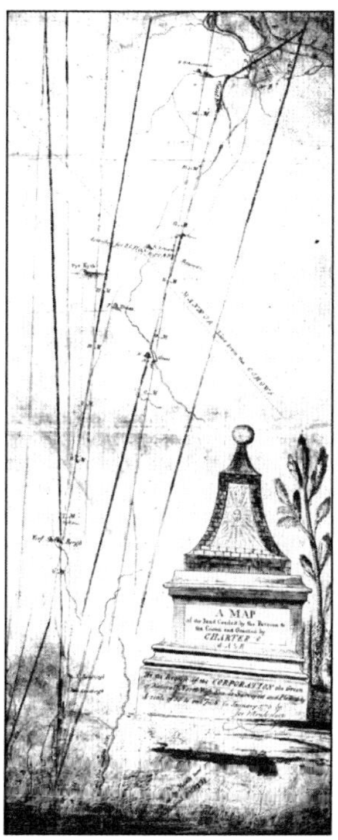

The 1773 Van Rensselaer map shows how Albany controlled the trade and transportation route between Albany and Schenectady. When the city was chartered in 1696, it was given the boundaries making it 1 mile wide and 16 miles long, struck at an angle to insure that Albany had control of the King's Highway. Schenectady was always considered secondary in importance to the fur trade as Albany had a monopoly over it. Schenectady was supposed to be an agricultural community. This map shows various boundaries of Albany over time.

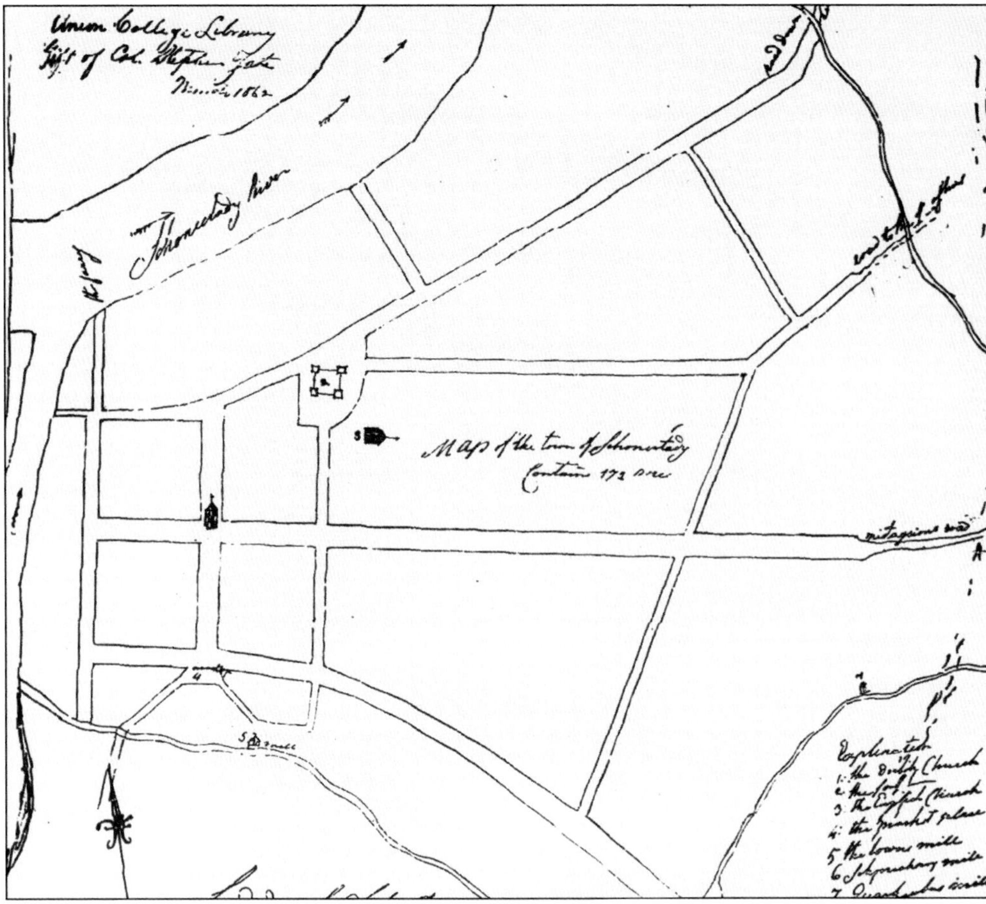

The Vrooman map of 1768 shows the basic layout of the still Dutch village before the American Revolution, and Fort Cosby, along with the Dutch and English churches.

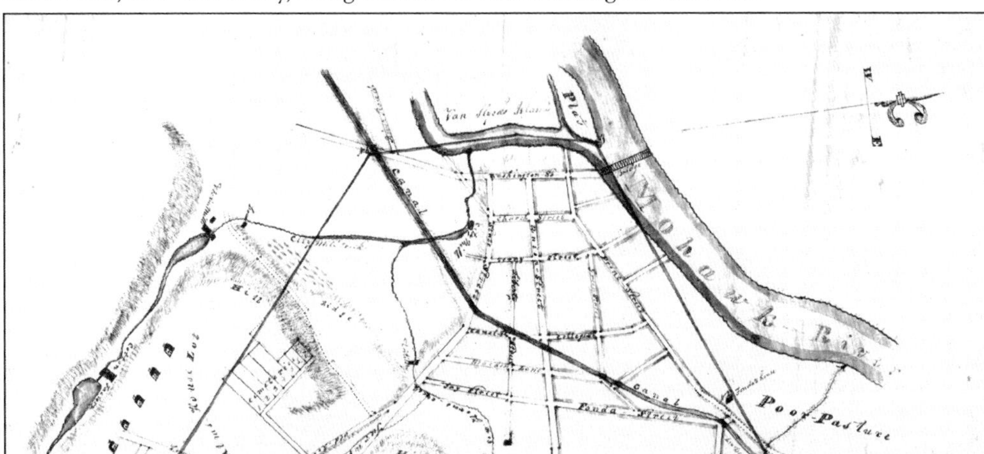

The Switts map of 1823 shows that little changed over the years in the basic layout of the stockade. A few new streets were laid out and the Erie Canal was being built, but the four-block stockade area remained unchanged. This map was made shortly after the 1819 fire that burned most of the warehouses along the river and Binnekill.

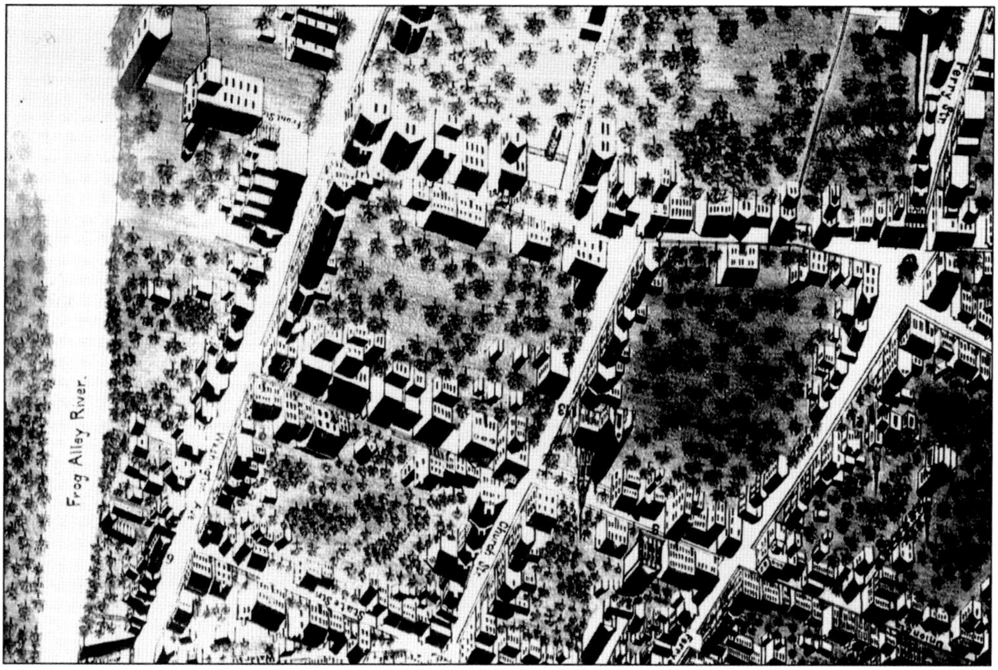

A panoramic view of the stockade area in 1875 shows an area still not heavily populated with homes or businesses. After the great fire of 1819, most industry and business moved further east to the banks of the new Erie Canal and left the Stockade to become more of a residential community that exists today. The Binnekill was called Frog Alley River at this time.

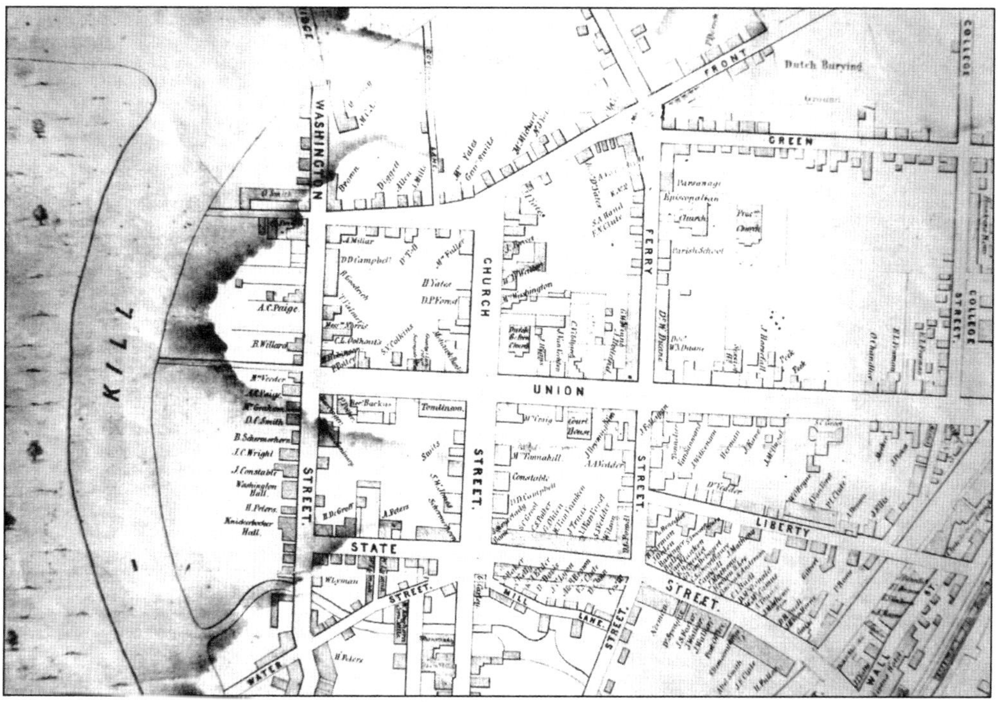

The Switts map of 1850 reveals some of the names of the residences at this time and the size and shape of the buildings. The stockade still retains its original shape.

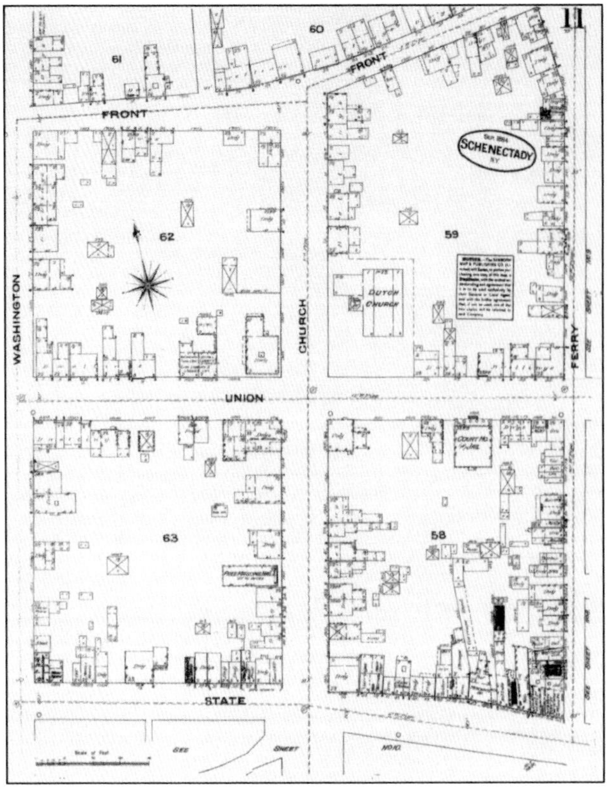

This 1894 Sanborn insurance atlas map shows the basic layout of the stockade before it moved into the 20th century. Parts of the outer limits of the stockade, State Street in particular, were changing from residential to commercial. The inner quadrangle however remained for the most part residential.

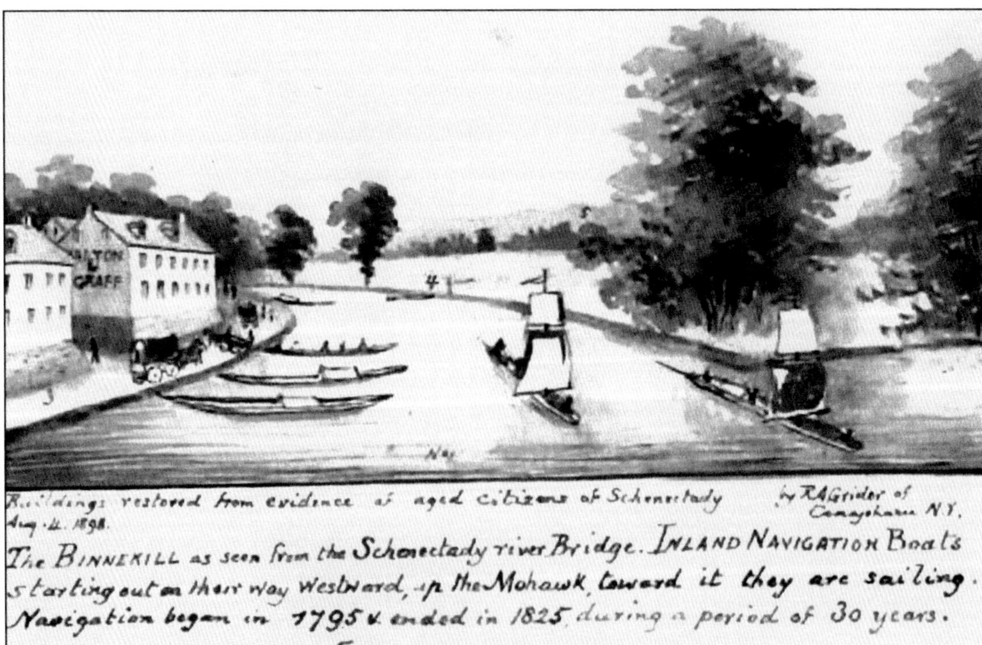

Rufus Grider painted this picture of the Binnekill and warehouses in the location where the community college now sits. Grider was an art teacher in Canajoharie and decided to record the history of the Mohawk Valley in ink and watercolors.

Two

Lower State Street

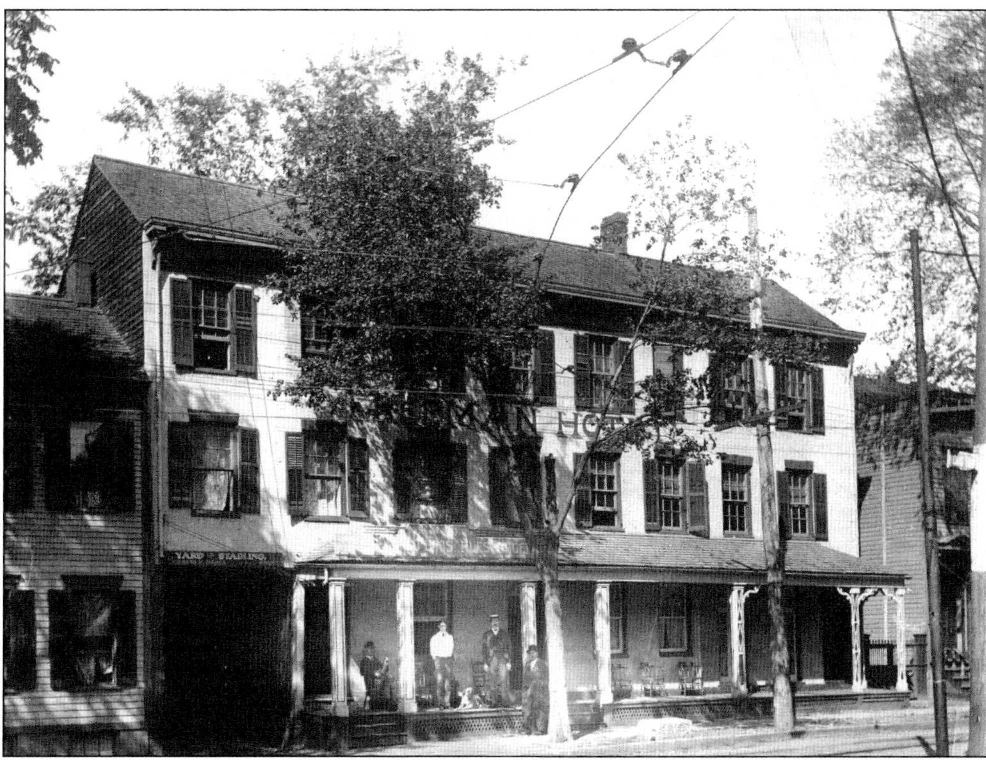

The Freeman House was located at the beginning of State Street on Washington Avenue. It marks the southwest border of the original stockade area. It was razed in the early 1920s to make way for the Western Gateway Bridge and the new Van Curler Hotel.

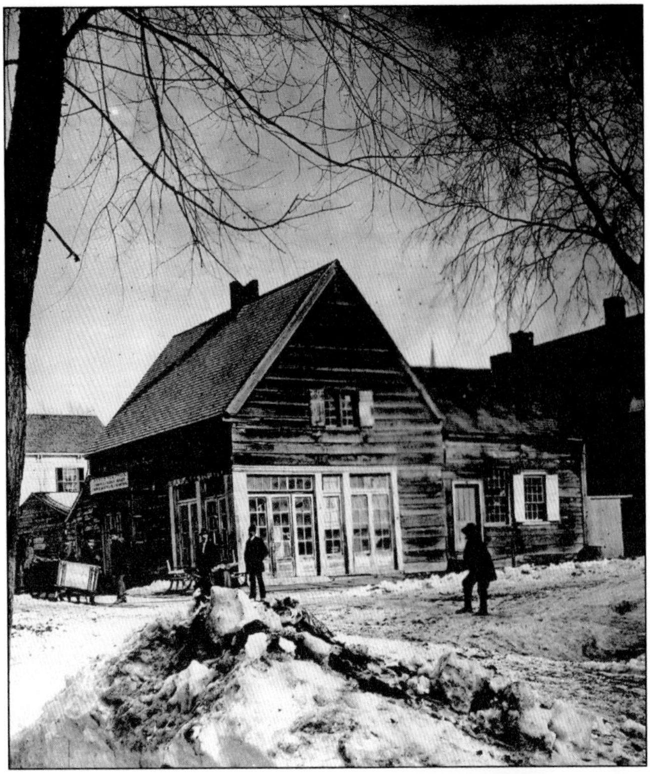

The northeast corner of State Street and Washington Avenue was occupied by James Simpson, a carriage and sleigh maker, around 1870. However, this building is also where Schenectady's first newspaper, the *Mohawk Mercury*, was published in 1795. An apartment building now occupies the site.

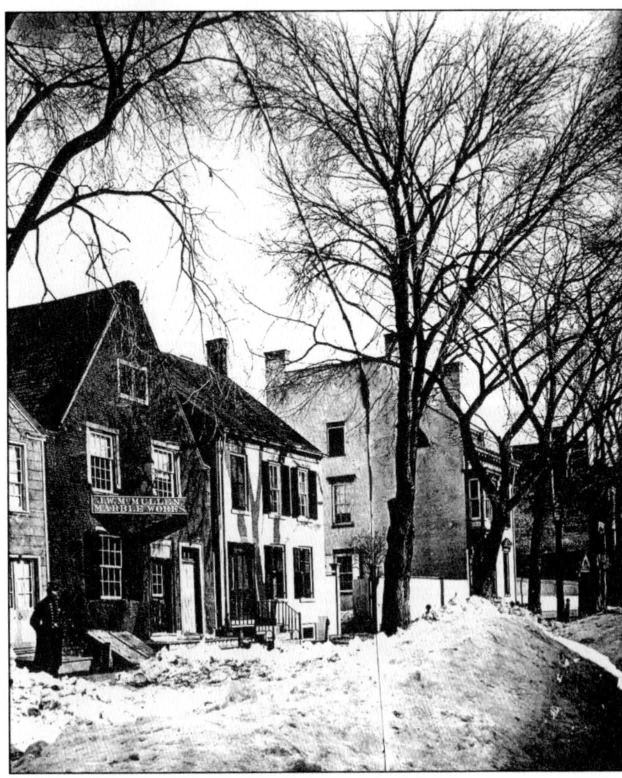

The building on the left belonged to Capt. Arent Brandt and this Dutch house was built in 1715 but was demolished in 1895. The YMCA building now occupies the site. Brandt's father, Arendt, was an original founding member of Schenectady in 1661. This Arent was a brewer at this location. Brandt was a member of the Provincial Assembly in 1745 and a Schenectady trustee for 52 years until he died in 1767. This photograph is from around 1880. Martin Lodewijk, a Dutch cartoonist in the 1950s, drew a comic series of a pirate called "Arent Brandt," later changed to "Captain Kidd."

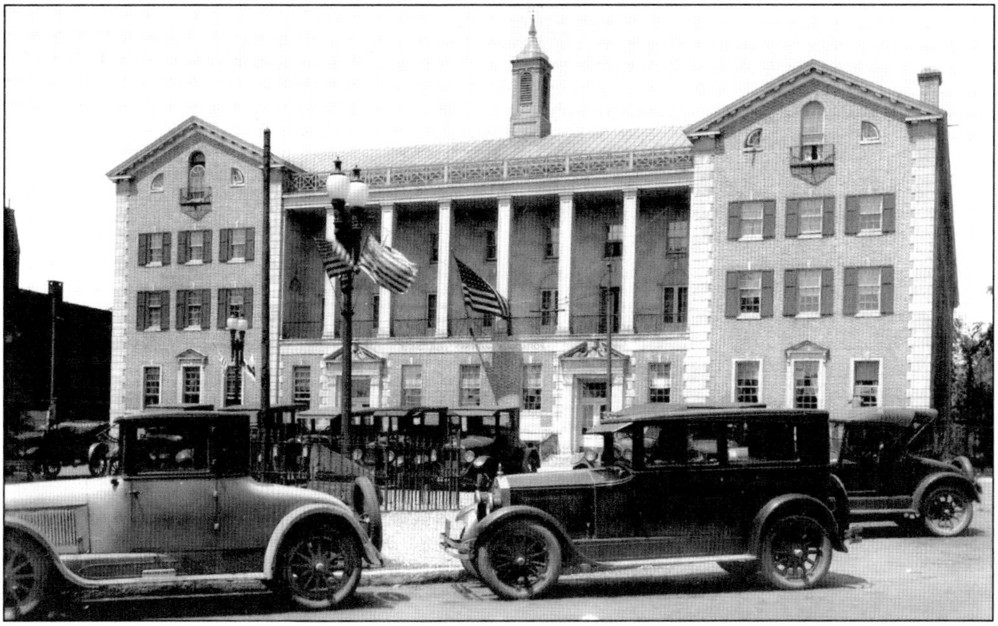

The YMCA once stood on the corner of State Street and Washington Avenue just a few feet west of here and earlier a block east on State and Ferry Streets. This currently used building was built in 1927. The first meeting of the YMCA was held in 1857. This photograph is dated 1930.

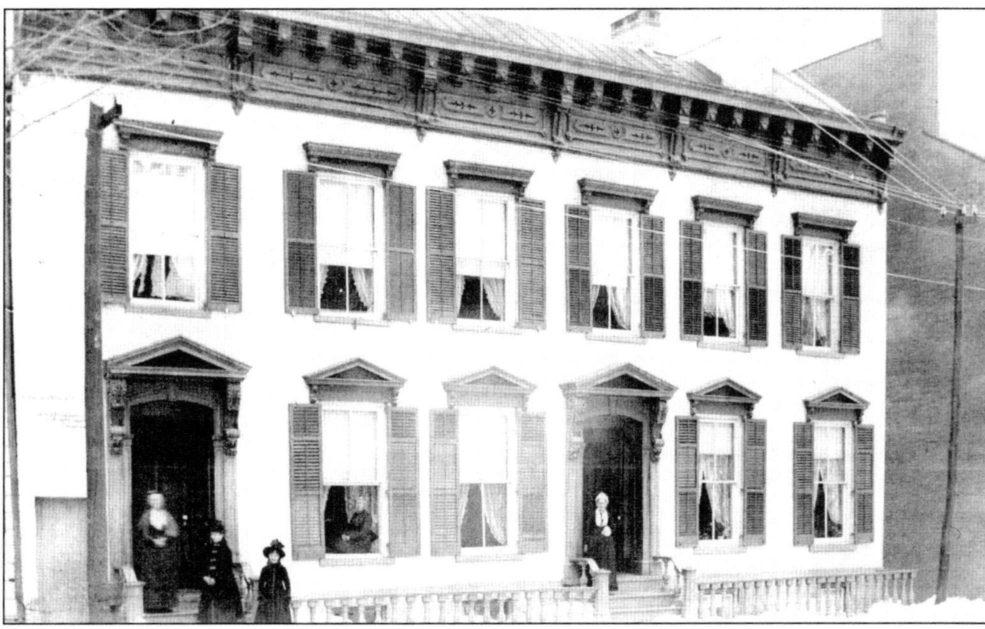

The George Westinghouse Residence is now a bus stop across from the YMCA. George Westinghouse Sr. moved his agricultural works to Schenectady in 1856. His son George Jr. lived here and developed the first air brake for trains and later went on to form the Westinghouse Electric Company in Pennsylvania in 1886. The battles between Westinghouse and Thomas Edison over the preferred use of AC versus DC was known as the "Battle of the Currents." Westinghouse eventually won since Edison's Charles Steinmetz championed AC current by solving some of the problems associated with its transmission over long distances.

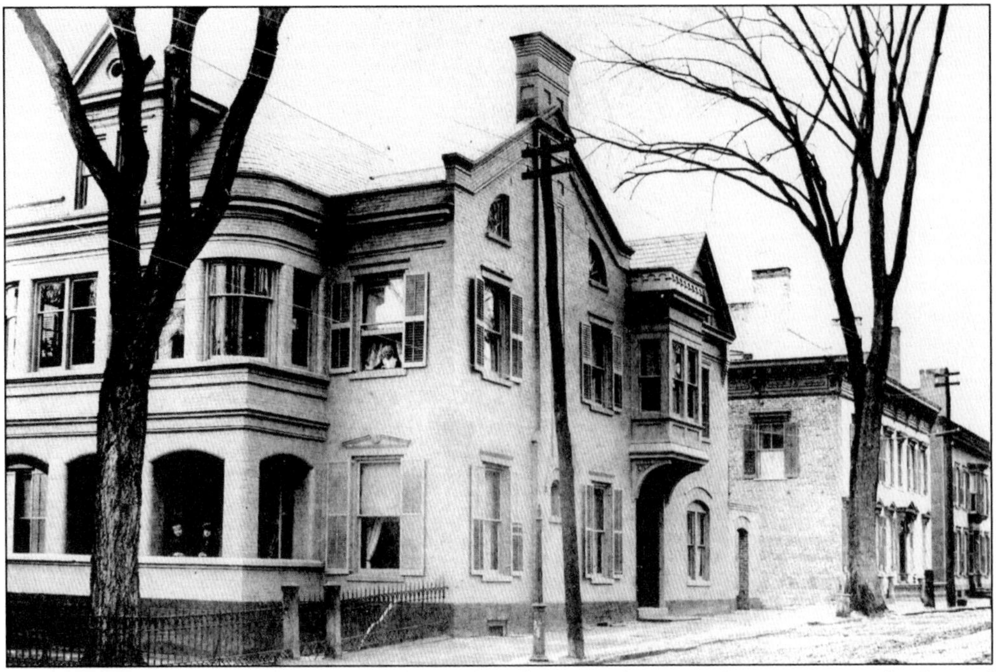

The south side of lower State Street from Church to Washington Avenue is completely void of homes today. George Westinghouse Sr. and Jr.'s home can been seen on the right and the mansion on the left was also occupied by a Westinghouse family member (this is also known as the Mitchell Carley-Westinghouse-Ford house).

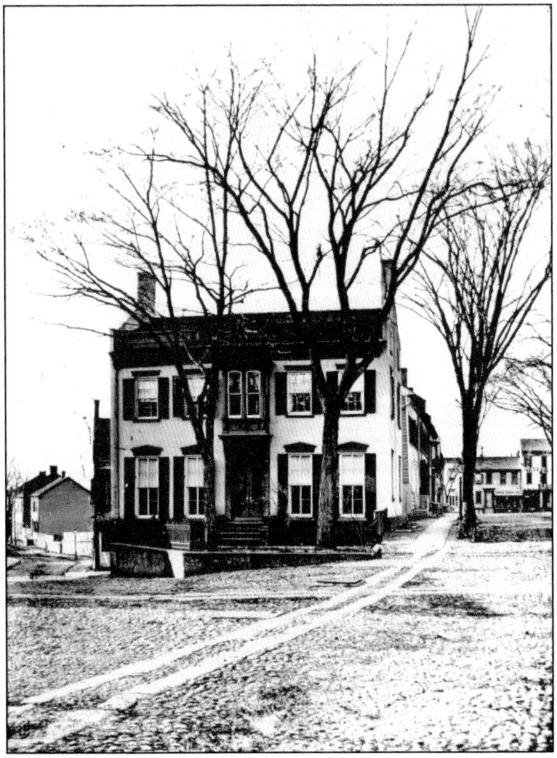

This Westinghouse mansion was located at the intersection of State, Water, and Church Streets. It is now a bus stop. The road to the left was an important military road to the west during the French and Indian War and the Revolutionary War.

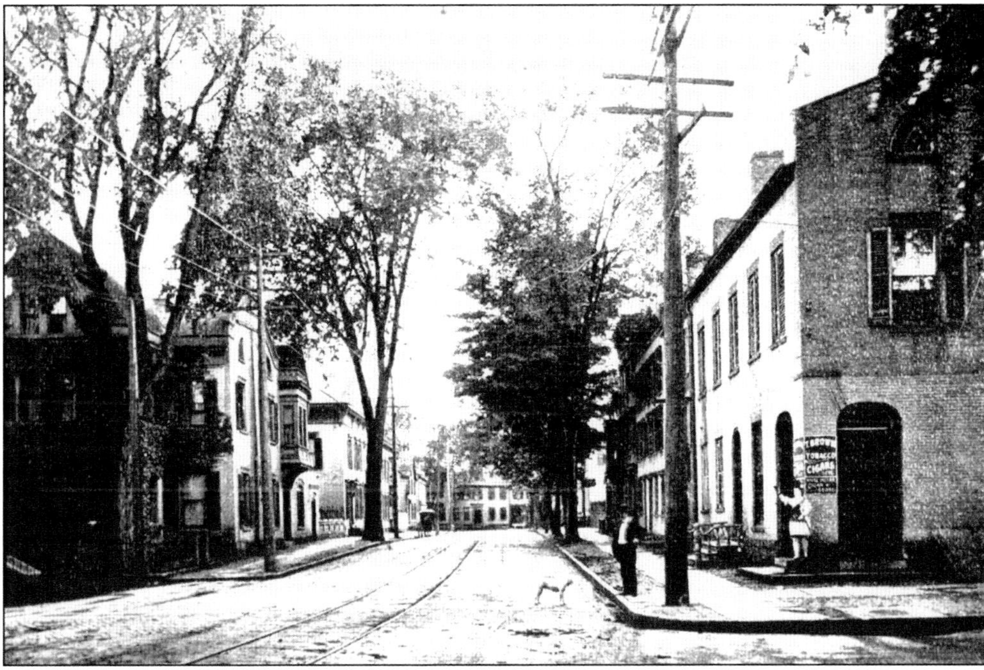

Martyr Lane is the early name for lower State Street between Church Street and Washington Avenue. Many of the early residents were killed and buried here during the massacre. Judge John Sanders's residence is on the right. The Westinghouse home can be seen on the left and the Freeman Hotel can be seen at the end in the center of the street. Not one building remains.

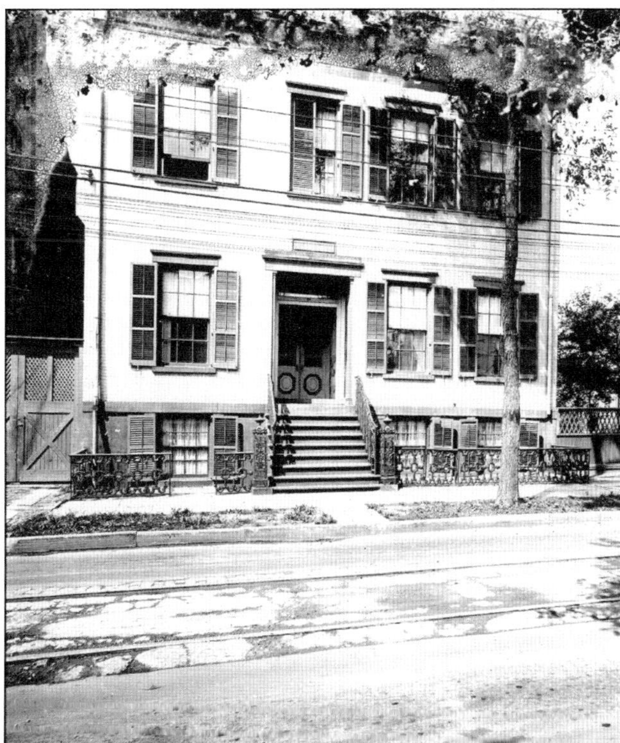

This is an example of an early 19th century home on lower State Street. This part of lower State Street was the first area settled after stockade citizens started moving out of the palisaded village. There is virtually no indication today that this area was once a substantial residential community.

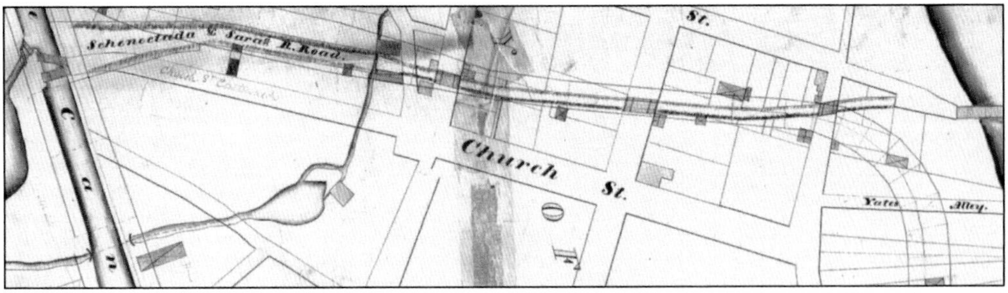

The first railroad tunnel in America was carved through the stockade in 1831 and opened with the Saratoga and Schenectady Railroad in 1832. This 15-foot-deep-by-25-foot-wide tunnel, flanked on both walls with fieldstone, took train cars, modified stagecoaches, by horse through the tunnel and over the Washington Avenue Bridge where a little steam engine would take it the rest of the way to Saratoga. This tunnel was used from 1832 to about 1838 and then filled in. The author will be excavating part of the tunnel to reveal its hidden secrets. This map shows the original route of the tunnel and bridges over State, Union, and Front Streets.

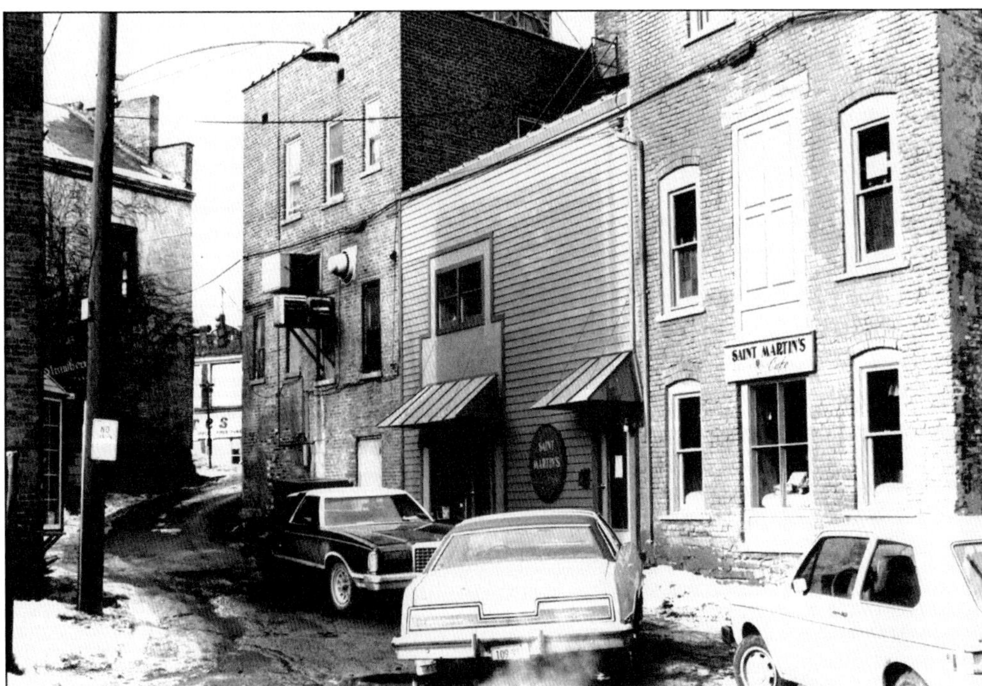

Mill Lane is one of the original paths of the early settlement leading out of the south gate, and it is here where Sweer Teunise Van Velsen built the first gristmill in the Mohawk Valley. He was killed in the 1690 massacre, but a mill had been on this site until the 1970s.

This is the old mill on Mill Lane. This building, 18th century in origin, was standing until the 1970s. This site represents the first gristmill in the entire Mohawk Valley.

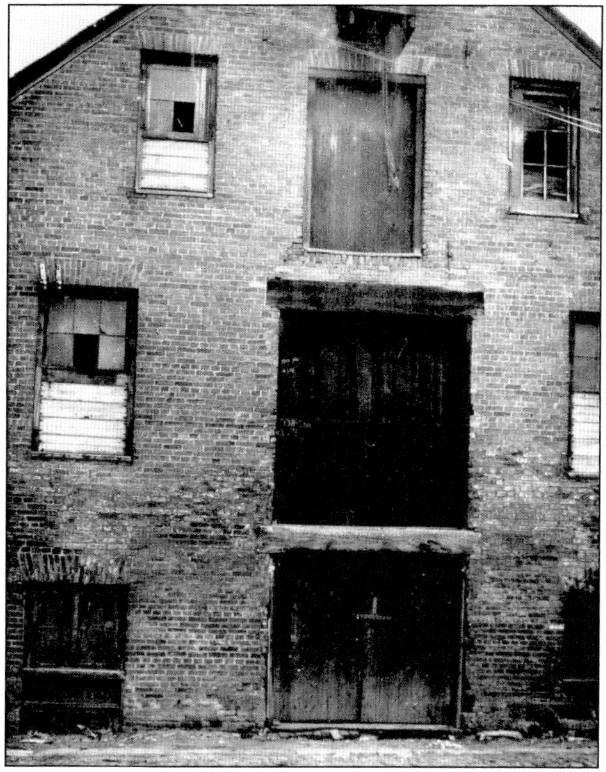

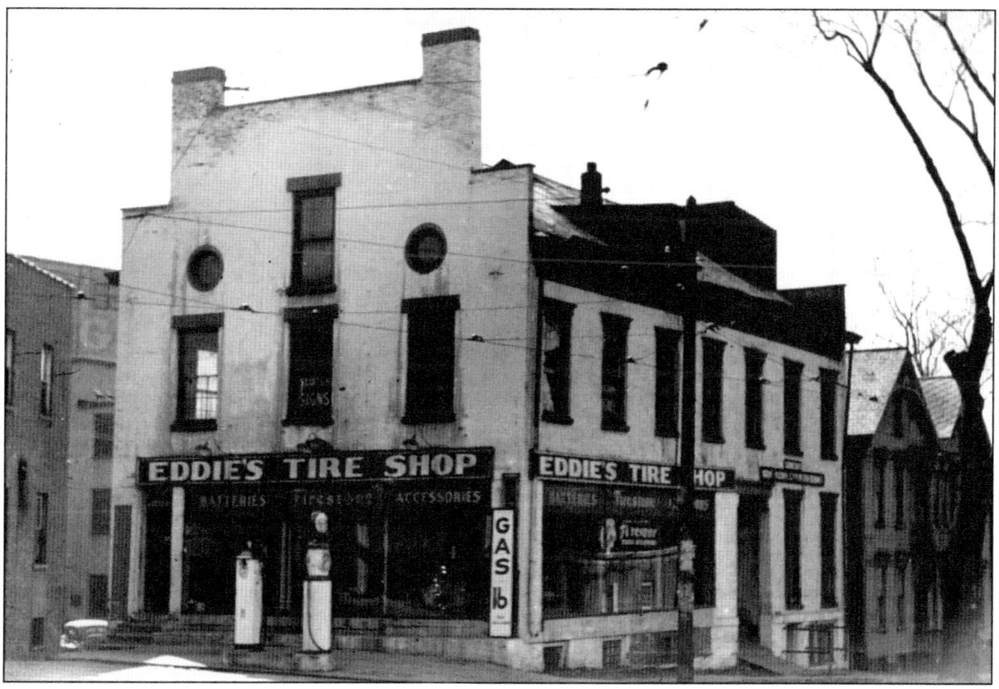

The Block House actually was never a blockhouse but a residence that was later converted to commercial enterprises as seen here in the 1930s. It is currently being renovated to serve as a tavern.

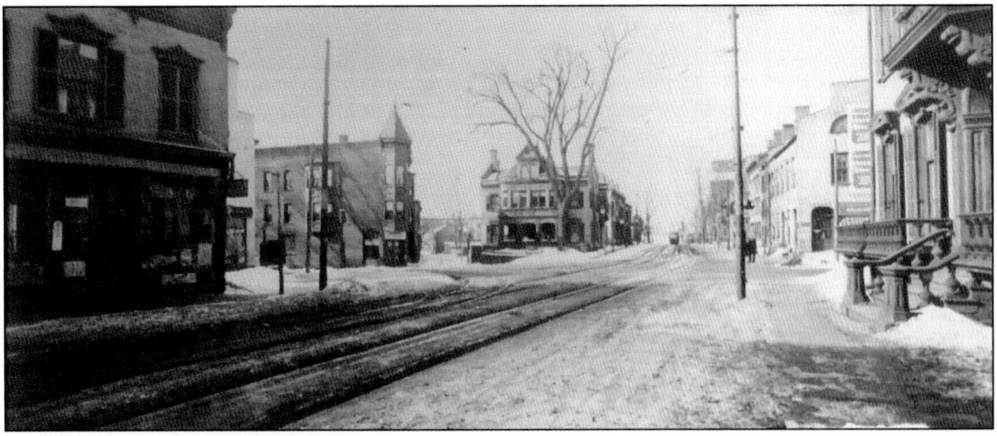

A view of lower State Street just past Church Street looking towards the river reveals the residential character of the region. A trolley can be seen coming up the street. Water Street is to the left. The Daniel Campbell mansion is on the right in this 1890s photograph.

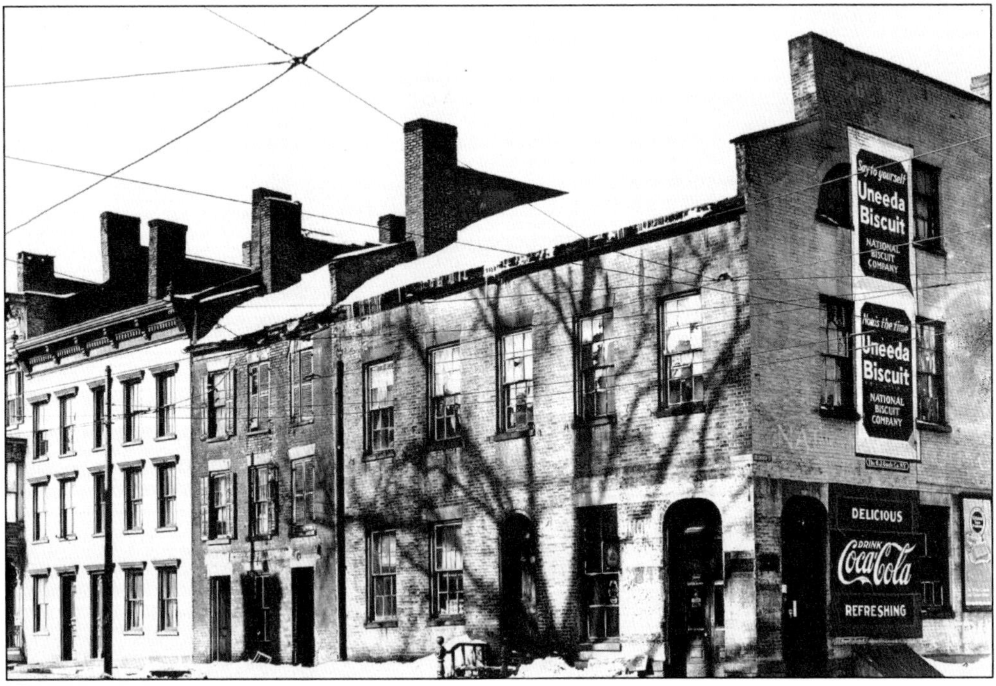

This is a close up of Judge John Sanders's home at the corner of State and Church Streets then being used as a store. Sanders was a county court judge from 1855 to 1860 and an author of the history of the county.

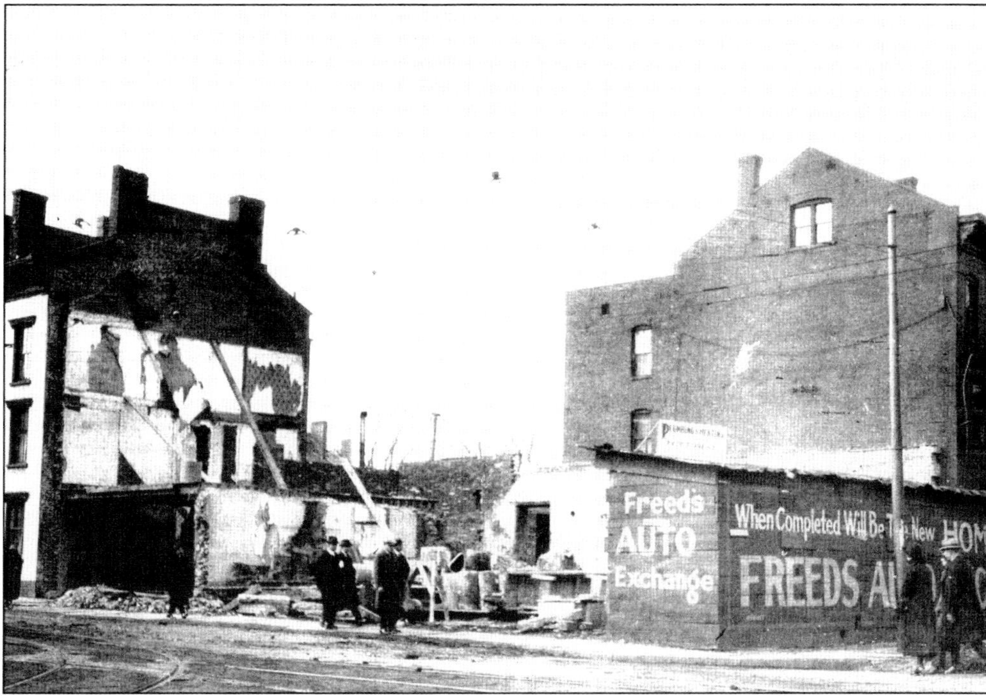

Sanders's mansion was demolished for one of Schenectady's first auto dealers, Freeds Auto Exchange, in the first quarter of the 20th century.

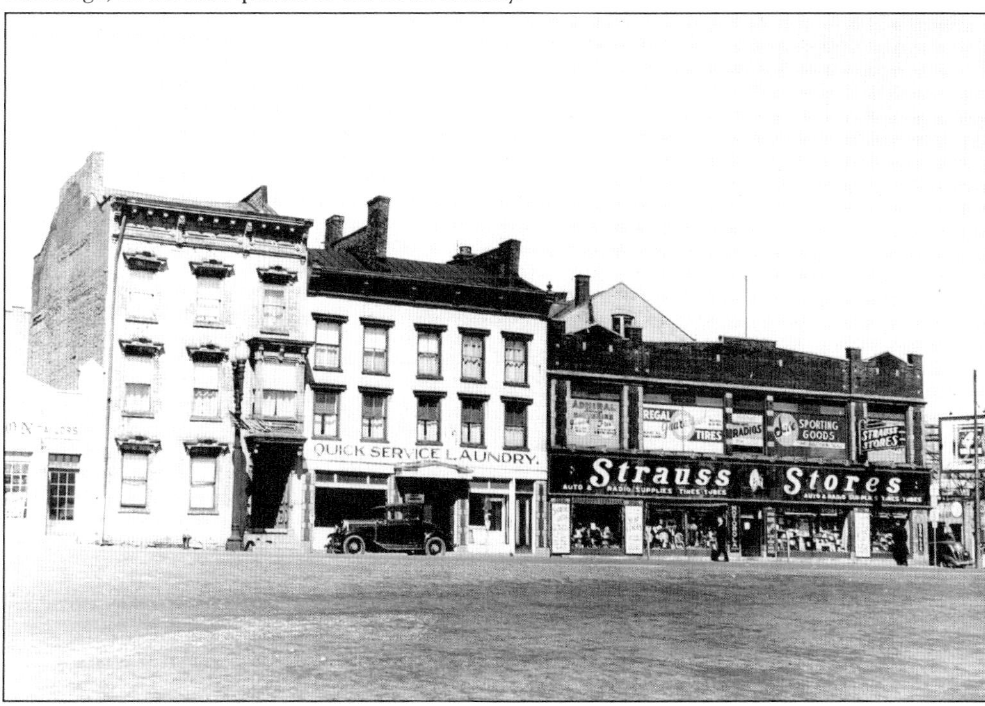

Unfortunately, Freeds Auto Exchange did not last that long and was replaced by Strauss Stores, an early automobile supply company founded in 1929, the date this photograph was taken. The former residences to the left are now commercial enterprises.

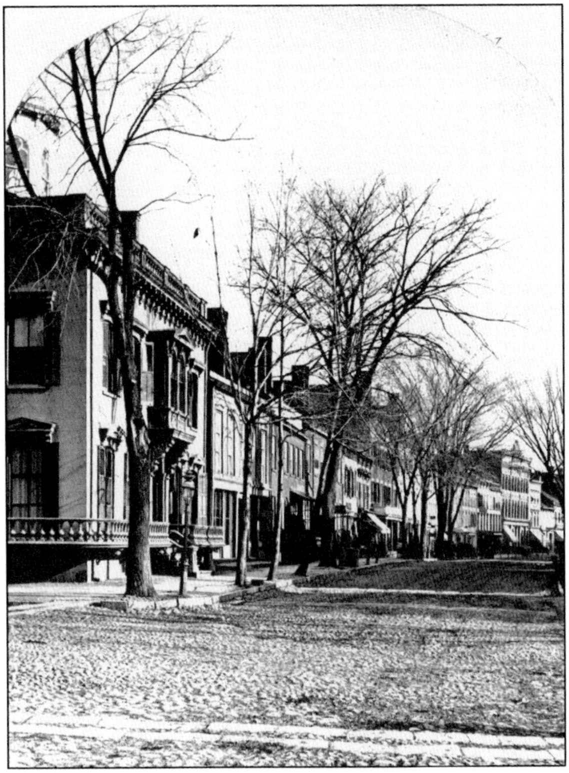

A view looking east up lower State Street around 1890 from Church Street shows the Daniel Campbell mansion on the left and the cobblestone street and stone crossing. This view is drastically altered today as most of the buildings have been torn down.

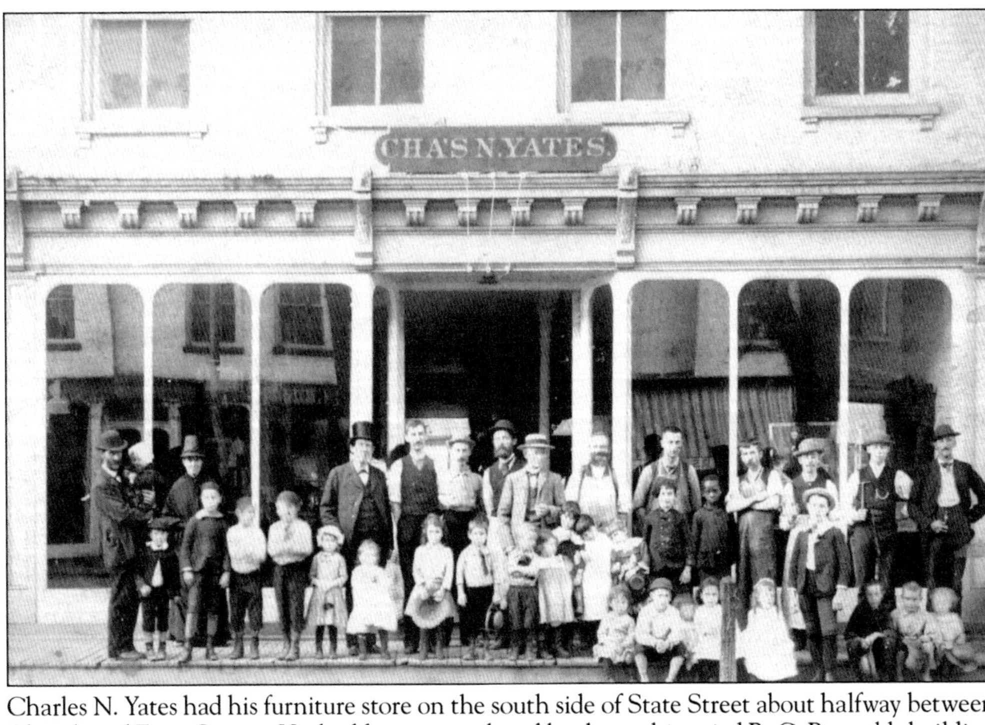

Charles N. Yates had his furniture store on the south side of State Street about halfway between Church and Ferry Streets. His building was replaced by the multistoried R. C. Reynolds building that is still standing there today.

Seen here is another view looking east on lower State Street on the south side from Church Street around the 1880s. The area had become mixed residential commercial strip even earlier. Mill Lane is on the right.

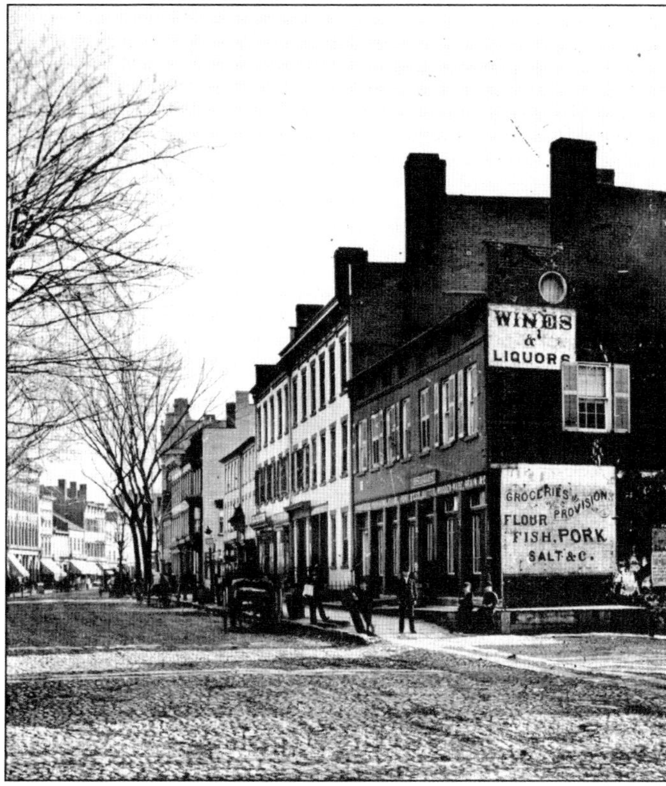

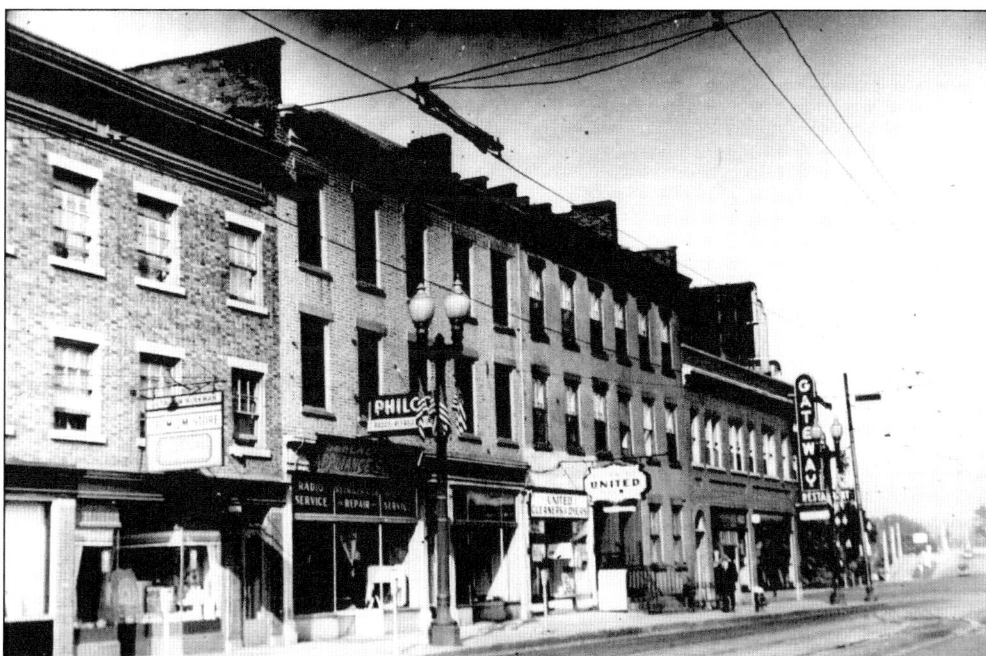

Here is a view of the same area as the previous photograph but looking west and about 125 years later (1923). These homes have had their first floors converted to businesses while people still lived in the upper floors.

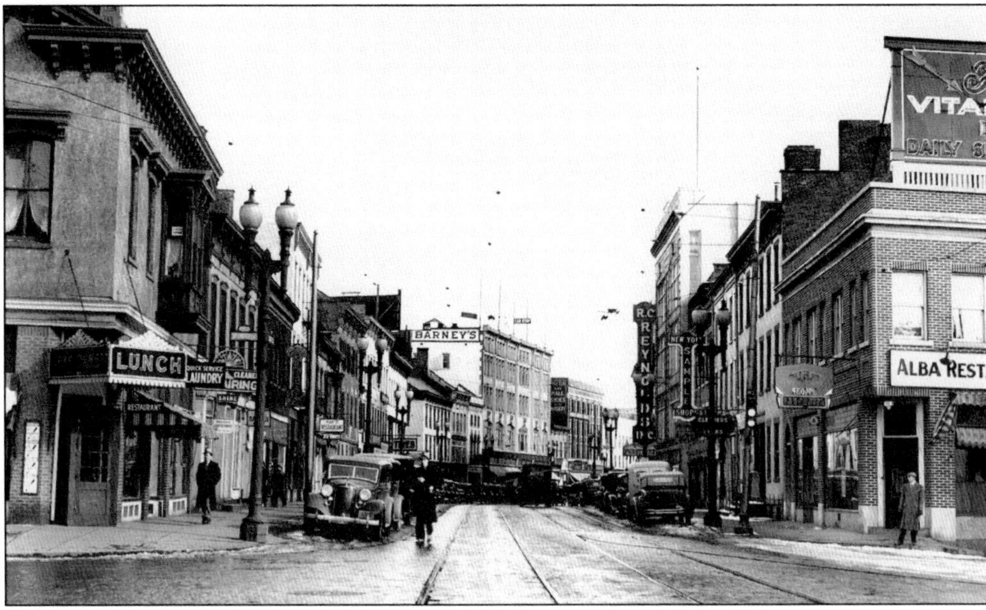

This is a view looking east up lower State Street from Church Street during the 1920s when this section was a busy commercial area. Restaurants on every corner and trolleys and cars shared the road. Lower State Street was a vibrant and busy part of downtown Schenectady. The Campbell mansion, where Sir William Johnson visited in the 18th century, is seen as a place to buy soda and candy and have lunch. It looks nothing like its former 18th-century glory; note the R. C. Reynolds furniture store and Barney's department store.

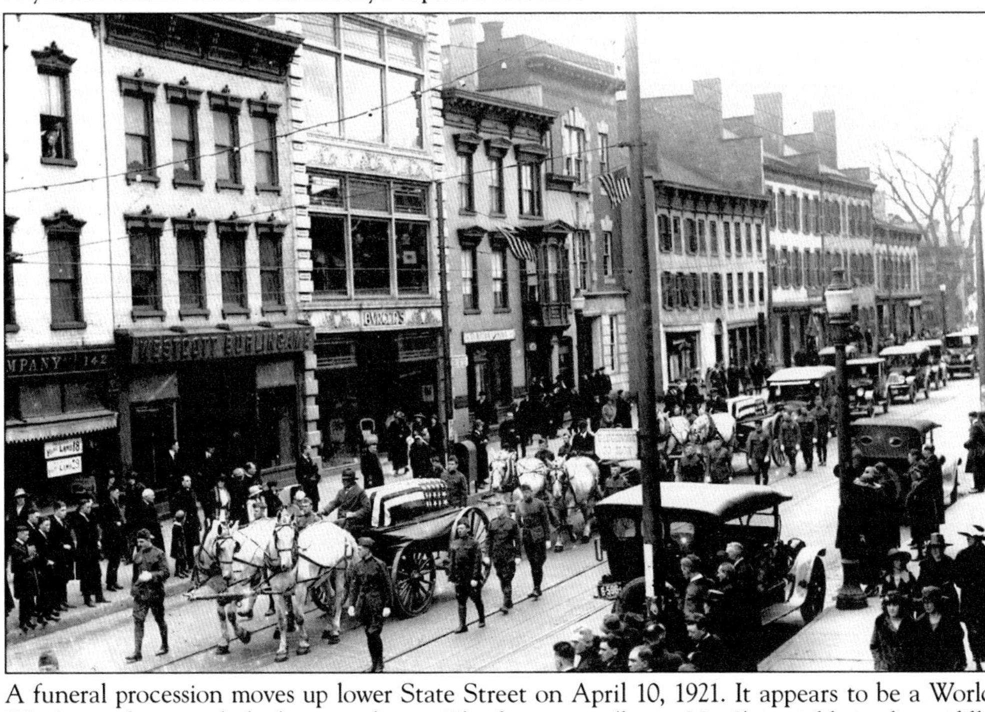

A funeral procession moves up lower State Street on April 10, 1921. It appears to be a World War I–era photograph, looking southwest. The fire station (house No. 2) is visible in the middle of the photograph.

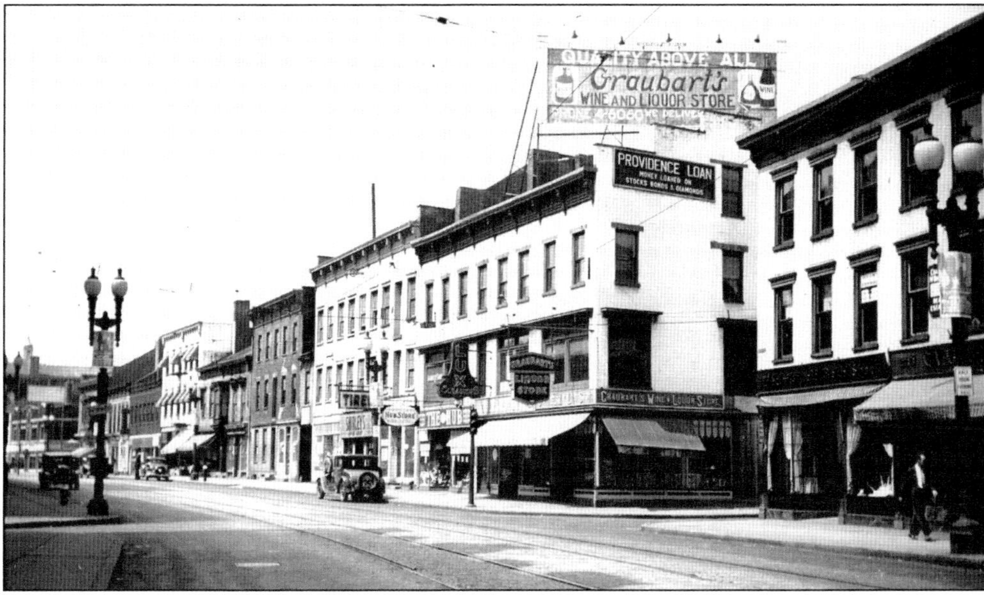

This view, to the northwest side of State Street up from Ferry Street in 1930, no longer exists. Ferry Street represents the eastern border of the original stockade area, and in fact, the street was called a *rounwaag*, or "walkway." Many of the buildings seen here were demolished.

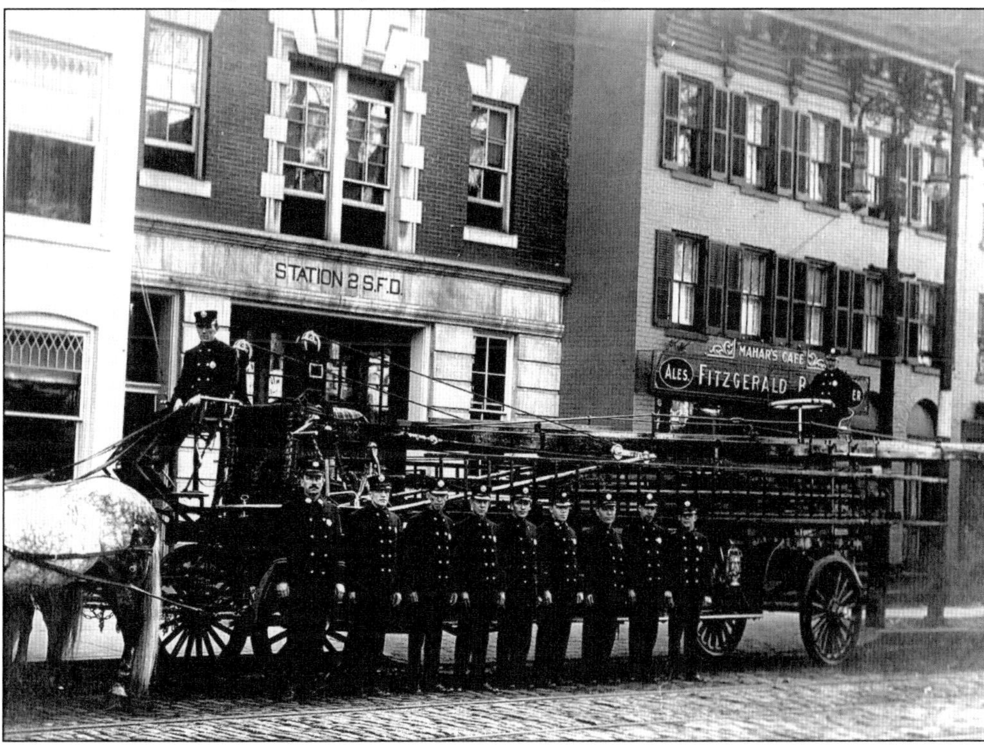

Station house No. 2 of the Schenectady Fire Department was built here between Church and Ferry Streets on the south side in 1904 and closed in 1929. The stockade was also protected by the Van Vranken Hose No. 2 station on 107 South Church Street and the old Hose No. 4 station at South College Street.

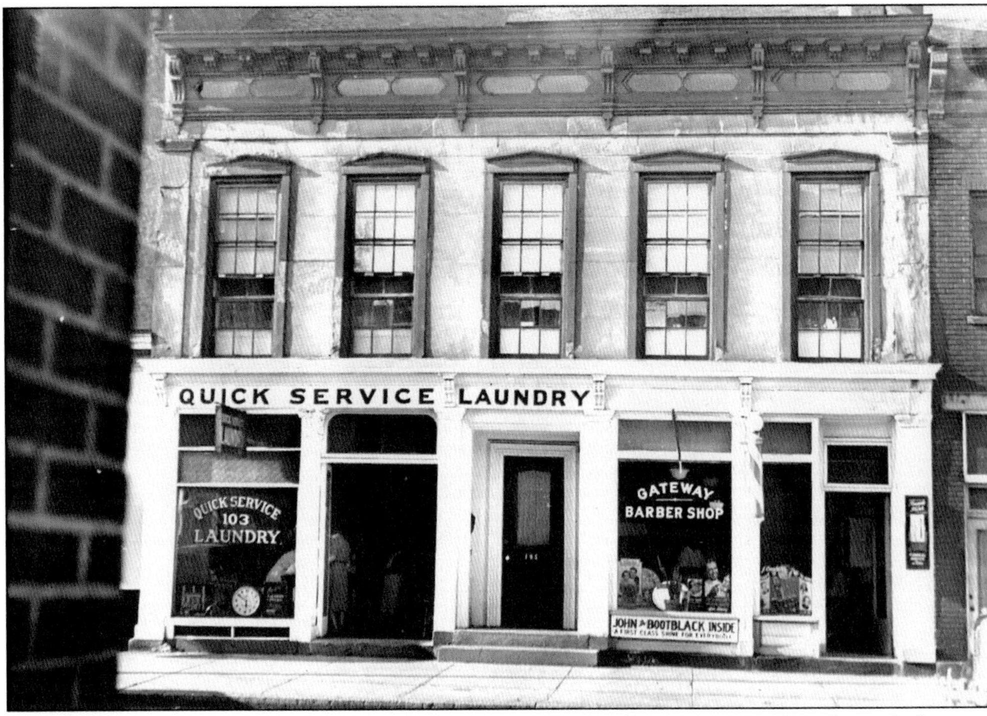

Slowly stately homes on lower State Street were converted to commercial and retail shops as the city grew eastward, as seen here at 103 State Street on the north side above Church Street around 1900.

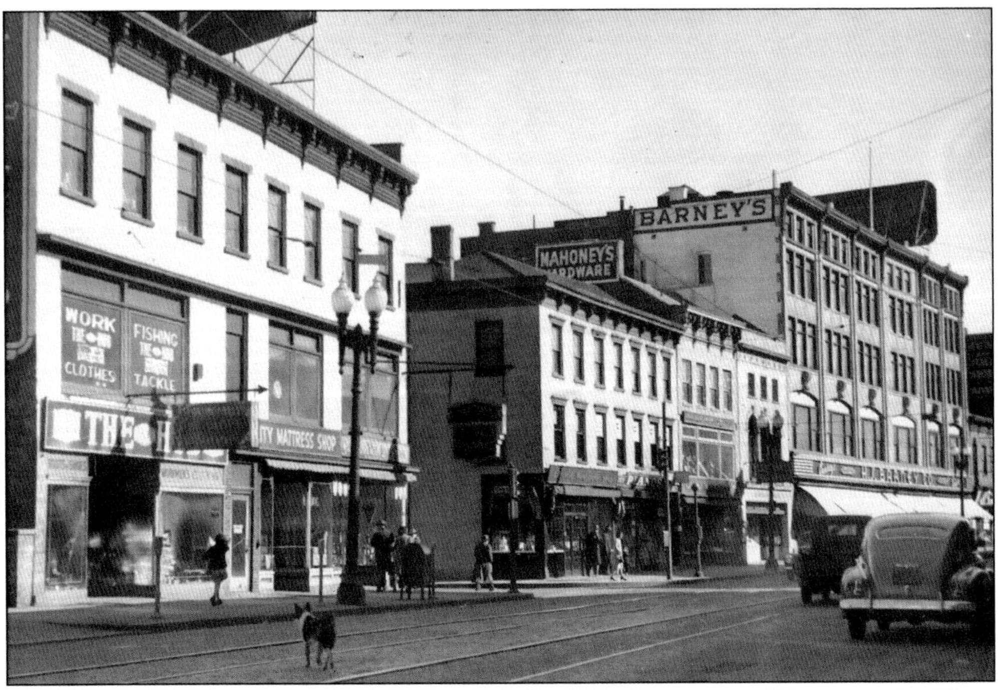

State Street at the intersection of Ferry Street in the 1930s shows many 19th century buildings converted to commercial businesses.

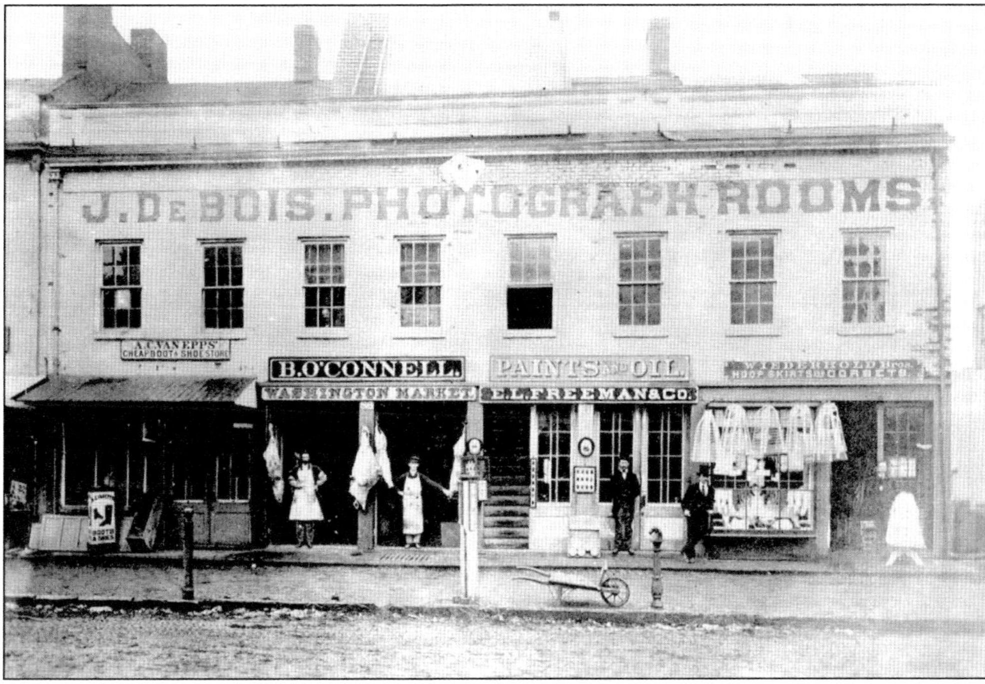

The southeast corner of Ferry and State Streets was the home of J. DeBois, a photographer, in this 1874 photograph. Many early photographs of Schenectadians were captured here. Notice the hanging meat at the butcher shop. One could not do that today with current health standards.

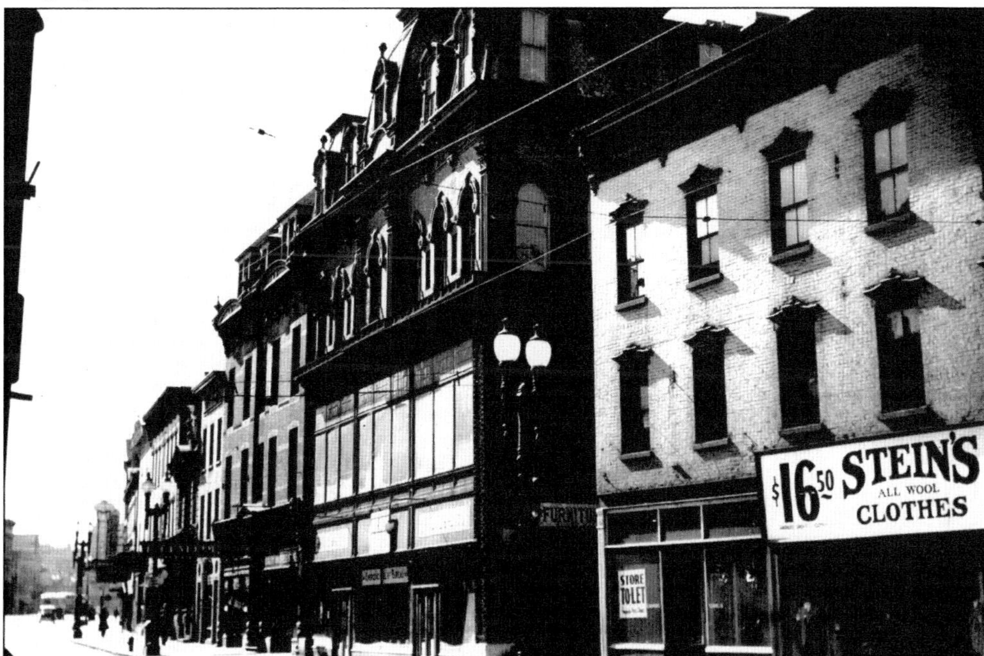

The YMCA replaced DeBois Studios in 1871 here at 203–204 State Street. The YMCA actually started in 1857 and met at the Clute Building at 202 State Street. Parts of this building exist in the present structure at the site.

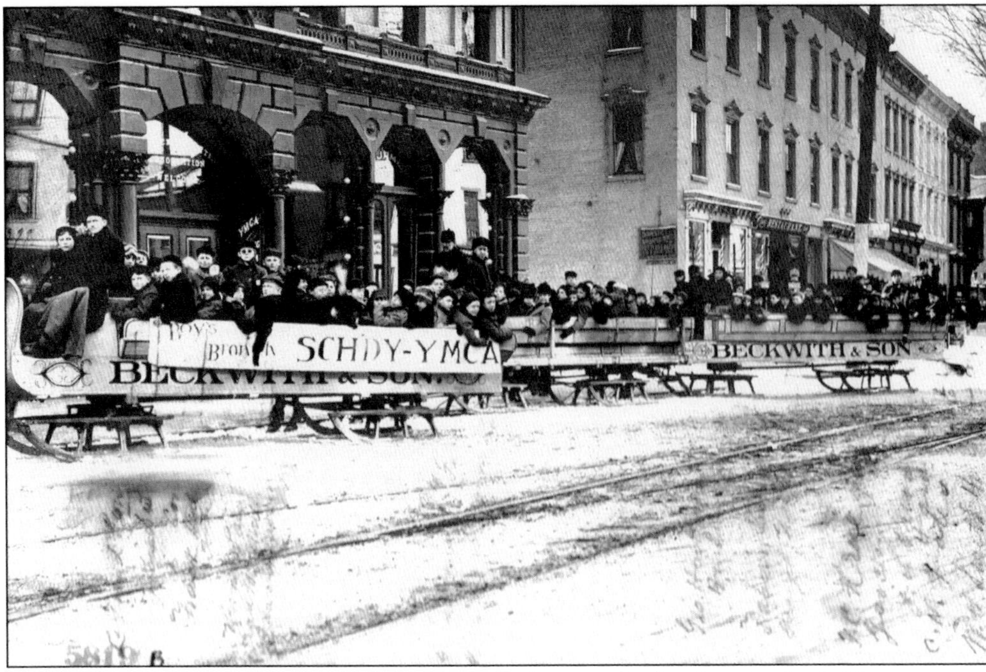

Here is a winter view of the YMCA with kids ready to go sleigh riding in the 1890s courtesy of Beckwith and Son, a sponsor.

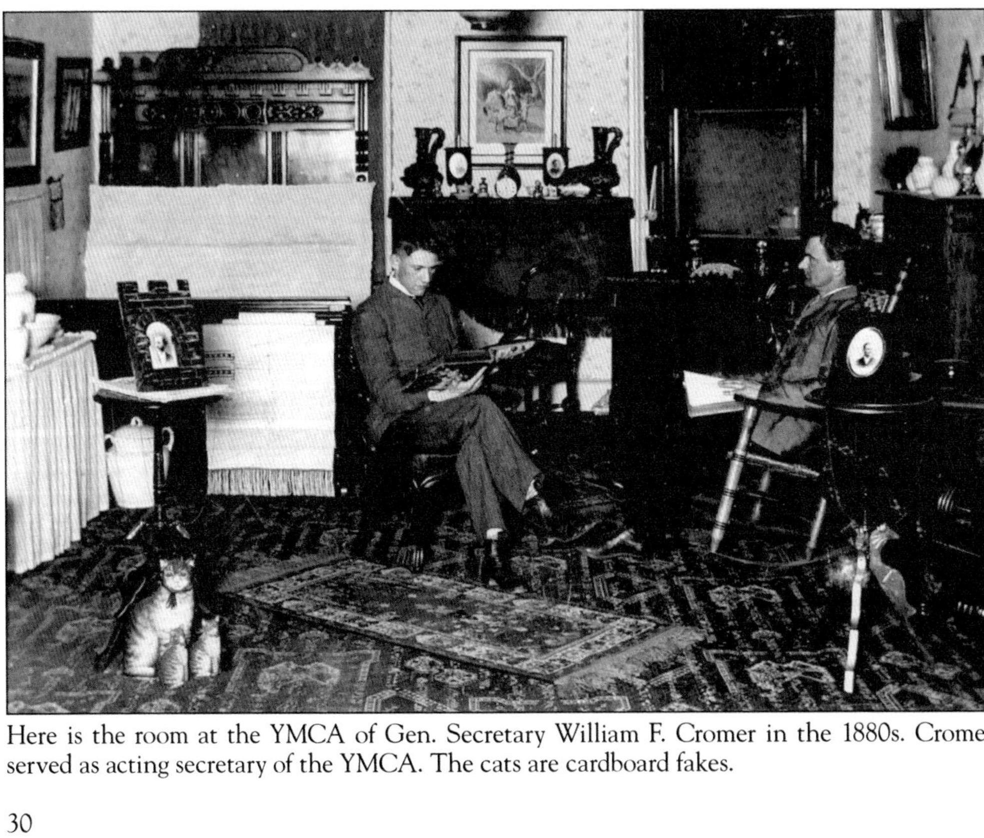

Here is the room at the YMCA of Gen. Secretary William F. Cromer in the 1880s. Cromer served as acting secretary of the YMCA. The cats are cardboard fakes.

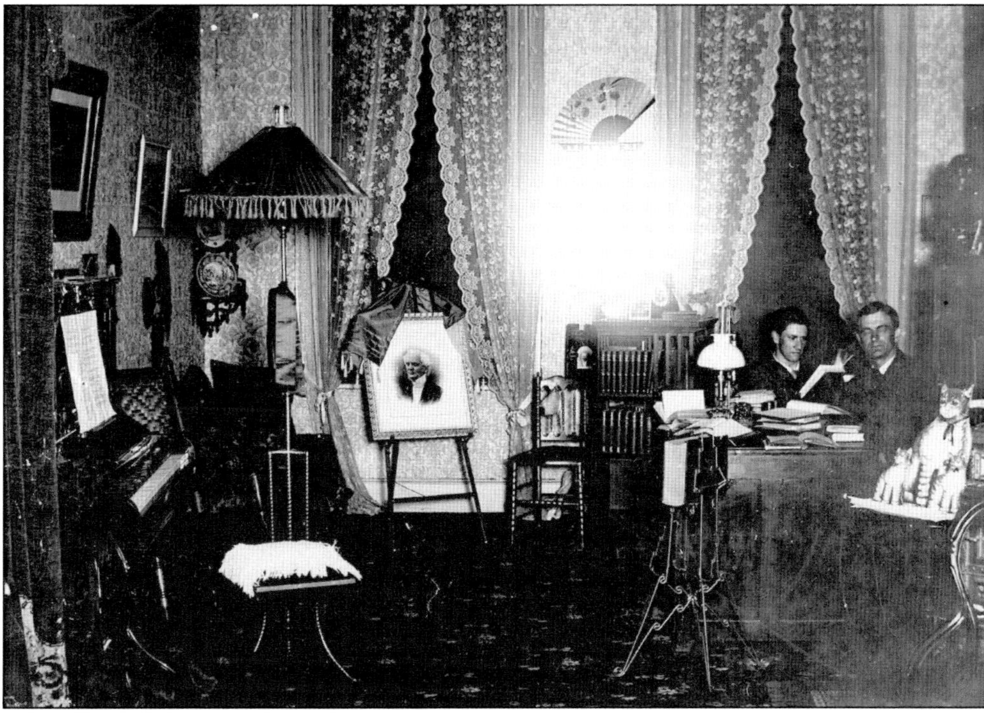

Here is another view of William F. Cromer's YMCA room. Look where the fake cats are sitting.

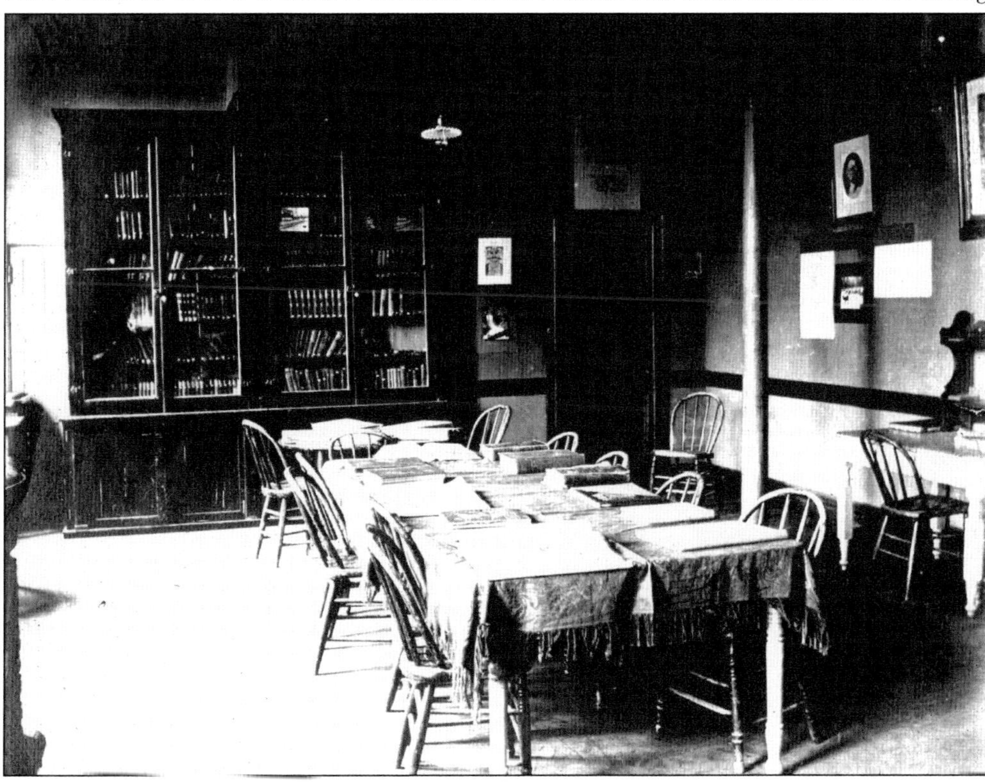

Here is a view of the reading room at the YMCA.

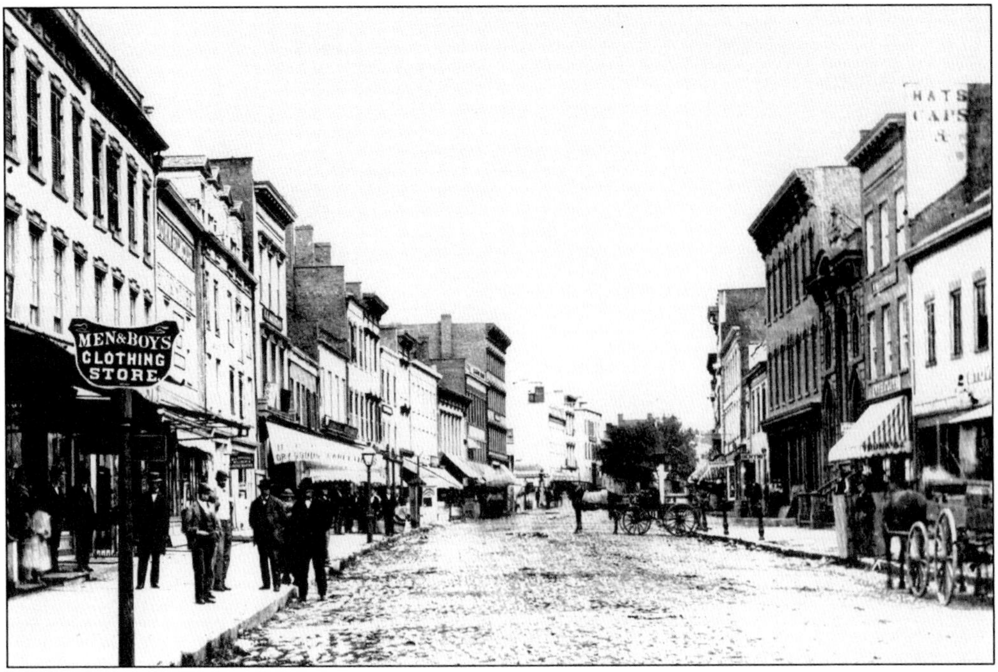

This is a view looking east from Ferry Street towards the Erie Canal in 1865. Ferry Street was the eastern border of the original stockade. Here one can see a cobblestoned State Street with several horse and wagons. H. S. Barney's department store was just a small, three-story building on the left.

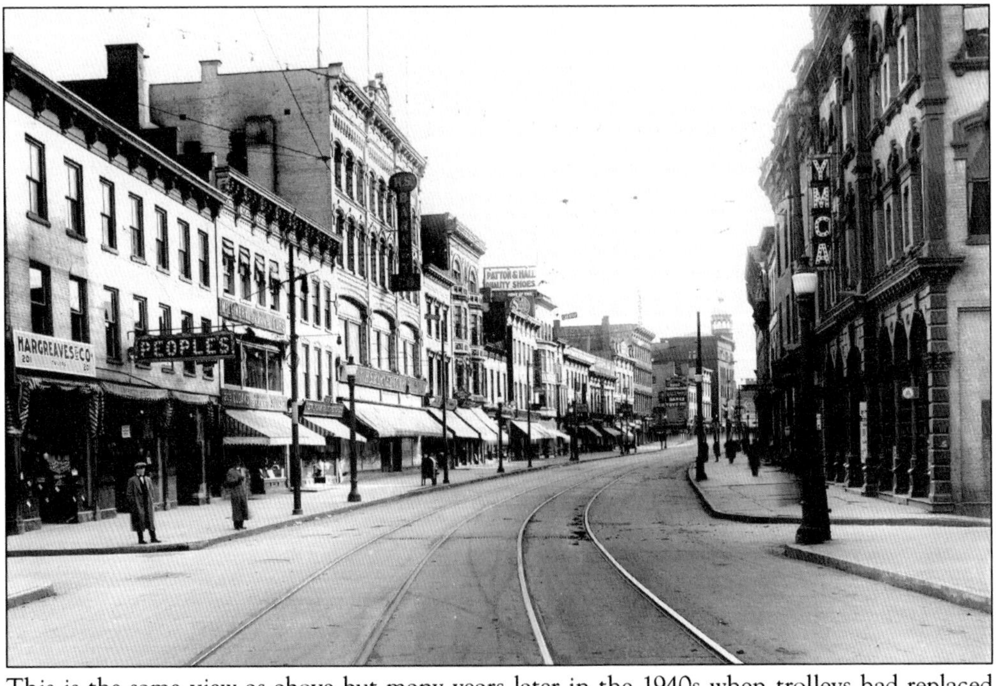

This is the same view as above but many years later in the 1940s when trolleys had replaced horse and wagons. Barney's department store has expanded and prospered and was getting ready to expand again.

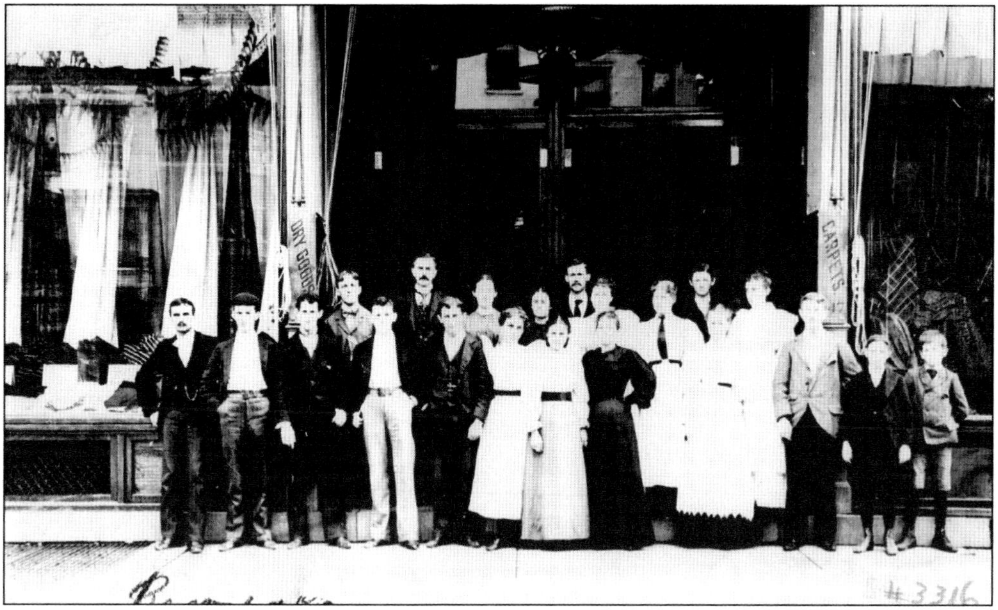

Reeves and Company dry goods store was located just above Ferry Street on the north side of State Street, later taken up by Barney's department store. Founder Howland S. Barney came to Schenectady in 1836 at age 14 and founded the company in 1855. His store on State Street near South Ferry Street soon became a landmark business.

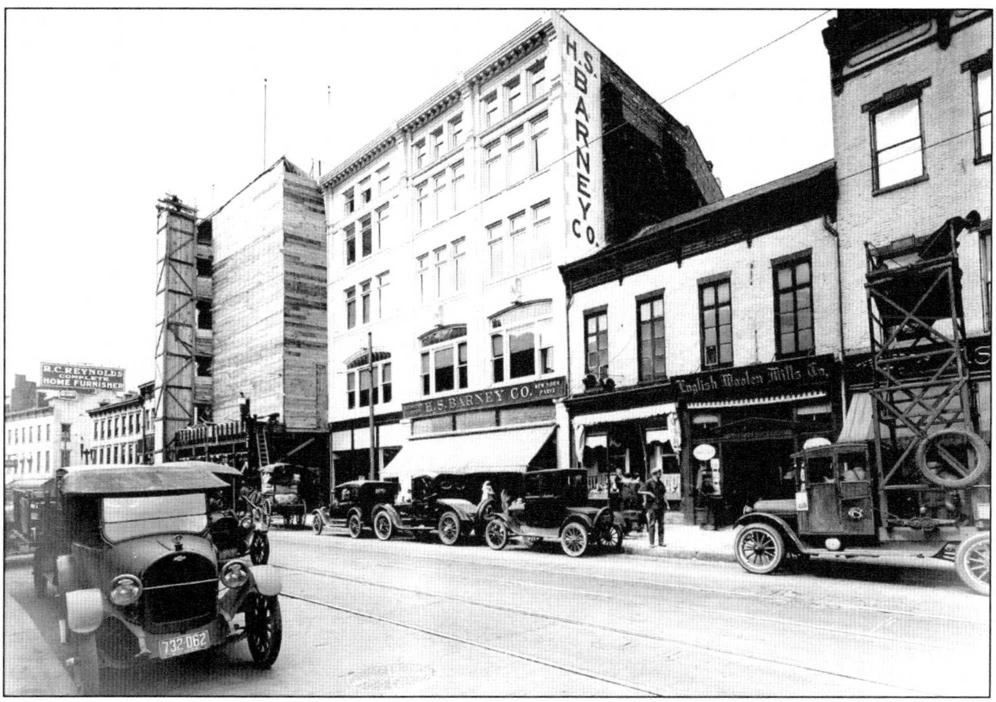

Barney's store was one of the biggest department stores in the city since the 1840s. Here it is expanding again to the west but like most urban department stores, competition from the suburban malls forced them to close their doors in 1973. It is now called Barney Square, an apartment complex created in 1980.

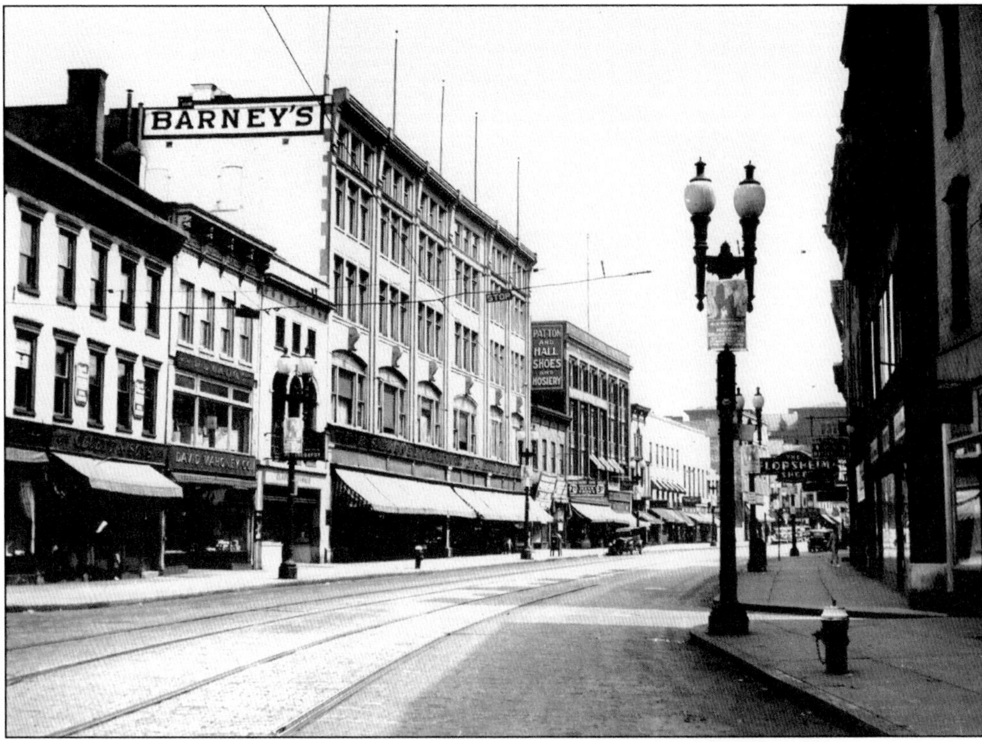

Here is a Sunday view of lower State Street from Church Street during the 1930s. Schenectady was in its heyday with more than 95,000 people living and working in the city.

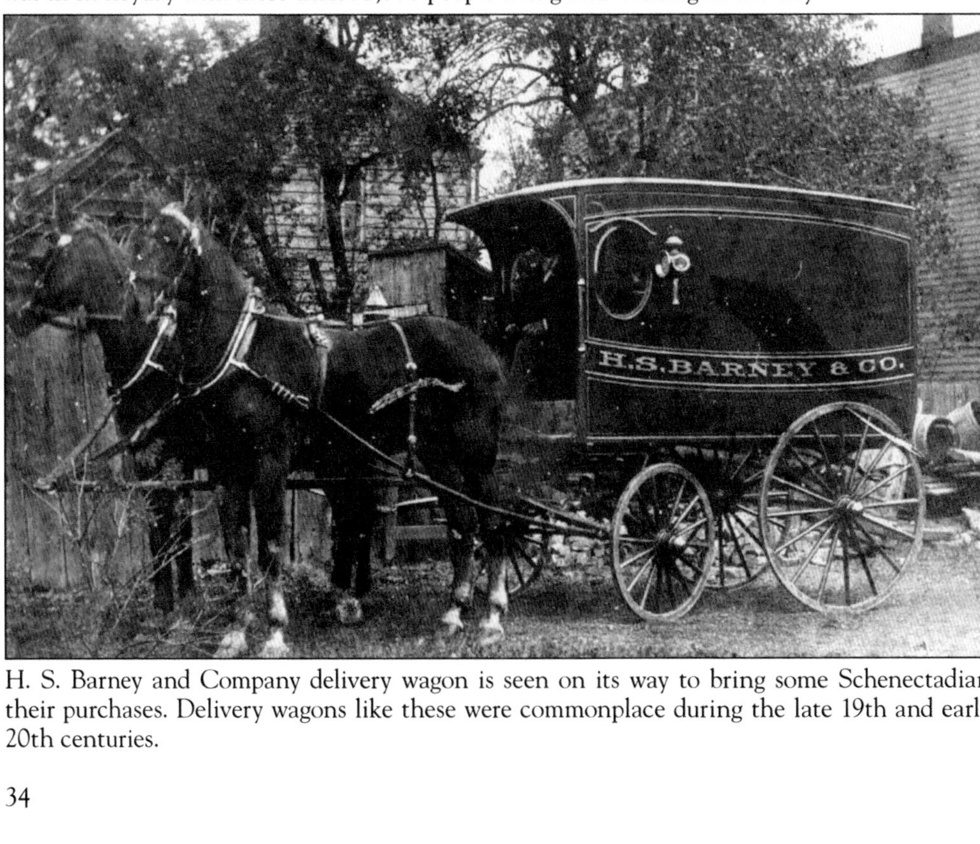

H. S. Barney and Company delivery wagon is seen on its way to bring some Schenectadian their purchases. Delivery wagons like these were commonplace during the late 19th and early 20th centuries.

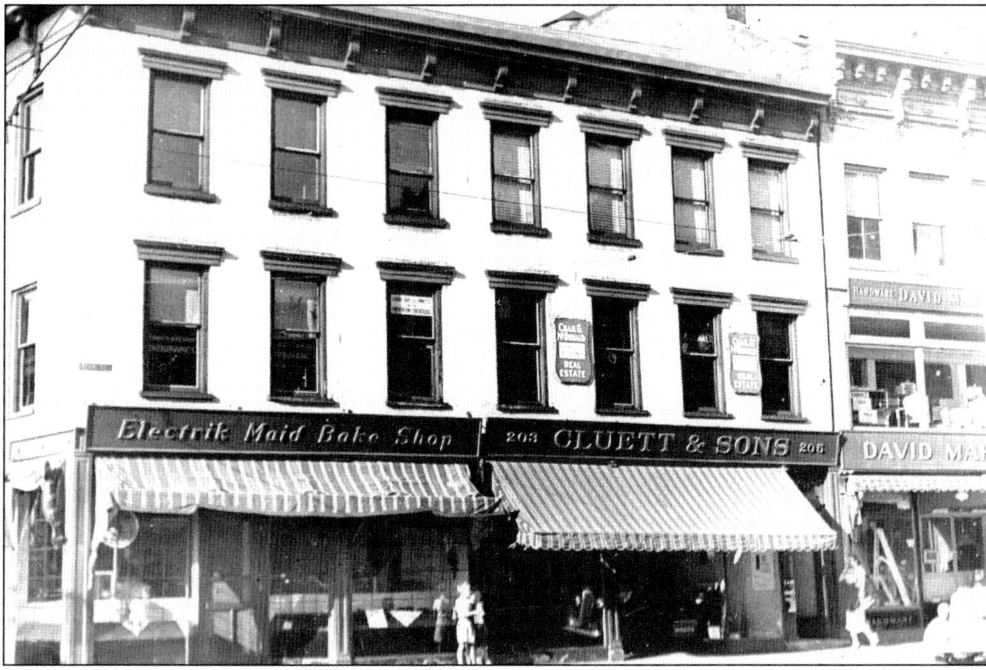

The Furman block, at the northeast corner of Ferry and State Street, was owned by Robert Furman, a successful clothing dealer of the 19th century. It was the former Van Guysling dry goods store. Furman helped form Vale Cemetery, was an early supporter and founder of the YMCA, and was one of those responsible for bringing Thomas Edison to Schenectady.

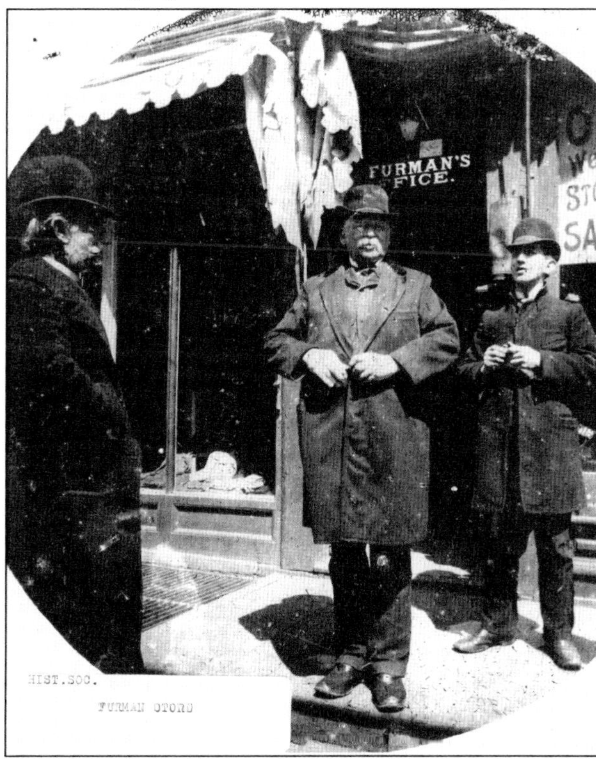

Here is Colonel Furman standing in front of his dry goods store on the corner of State and Ferry Streets. He received his colonel title for putting together the 83rd Regiment during the draft riots of 1863. His mansion is now the rectory for St Joseph's Church.

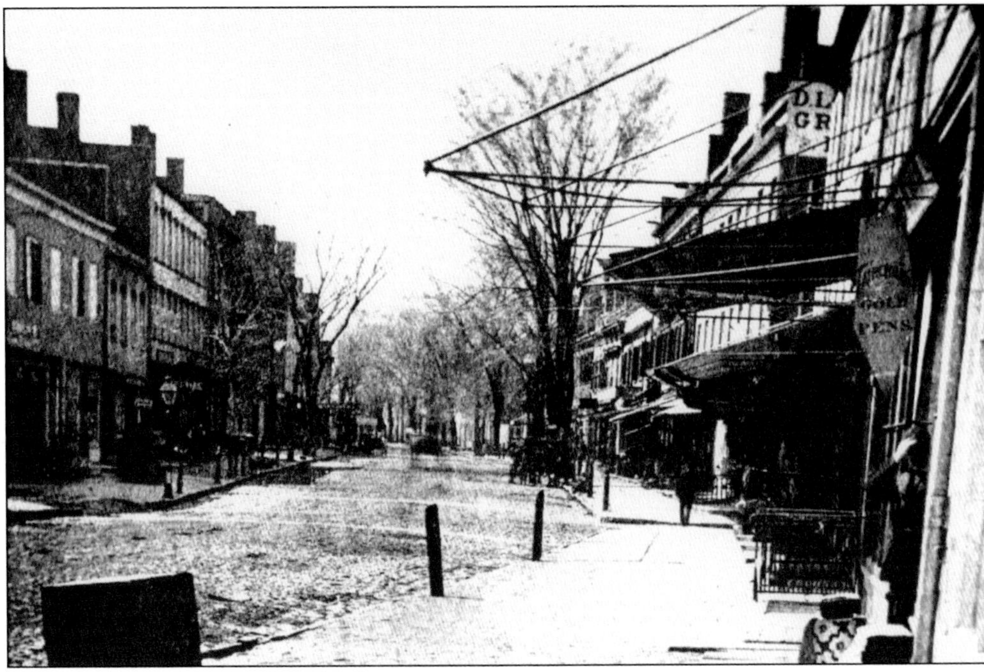

Seen here is a view to the west down State Street just past Ferry Street and Furman's building. Notice the cobblestone street and hitching posts. Compare that to the next photograph.

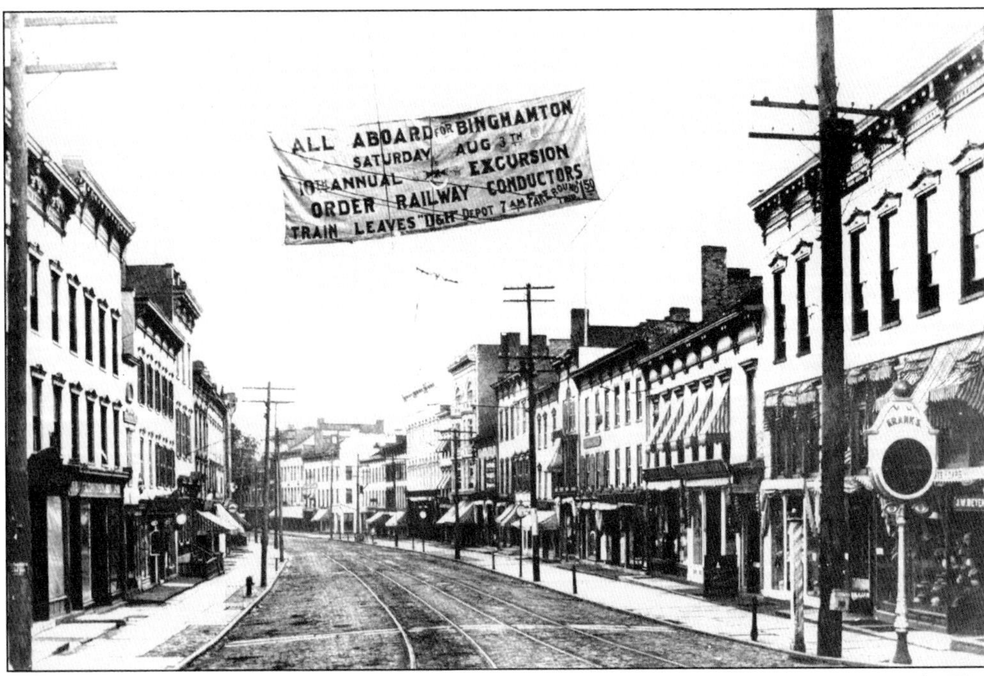

This is the same view but from further up State Street almost near the Erie Canal. This photograph shows the trolley tracks that started running in the city in the later part of the 19th century.

Three

WASHINGTON AVENUE

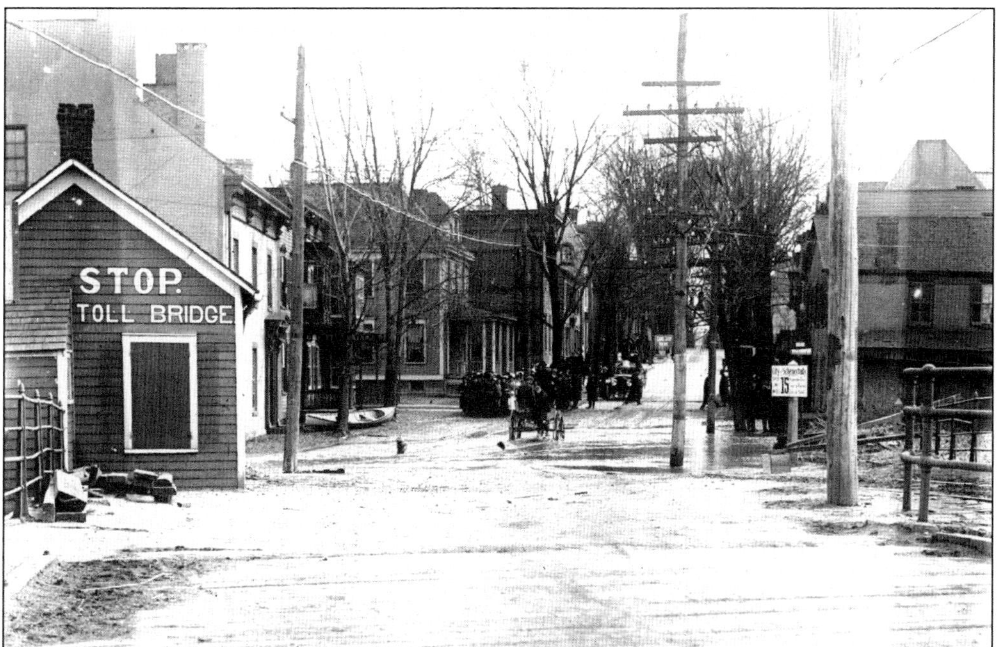

Washington Avenue was the western border of the original stockade and began at the intersection with Front Street but extended down to the river later on when a wooden bridge was constructed over the Mohawk River in 1808. This region was also part of the early industrial base when Schenectady built boats and made brooms. A fire in 1819 changed the course of history of the stockade forever.

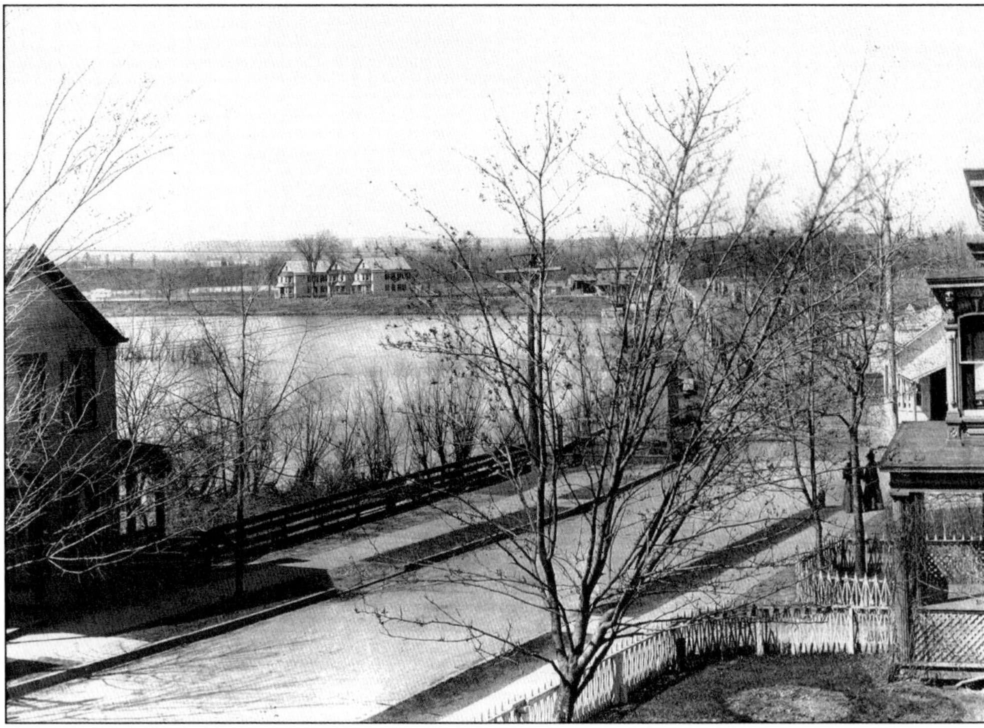

This is a view from one of the homes along Washington Avenue close to the river. Two women in Victorian garb are seen discussing the day, and a view across the river shows Scotia with a few homes on the riverfront.

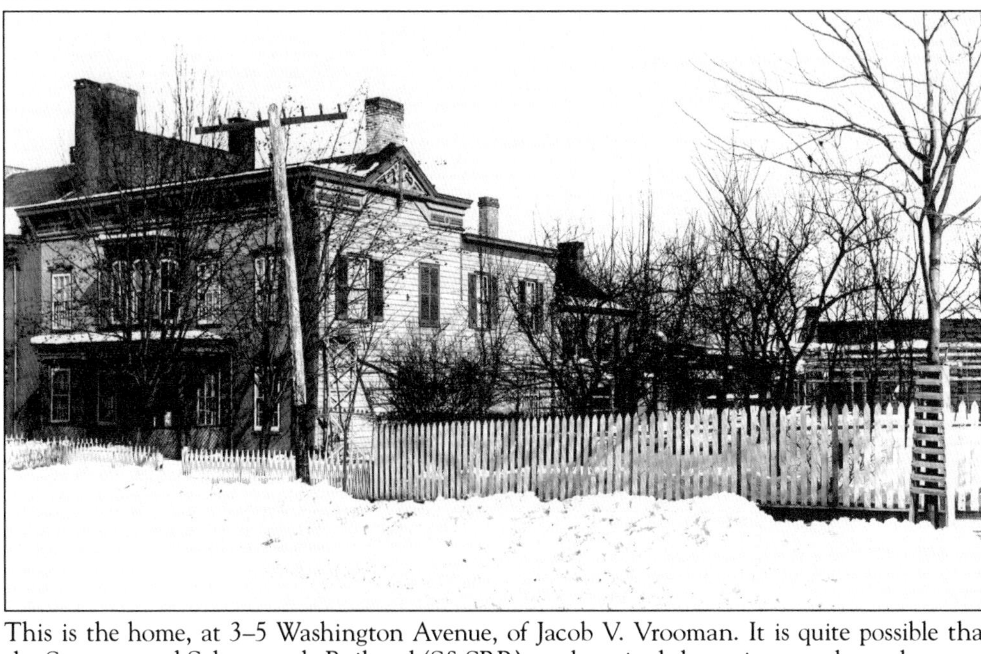

This is the home, at 3–5 Washington Avenue, of Jacob V. Vrooman. It is quite possible that the Saratoga and Schenectady Railroad (S&SRR) tracks exited the train tunnel near here and passed by this house before the train went over the Scotia Bridge. This home has been altered substantially today.

Across the street from Vrooman was the Hershey-Van Epps home at 3 Washington Avenue, built in 1820. The residents in this house would have seen daily trips of the S&SRR going over the bridge from 1832 to 1838.

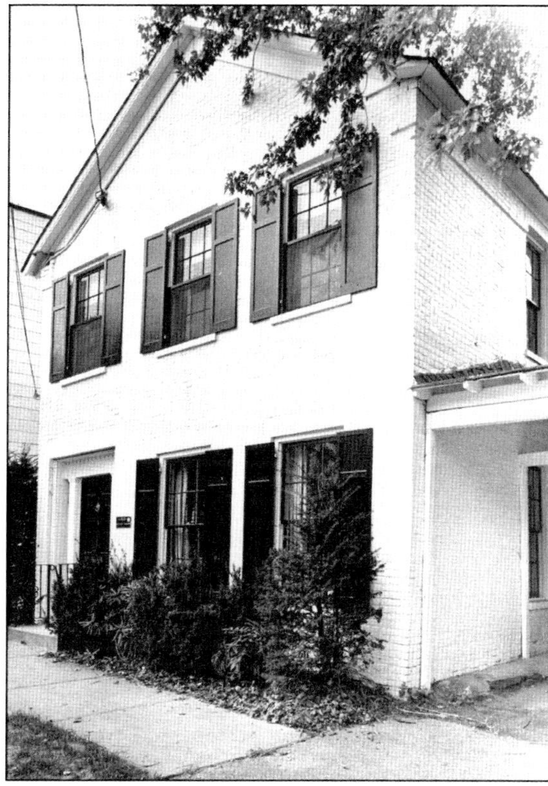

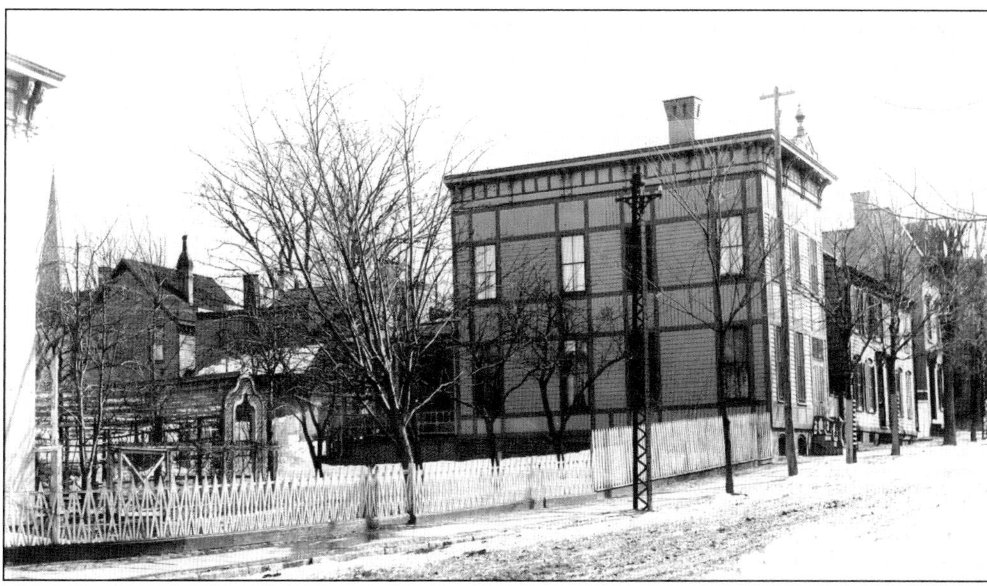

This is a view looking southeast up Washington Avenue to the William C. Vrooman house at 9 Washington Avenue in 1899. The home is still standing. Vrooman was on the Schenectady Board of Supervisors in 1894 and chairman of the New York League of American Wheelmen Division Highway Improvement Committee, a proponent of the Good Roads movement. He was the son of J. V. Vrooman, dealer in stoves and hardware, who started in 1854 and joined his father in the business.

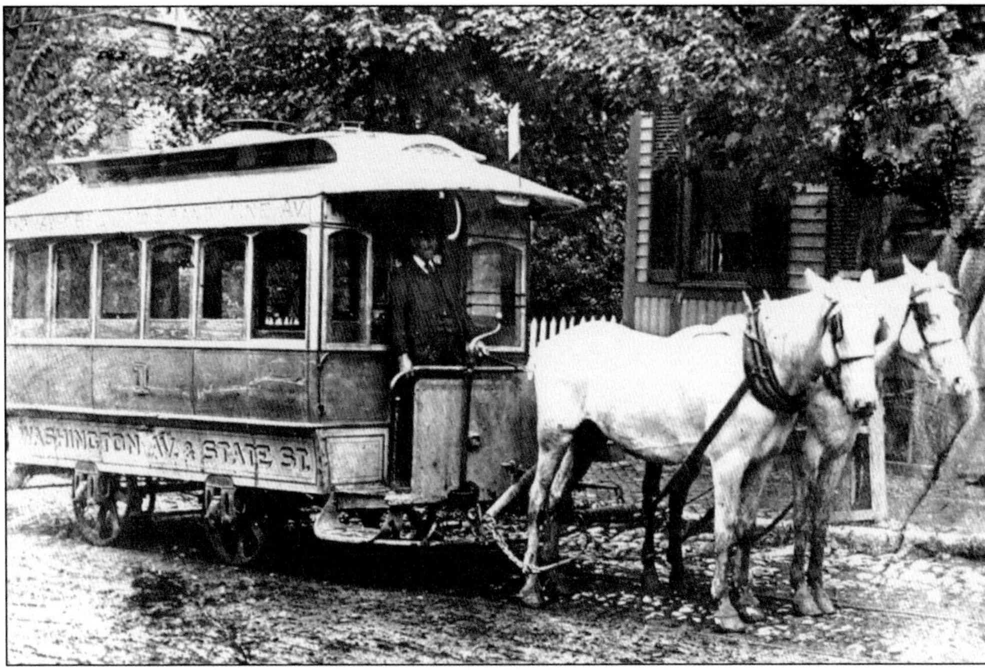

A horse-drawn trolley is coming off the Scotia Bridge and going past the W. C. Vrooman home at 9 Washington Avenue. This trolley went up State Street to Brandywine Avenue. This was the beginning of the Schenectady Street Railway in 1886.

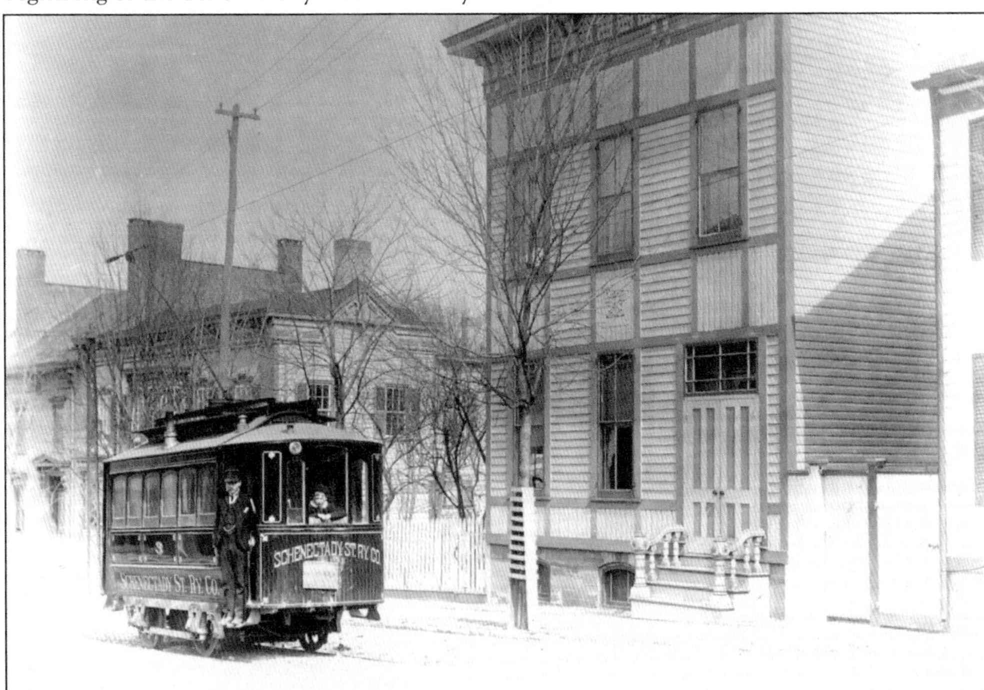

This is the same view as above although now electric trolleys are rolling by the William C. Vrooman residence. The Schenectady Railway Company opened an electric trolley service over the Scotia Bridge in April 1902.

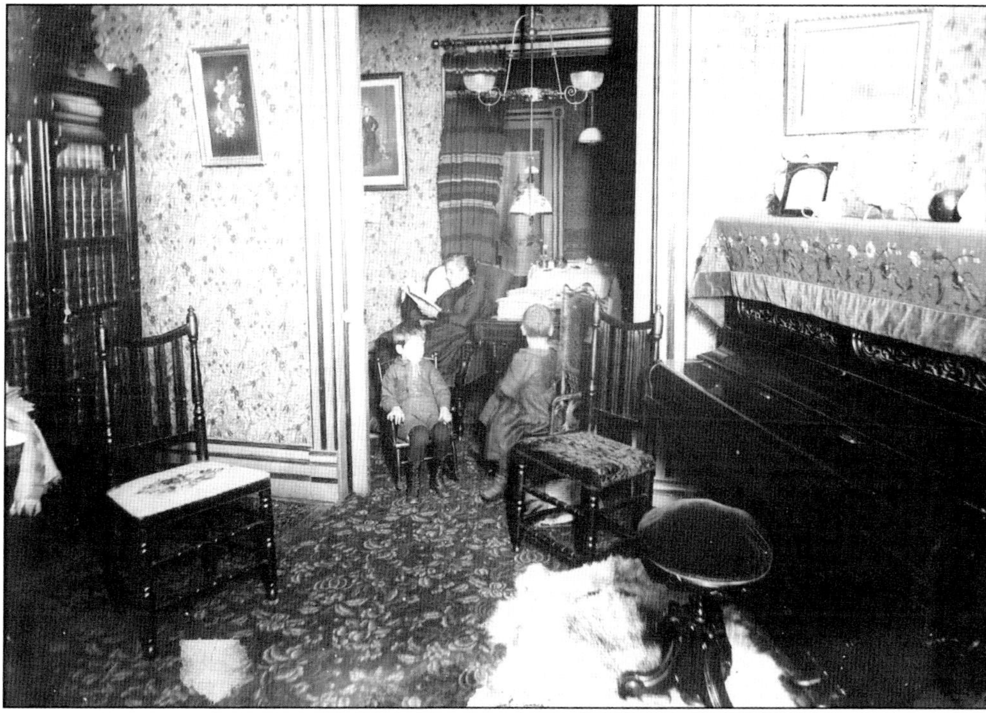

Here is a photograph taken with explosive powder flash in 1899. It shows the interior of the William C. Vrooman library at 9 Washington Avenue.

This is a view looking south on Washington Avenue from the intersection of Front Street on the left. This photograph was taken before 1886 since no trolley lines are visible in the cobblestone street.

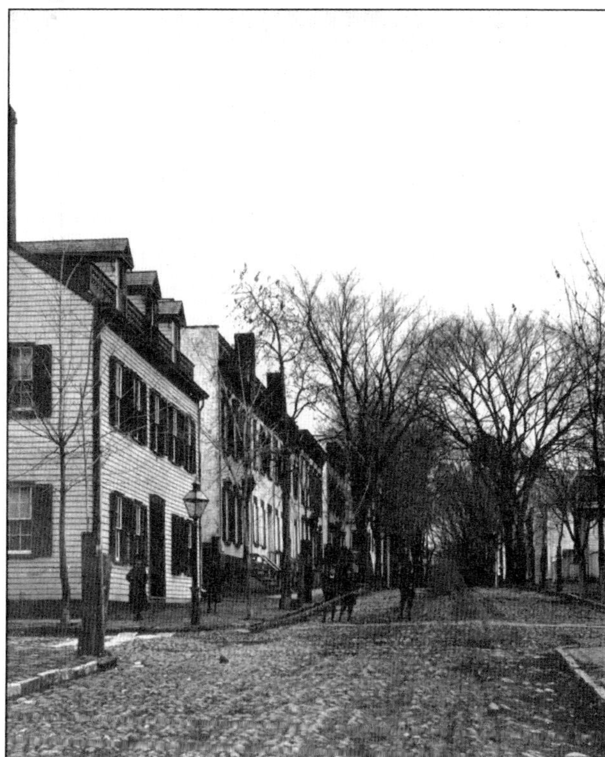

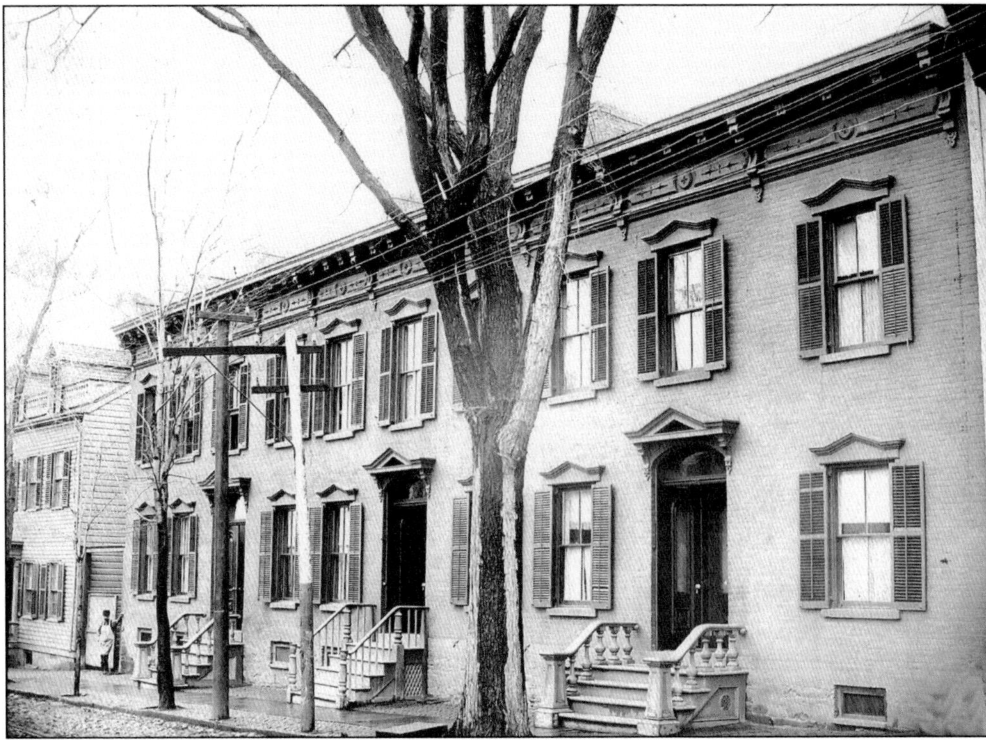

Here is a set of row houses along Washington Avenue. After the great fire of 1819, this part of the stockade was rebuilt with homes rather than businesses.

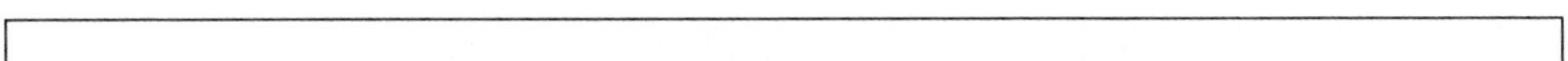

Here is a winter view of Washington Avenue from the rooftop of a home in 1891.

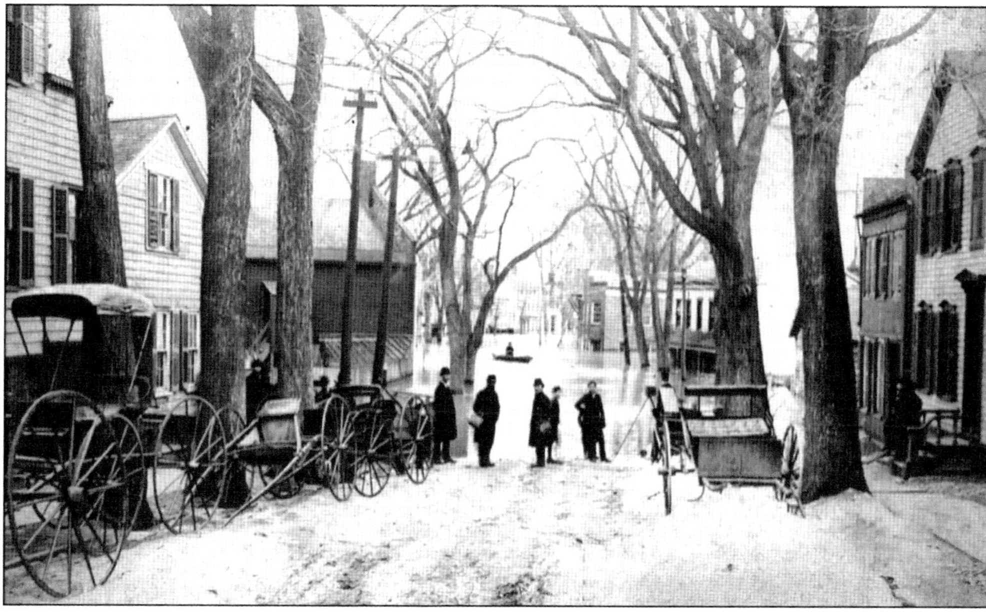

Floods have been a problem in the stockade since the earliest times. It seems almost every year or so, a flood makes it way almost up to about Front Street. One of the earliest records of a flood here was on February 24, 1792, when the floodwaters took away the wharf and bateau house of John Visger Jr. This flood scene is from the 19th century. This photograph shows Washington Avenue looking towards State Street from the Union Street intersection.

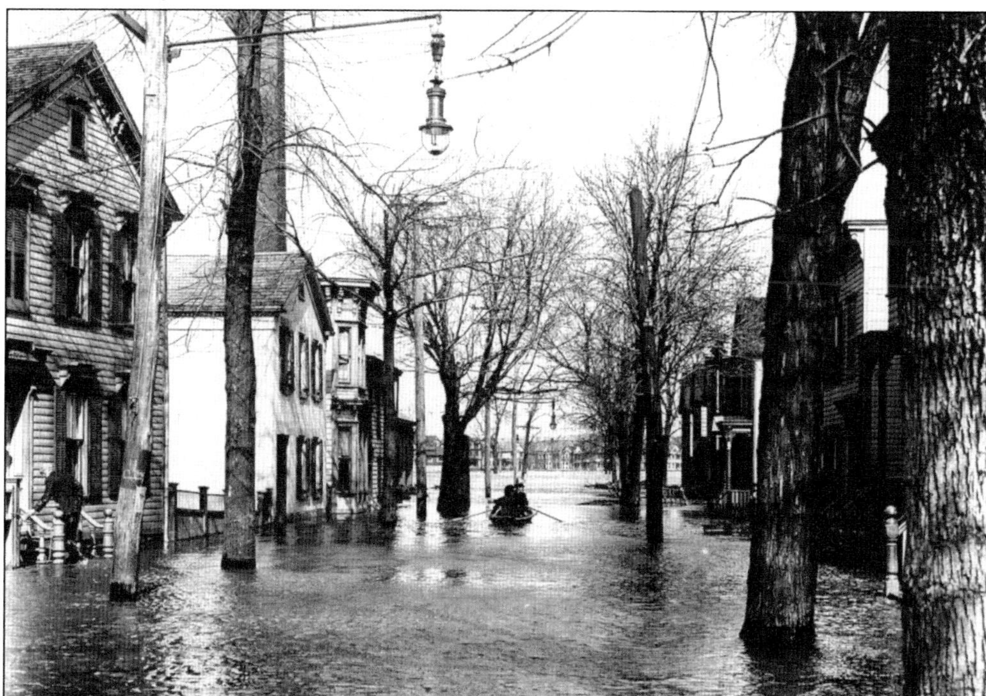

Here is another flood scene looking west down Washington Avenue into the Mohawk River, also in the 19th century. Notice people in a canoe trying to get to their home.

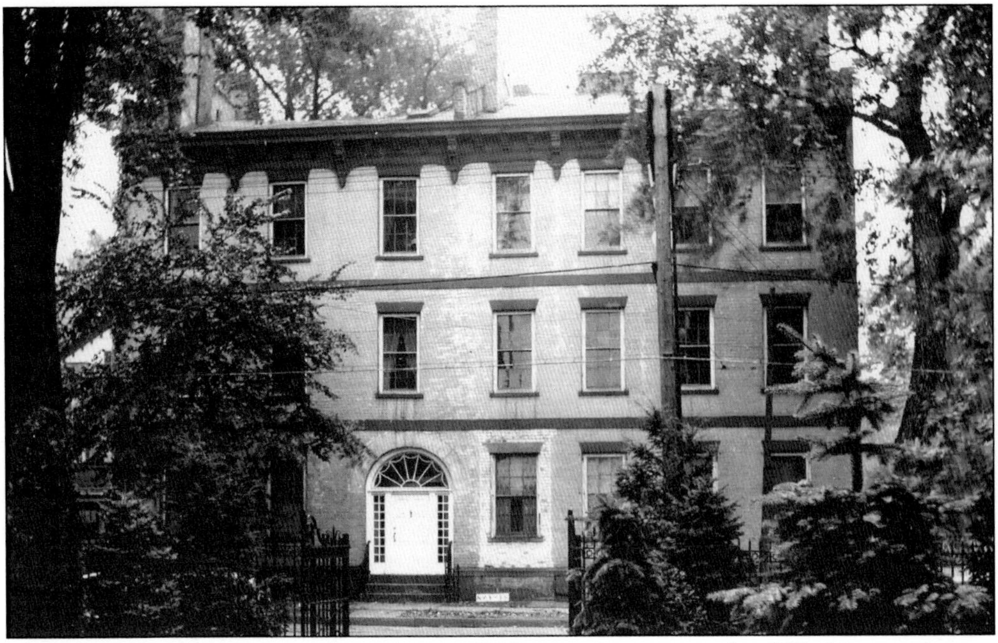

The Robert Sanders mansion, shown here in 1937, is on the eastern side of Washington Avenue between Union and State Streets and built in 1750. Robert Sanders was the son of Thomas Sanders who settled in Albany and became a trader. He attained considerable prominence as a man of wealth and through his dealings with the Native Americans. He was a great landowner before his death. In 1667, he was a silversmith like his father and probably did his apprenticeship under him. In 1692, he is listed as a merchant. George Washington had tea here at his house in 1775. His home later became a school for girls, and over the years, the students carved their initials in various places on the building.

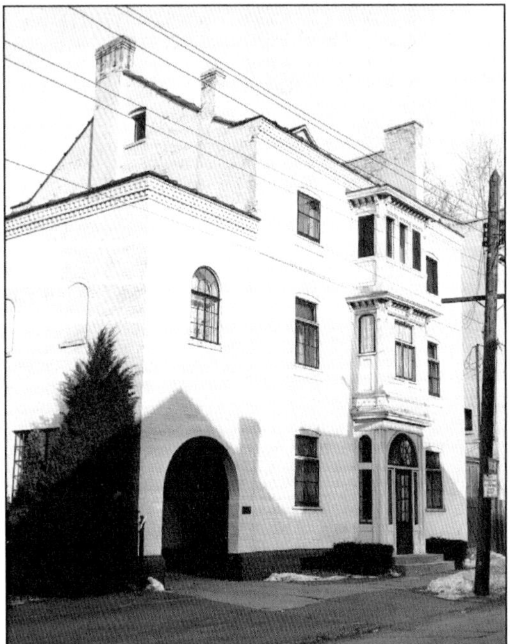

The John Glen house, at 58 Washington Avenue, was built in 1740 and is across from the Sanders mansion. George Washington stayed in the northeast bedroom on the second floor on his first visit to Schenectady in 1775. Glen was a quartermaster during the French and Indian and Revolutionary Wars. Both he and his father were friends of Washington.

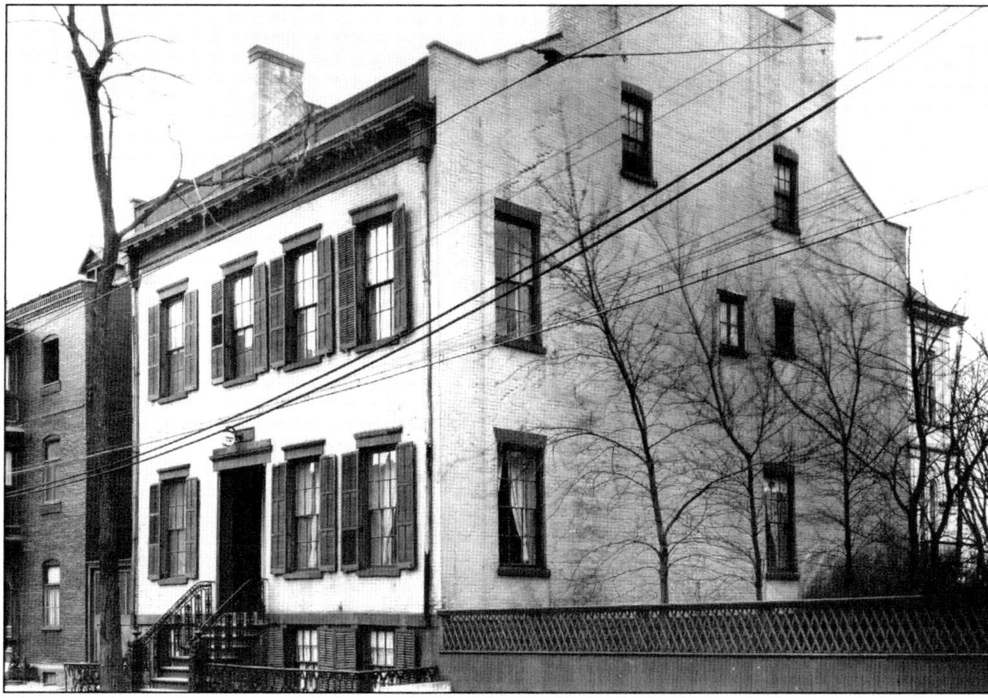

This historic building at 56 Washington Avenue was better known as the General Electric (GE) Women's Club. They later purchased the building at 32 Washington Avenue and then donated it to the Schenectady County Historical Society in 1959. The society still owns 32 Washington Avenue.

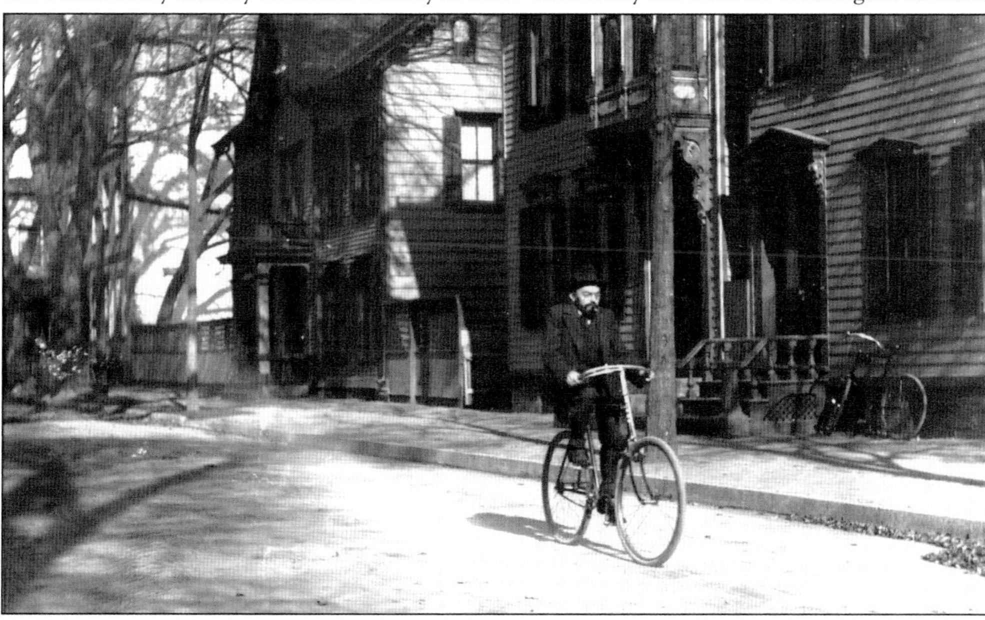

World-famous scientist Charles Steinmetz is seen here riding his bicycle near his home at 56 Washington Avenue. Steinmetz came to Schenectady to work for Thomas Edison and GE in 1893. When he died in 1923, he had already begun making some of the first electric cars with his Steinmetz Electric Car Company. He was an avid photographer and took many early pictures of Schenectady.

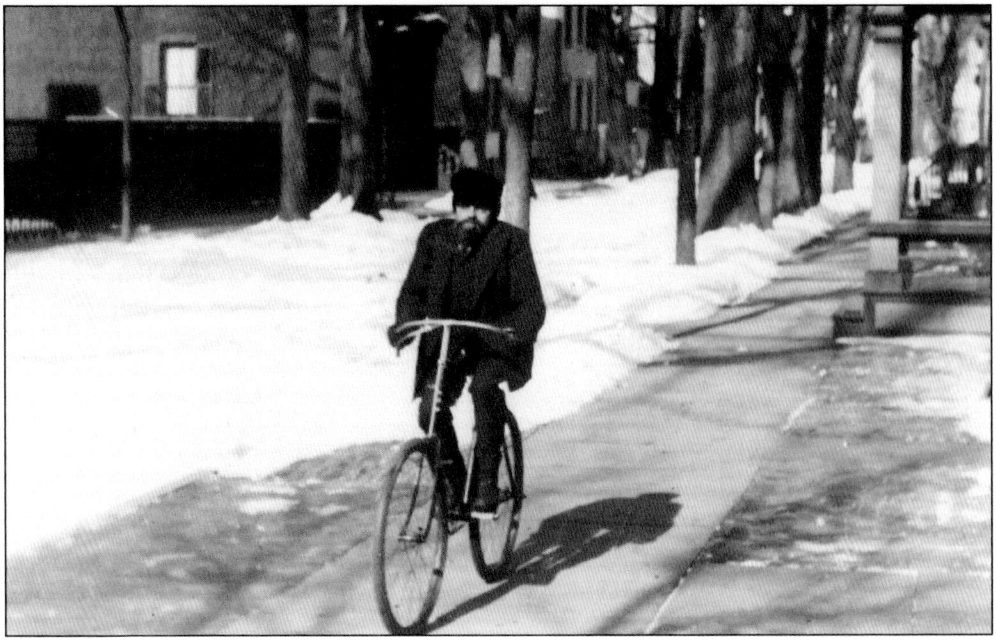

Steinmetz was a giant of a pioneer in the field of electrical engineering, who invented a commercially successful AC motor. He invented artificial lightning after watching the results of a lightning strike at his camp in Scotia. He was only four feet tall in real life. He became the president of the city council and the board of education. He was instrumental in making sure every child in school had a desk, and he helped make the city parks. This photograph was taken around 1894.

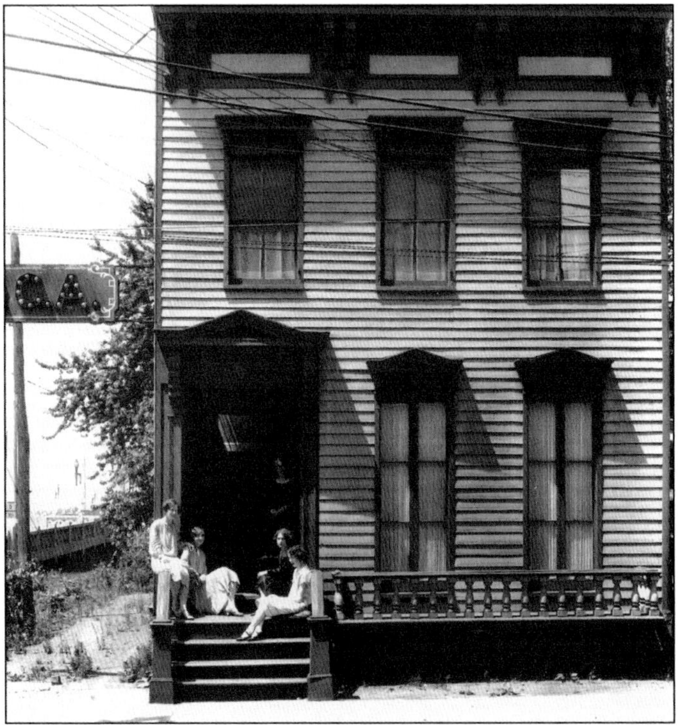

The YWCA was organized here in 1888. The YWCA purchased property on Washington Avenue in 1926, and this building, shown here in 1928, was located at the corner of Washington Avenue and State Street. The present Colonial-style building at 44 Washington Avenue opened in 1931.

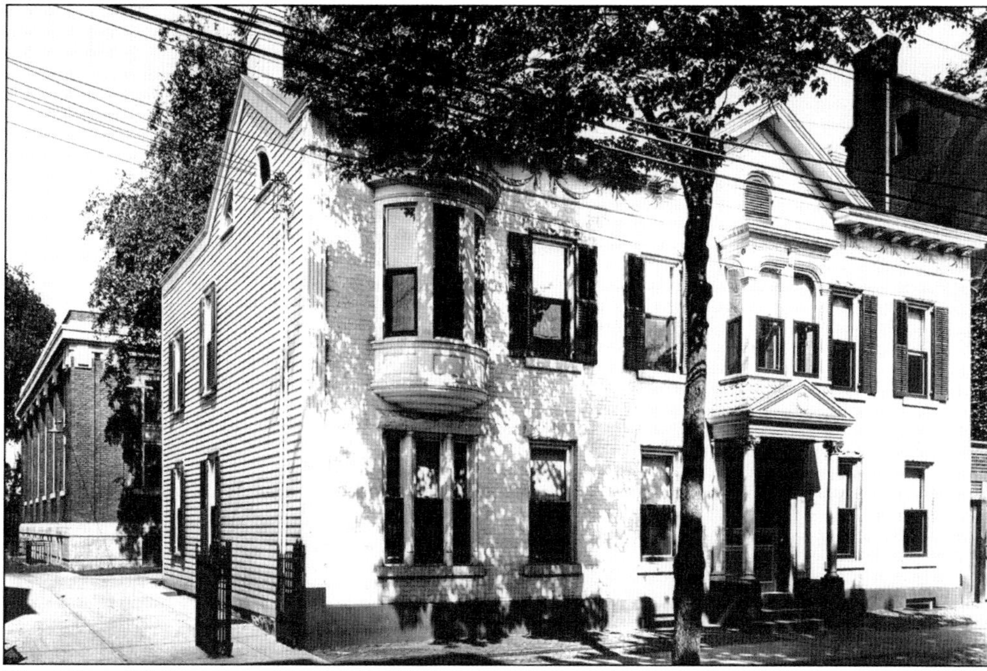

The Edison Club, as seen here at 60 Washington Avenue but now demolished, was founded by GE workers in 1903. They moved here in 1907 using the frame building as a lounge and library and built a brick structure in the back used for bowling and a gym for workouts. GE took over the club in 1925 and moved it to Rexford. The frame building came down, and the brick building became the first television station in the world.

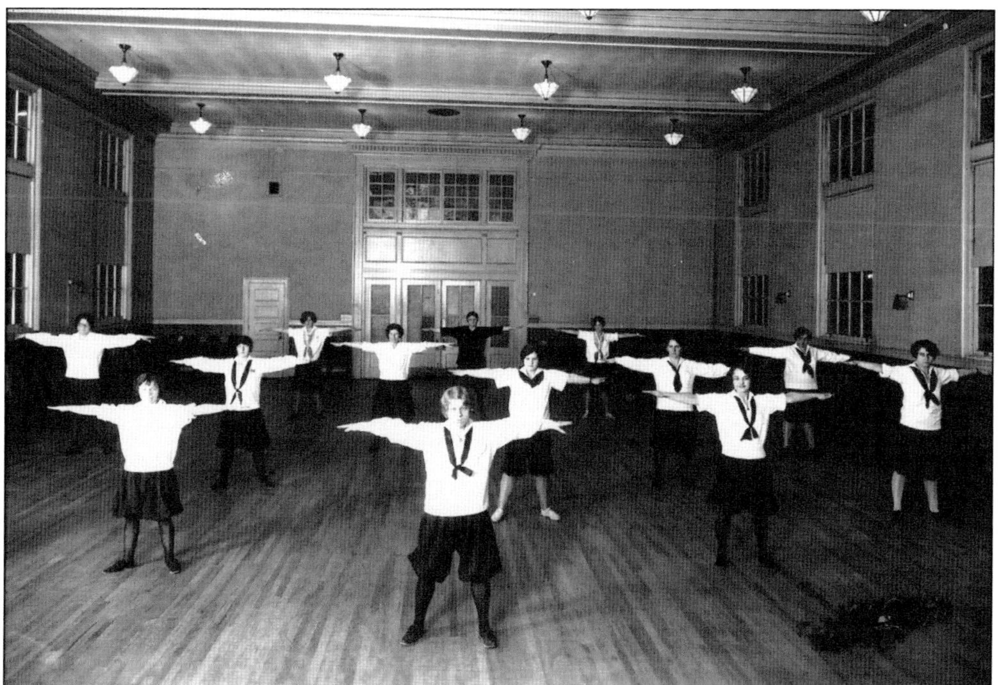

Here one can see girls from the YWCA using the GE Edison Club gym for a workout in 1928.

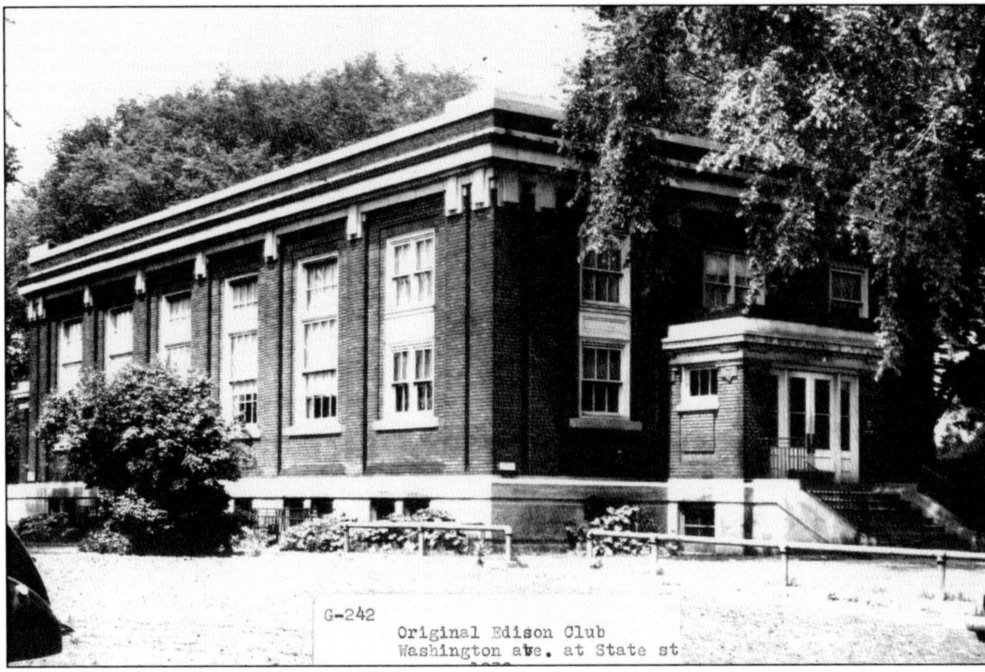

The Edison Club was converted on May 11, 1928, to the first television station in the world. WRGB, channel 6, occupied this building on December 19, 1941, and it was heralded as the most modern television production facility in the country and the first building created solely for the purpose of television. WRGB continues to broadcast in nearby Niskayuna, making it the oldest television station in the world. This building is now the Center for Science and Technology and belongs to the Schenectady County Community College.

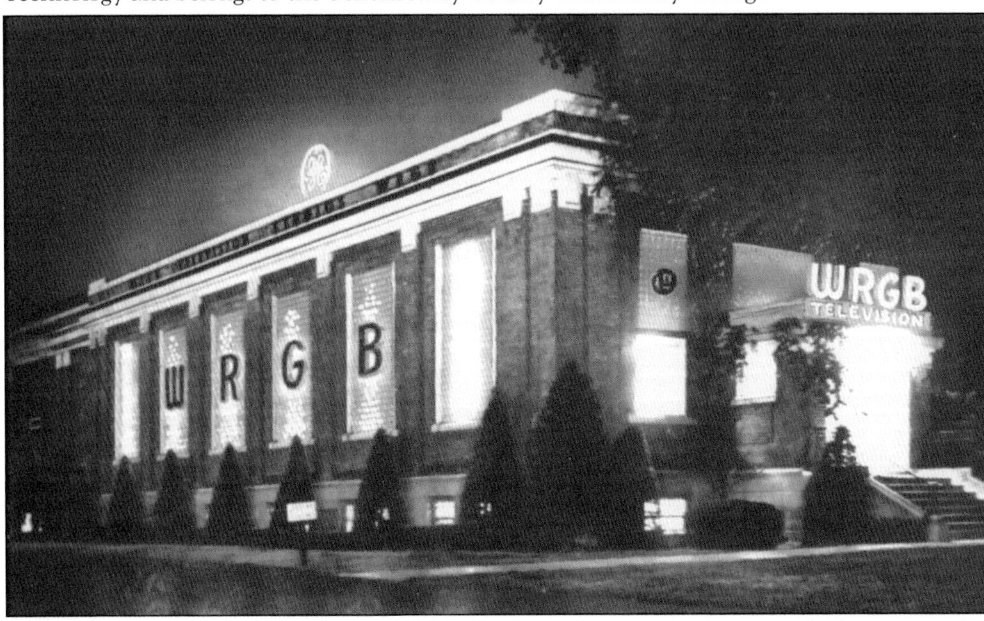

Here is a photograph from when WRGB was in its glory, during the 1950s and 1960s. Today, while still located in Schenectady County, it calls itself CBS6 and does not even mention its Schenectady roots.

The Freeman House was located where the Western Gateway Bridge begins and was torn down to make way for the bridge in the 1920s. There were many hotels like this one throughout the city that catered to a very fluid population. This photograph dates to 1886.

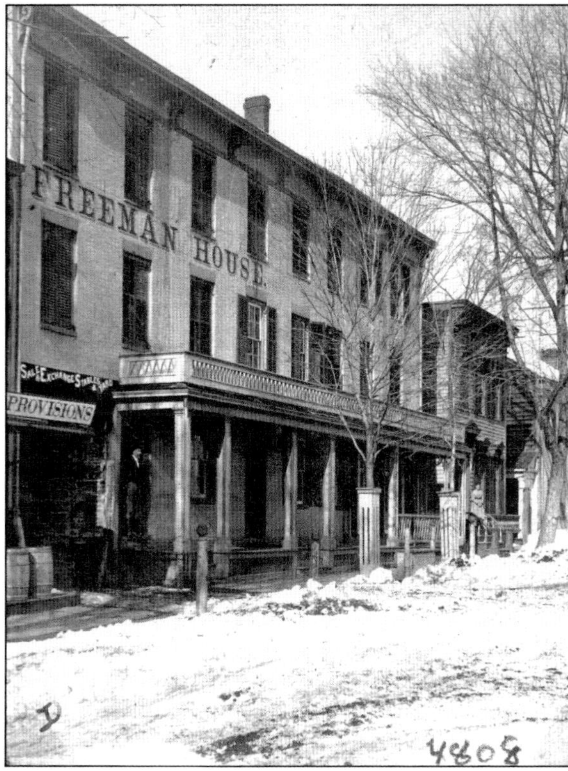

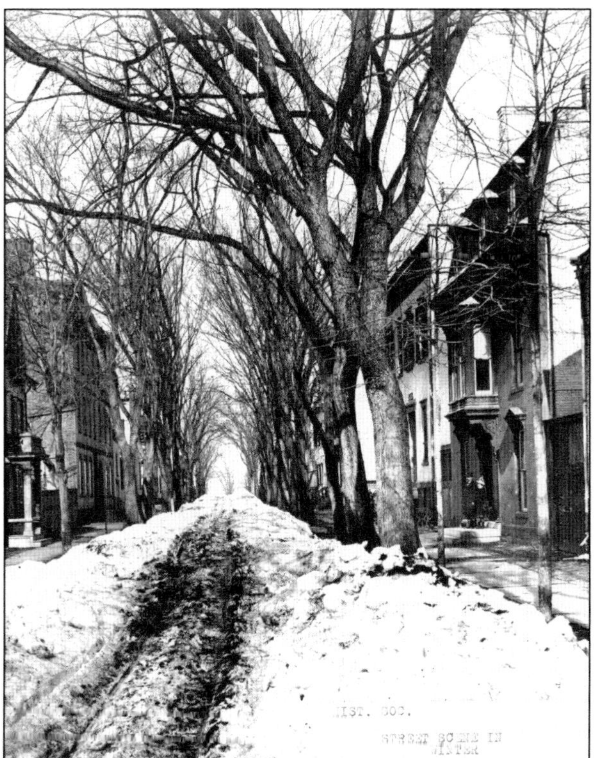

Here is a great view from the blizzard of 1888 of Washington Avenue from State Street looking towards the river. The snow did not stop the trolley from its destination, as seen by the pushed snow along the rails. The Robert Sanders house can be seen on the right.

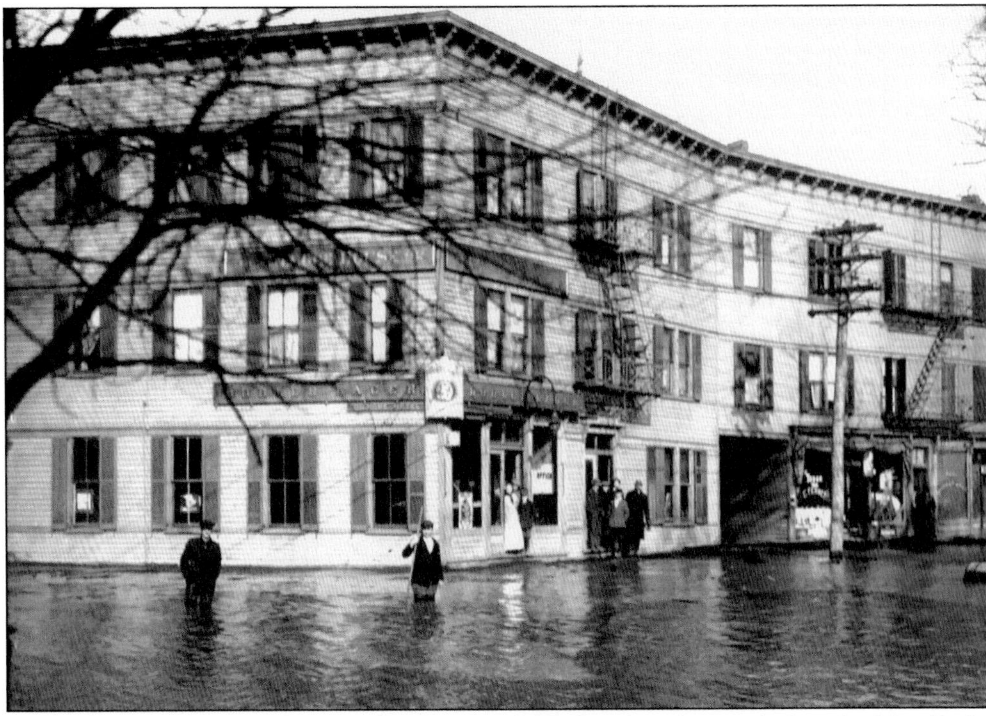

This is the southwest corner of State Street and Washington Avenue before the Van Curler Hotel was built. Notice it was a time of flooding (probably the flood of 1913).

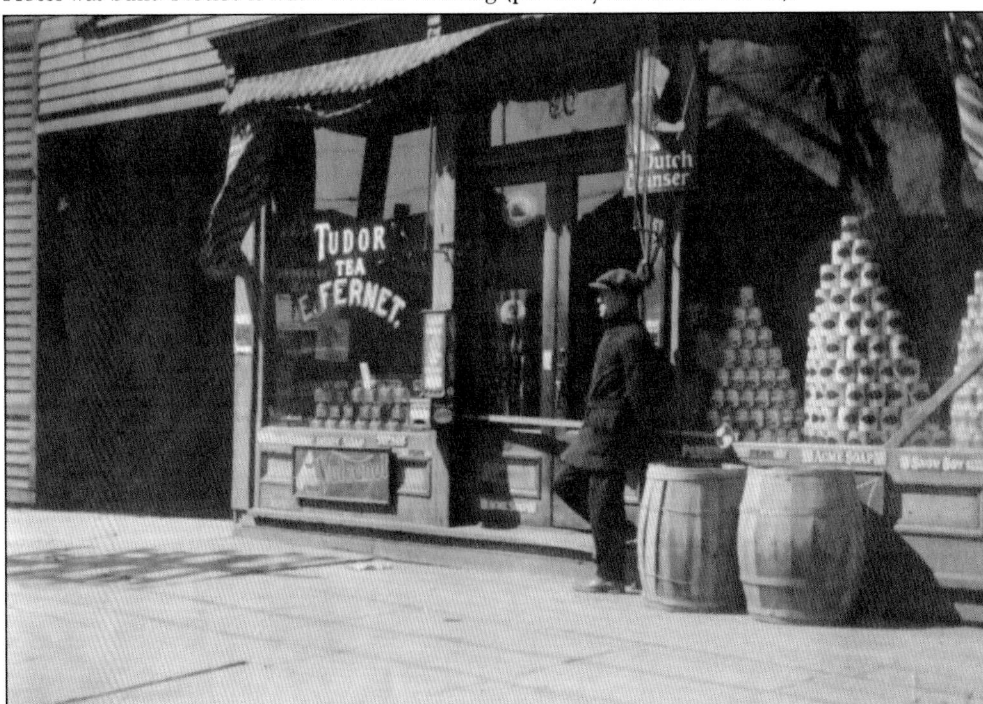

This small mom-and-pop store was located where the Van Curler Hotel was built in 1925. This photograph shows the aftermath of the 1913 flood.

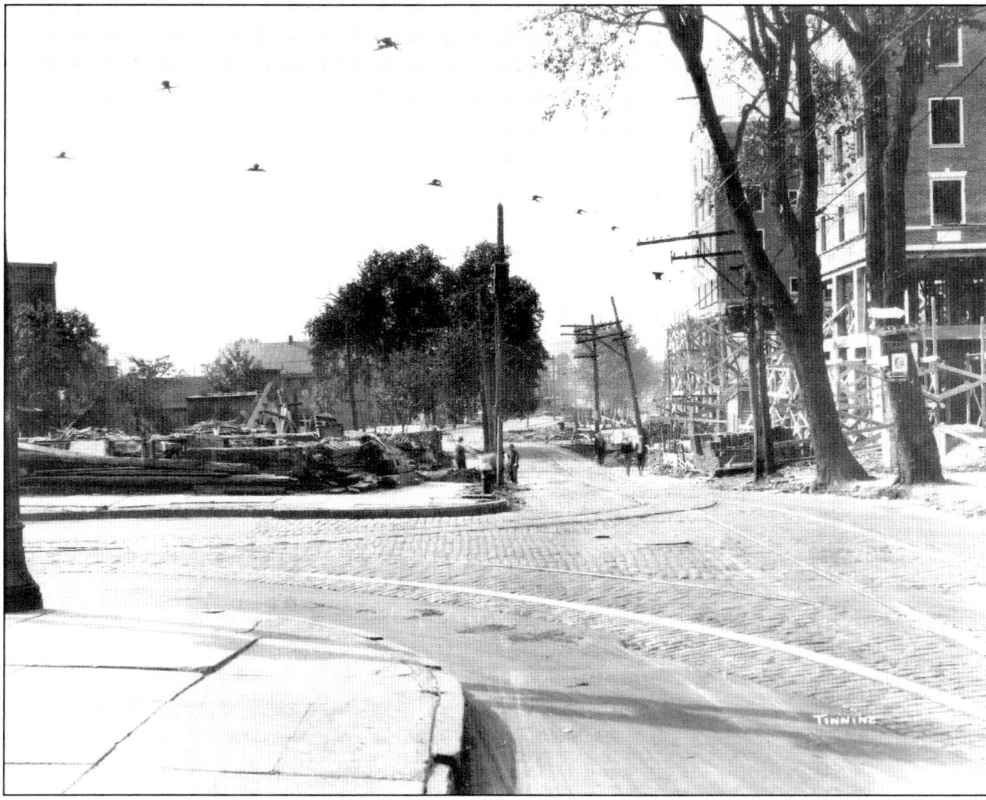

Here is a photograph taken in 1924 when the new Van Curler Hotel was being built. Many of the buildings on the south side of State Street were torn down, and this little park was built in its place.

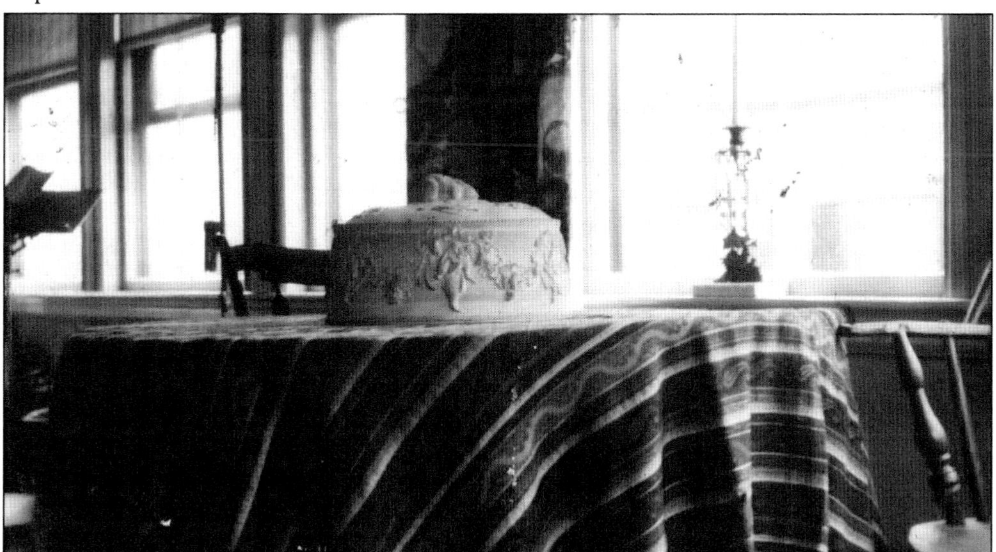

Clench's Hotel was at the southeast corner of State Street and Washington Avenue, and George Washington visited the tavern on a trip to Schenectady. In his 1792 visit, Washington reportedly used this Wedgwood dish while he was here.

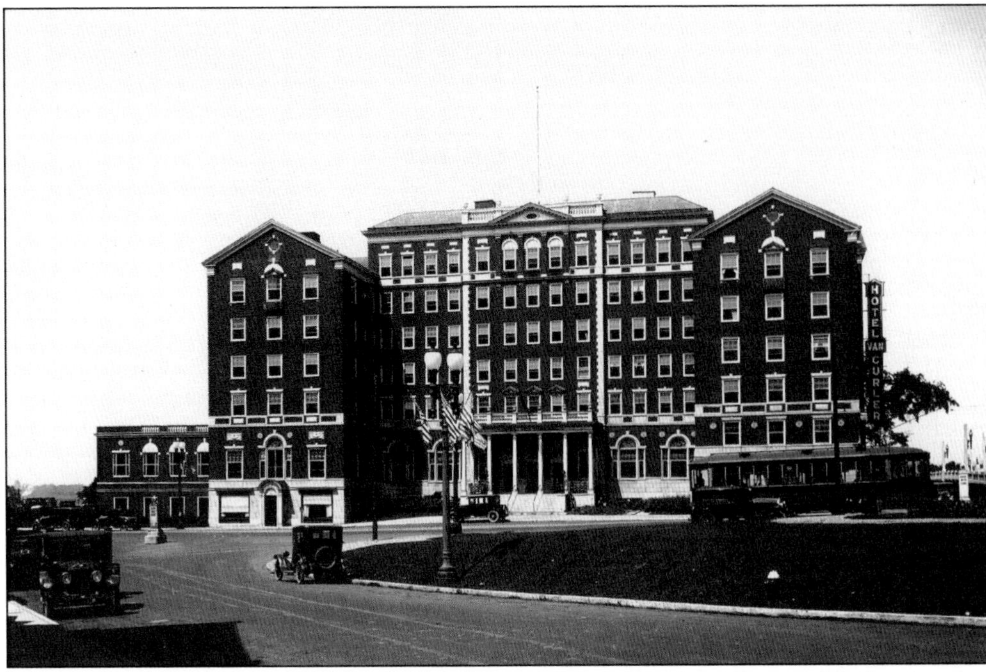

The Van Curler Hotel was built in 1925 and was a popular place for visitors and for local events. It had its own orchestra, a huge ballroom, and solarium, and while most of the local hotels closed and were demolished, the Van Curler Hotel was rescued form the wrecking ball by the county by purchasing it in 1968 and turning into the Schenectady County Community College, one of the finest community colleges in the country.

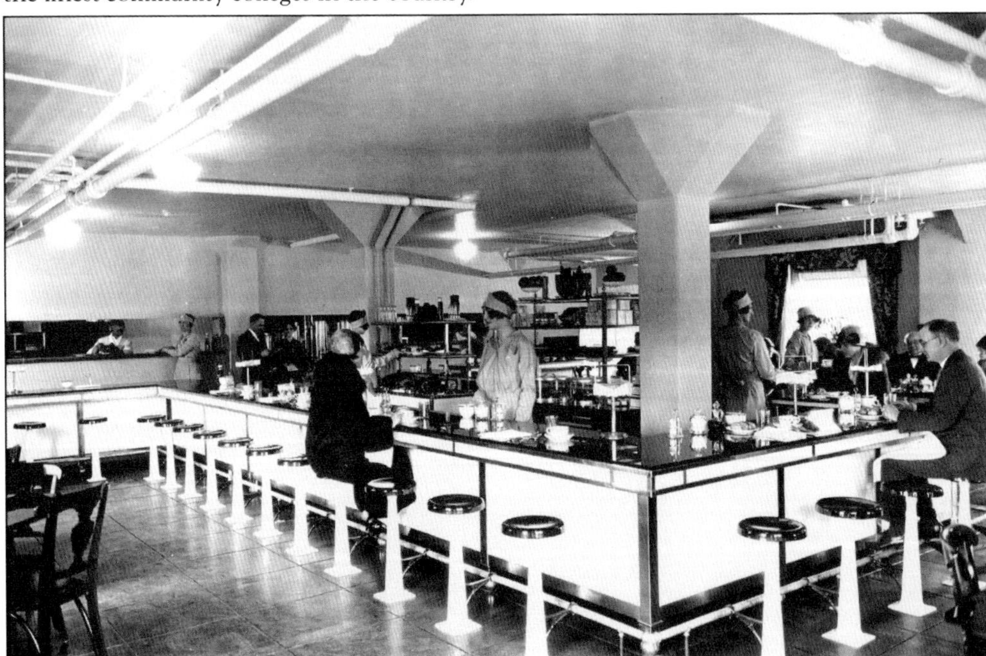

Here is a rare photograph of the Van Curler Hotel café located on the first floor. Many a story can be told here.

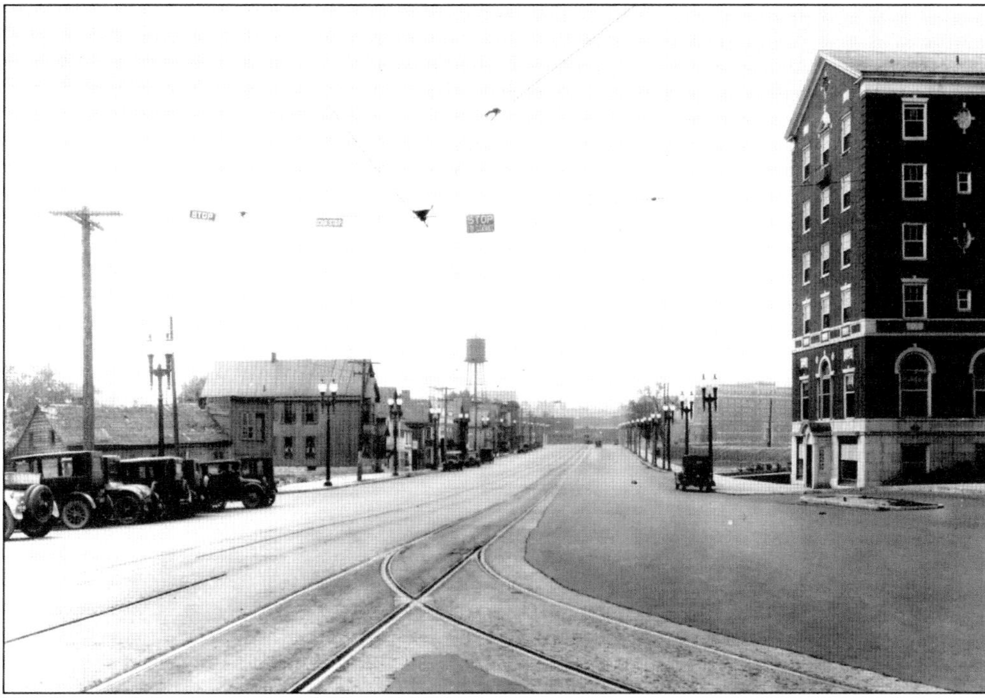

When the Van Curler Hotel was being built, Washington Avenue south of State Street was widened as well. Here one can see the trolleys that went to GE at the end of the street in this photograph that was taken on June 29, 1926.

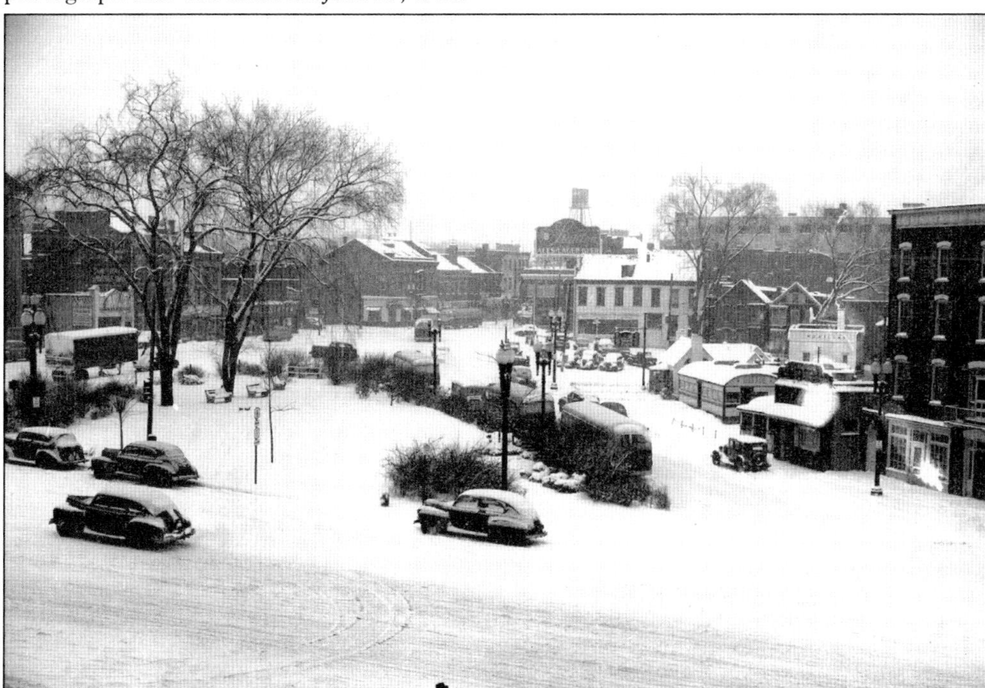

This winter view of lower State Street in 1946 from the Van Curler Hotel shows the park and diners that once made up the area.

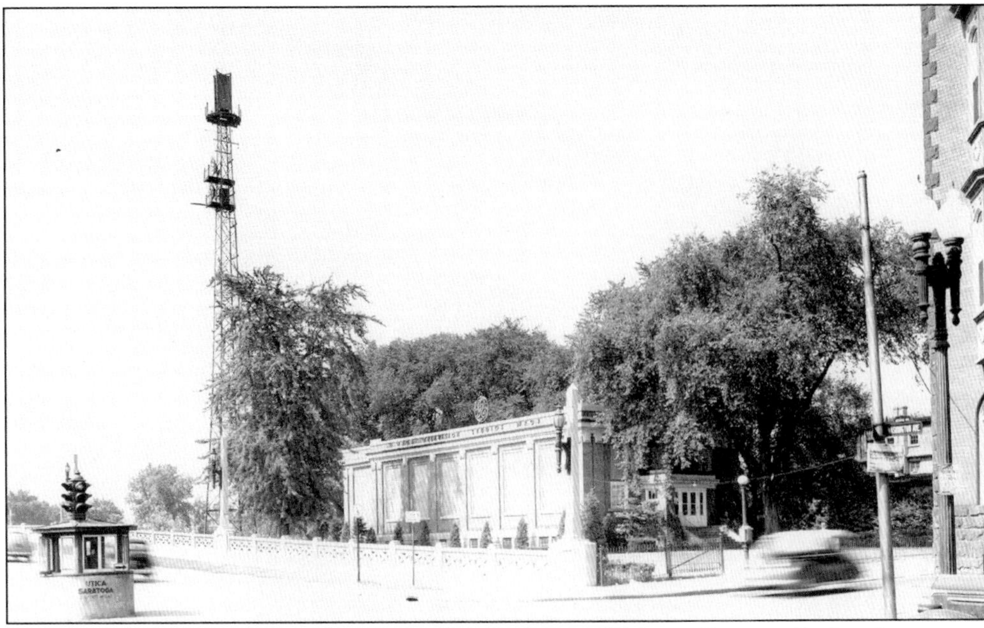

The Freeman house was torn down to make way for the Western Gateway Bridge that opened in 1925, the same year as the nearby Van Curler Hotel. It took three years to build the bridge. There were many problems building the bridge, including flash floods that wrecked equipment, and many accidents including deaths that delayed the work. Four men were killed on September 17, 1923, when 450 tons of concrete dropped. Channel 6 WRGB is on the right.

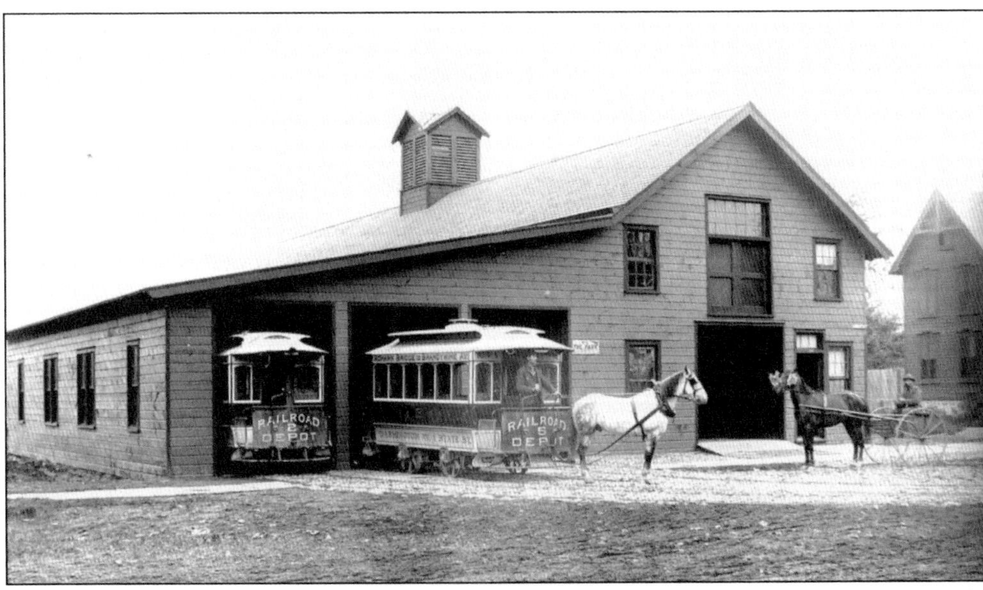

This trolley barn was located on Brandywine Avenue but housed the trolleys that went to the Scotia Bridge in the stockade. This was the beginning of the Schenectady Railway Company in 1886. The trolley system had 30 horses, 5 cars, and 4 sleighs. This photograph is from the 1880s.

Four

Front Street

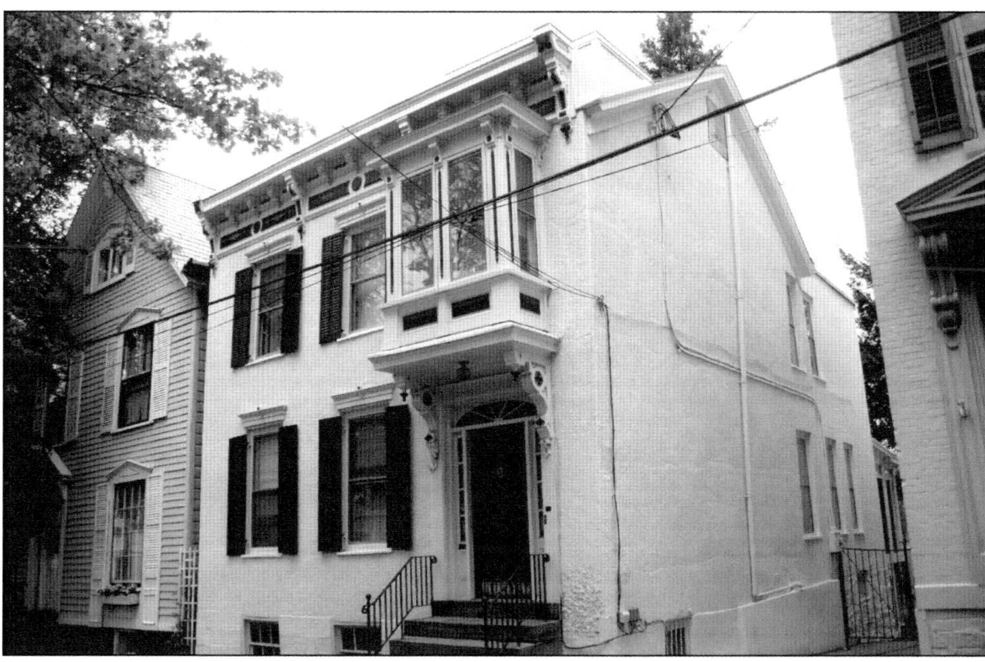

Front Street was the western border of the stockade. Here 9 Front Street looks like a typical late Victorian house. However, it has been revealed by the author through two years of research that it is actually a French and Indian War–era stone blockhouse dated by dendrochronology to 1727. This house was featured on the PBS show *The History Detective* in 2008.

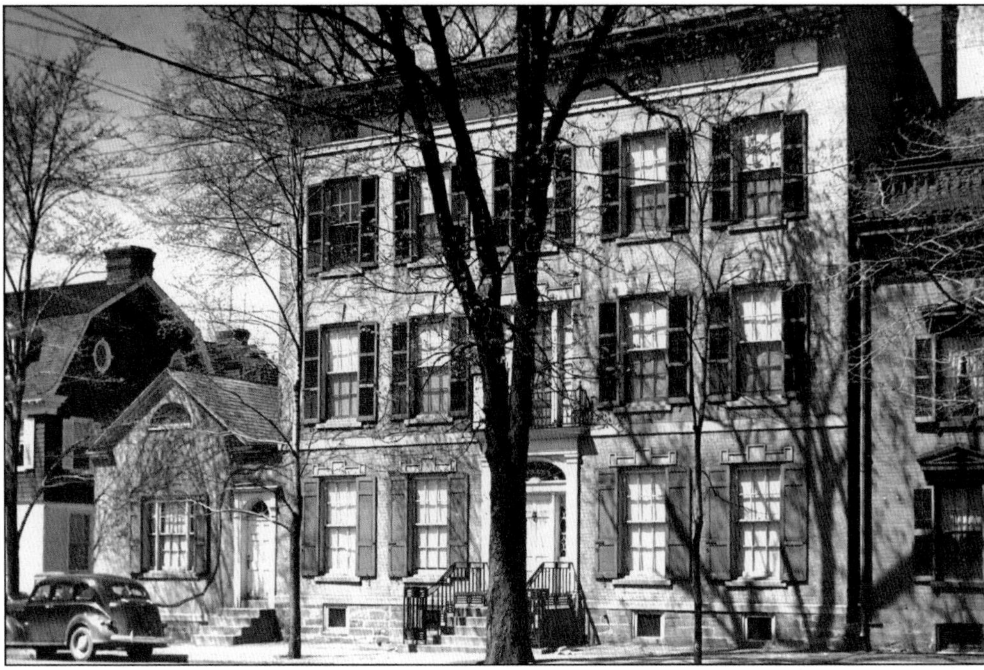

This is the Gov. Joseph Yates house and law office (smaller wing built in 1735) at 17 Front Street. Yates became the first mayor of Schenectady when it was incorporated in 1798. He became a state senator in 1805 and the governor of the state in 1823–1824. He was preceded by DeWitt Clinton and followed by him in the New York State governor's office. The Yates family played many important roles in championing Schenectady during colonial times. His summer mansion in Alplaus is still standing, and the home where he was born still survives as well. On June 11, 1825, Maj. Gen. Marquis de Lafayette stayed here as a guest.

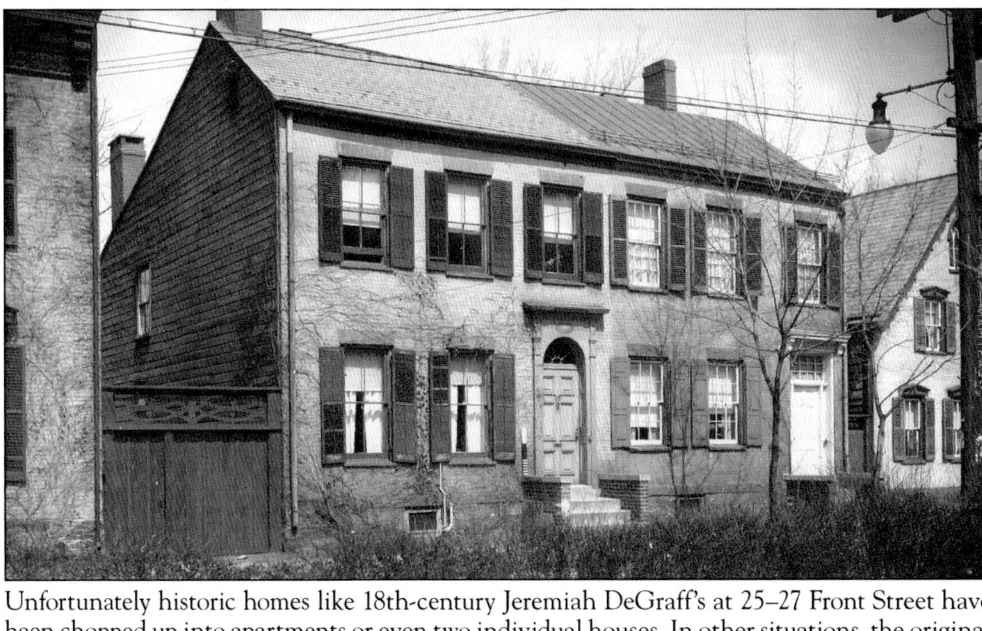

Unfortunately historic homes like 18th-century Jeremiah DeGraff's at 25–27 Front Street have been chopped up into apartments or even two individual houses. In other situations, the original family added on an extension to accommodate additions in the family or a married child.

Otis Smith was a broom maker and lived here at 21 Front Street. Brooms were one of Schenectady's biggest exports in the 18th and 19th centuries. Seen here in 1878 at the intersection of Front and Church Streets, cobblestones and hitching posts are now things of the past.

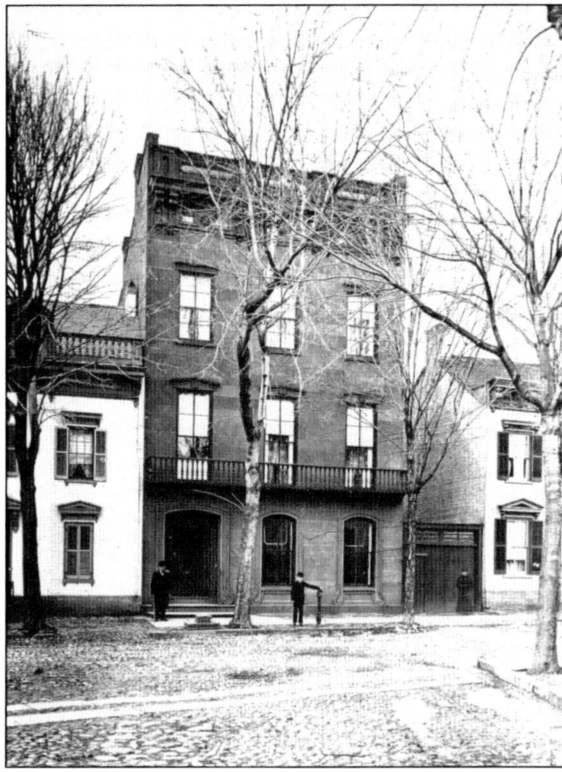

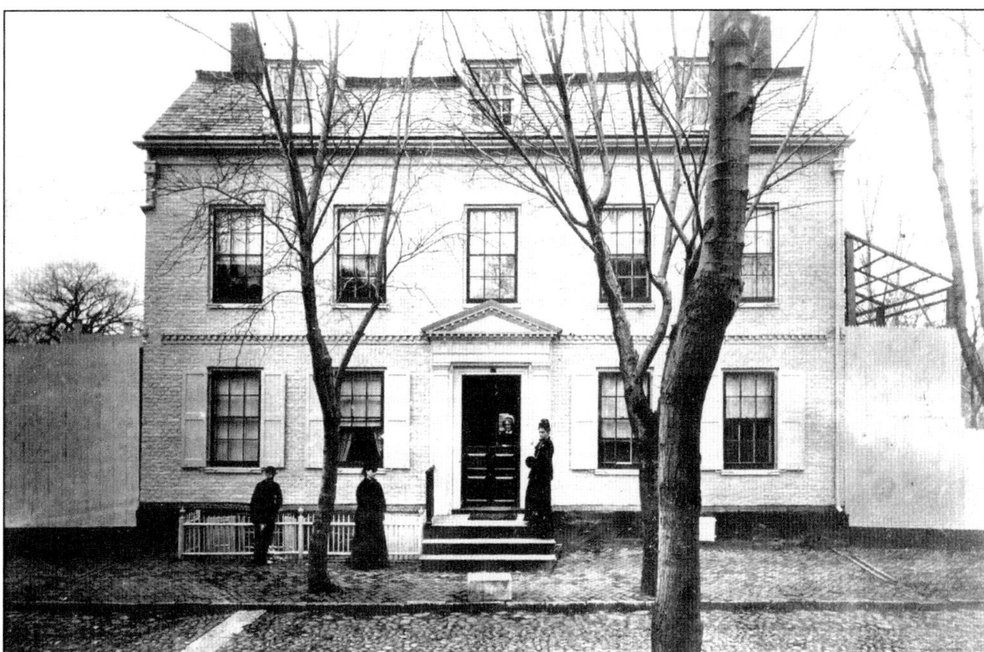

This house at 26 Front Street was the home of Christopher Yates, the father of Joseph Yates, governor of New York State. Joseph was born in this house. His father, Christopher, was a leader of the Sons of Liberty and chairman of the Committee of Safety, 1771–1776.

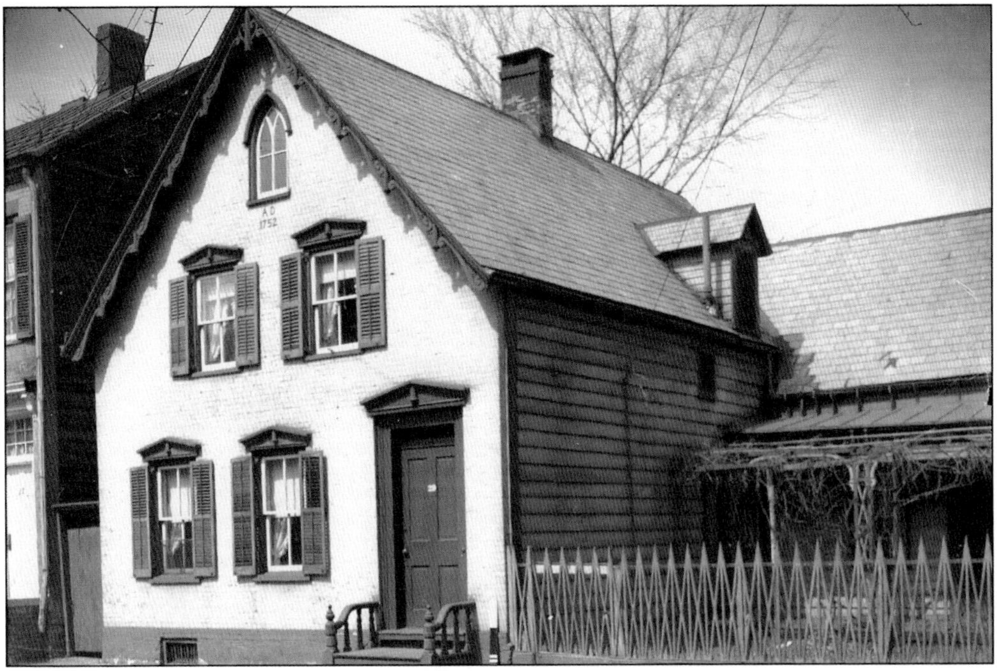

This Dutch house at 29 Front Street was built by Abraham Fonda in 1752 and was constructed of frame and brick-filled walls. During the 19th century, cast iron lintels were added above the windows and a carpenter gothic trim was added to the gables. All have been removed. The words "A.D. 1752," seen just below the attic gothic window in this photograph, were also removed sometime after the 1930s. The Gothic attic window is similar in style as the Dutch Reformed Church in Albany in the 17th century.

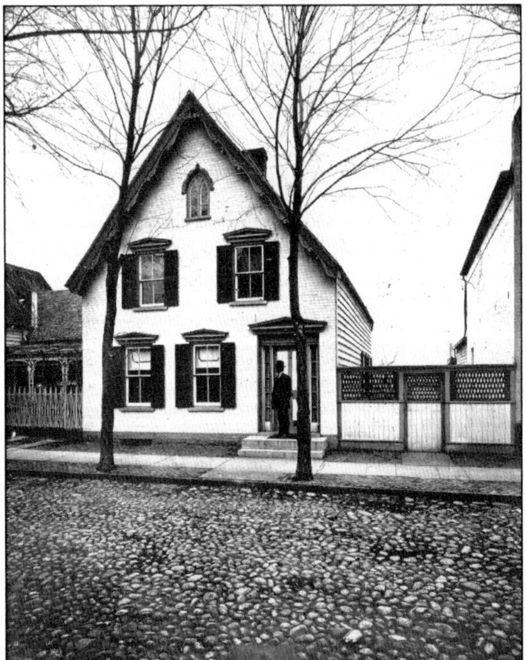

Next to the Fonda House is 31 Front Street where Isaac Vrooman lived since 1759. He was a large landowner and prominent citizen of Schenectady. He made several maps of the area including one for George Washington, who was a member of the general assembly 1759–1761, appointed mayor in 1765, and was a member of the New York State assembly from 1778 to 1782. This house is almost identical to 29 Front Street and had the same iron lintels during the 1930s. The gable trim is still intact, but the words "A.D. 1754," which previously appeared just below the attic window, have been removed. Here David Veeder poses in 1876.

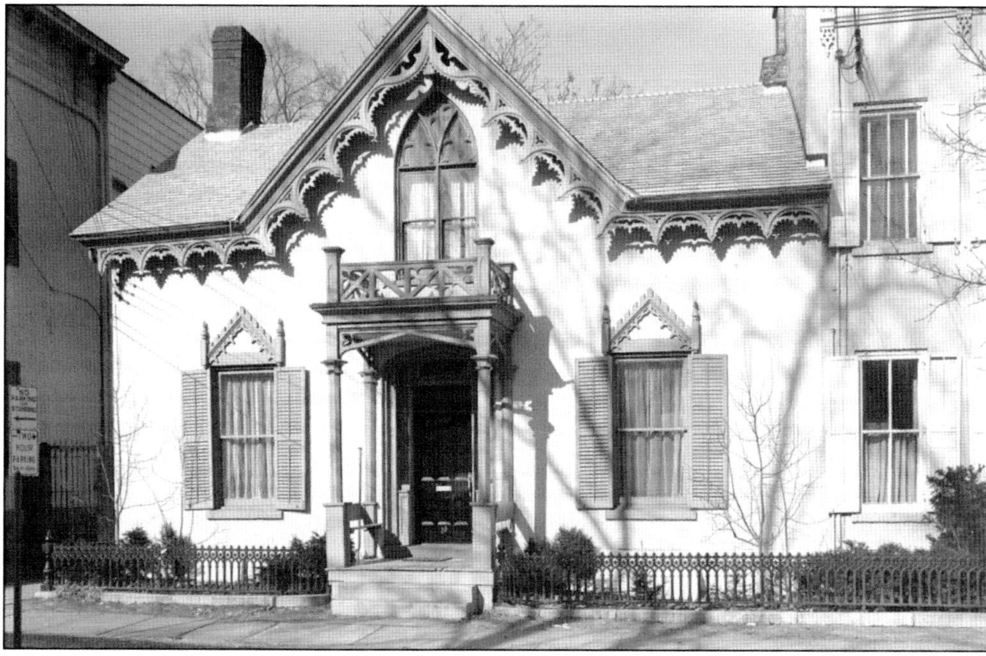

The David P. Forest house at 39 Front Street represents a style that is called Carpenter Gothic, an evolutionary English style popular in the late 19th century and promoted by architects Alexander Jackson Davis and Andrew Jackson Downing. It is well represented in the famous painting, *American Gothic*. This house was built around 1865. Interestingly the Dutch houses at 29 and 31 Front Street had some Carpenter Gothic trim attached to them, probably around the time this house was built.

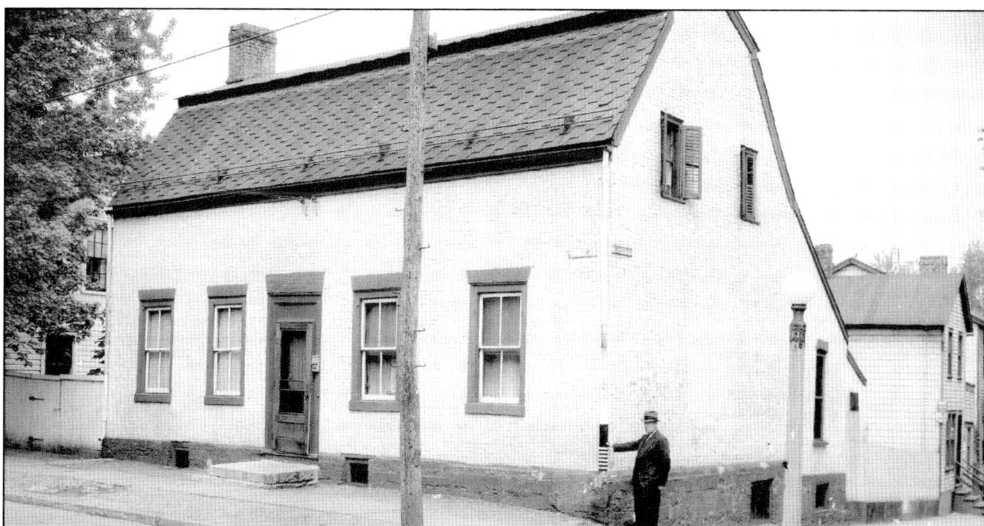

The Johannes Teller house is situated on the corner of Front and North Streets and represents a mid-18th century home. This one-and-a-half-story house has a rectangular floor plan and a gambrel roof. The house was constructed on a stone foundation. The bricks were predominantly laid in Dutch cross bond. It has "water table" bricks above the foundation as a way to prevent water from entering the basement—typical of this time period.

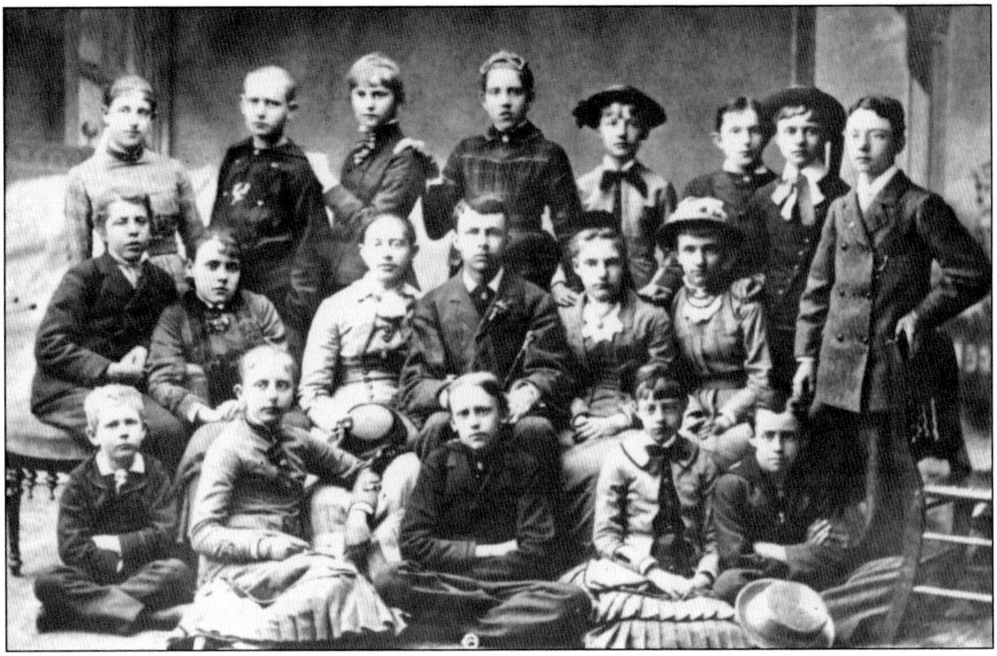

Clyde Fitch, second from left in the third row, poses around 1878–1880 in Alice Wood's private school at 145 Front Street. Fitch went on to write over 36 original plays, including *Beu Brummell* in 1890, and was the first American playwright to have his plays published.

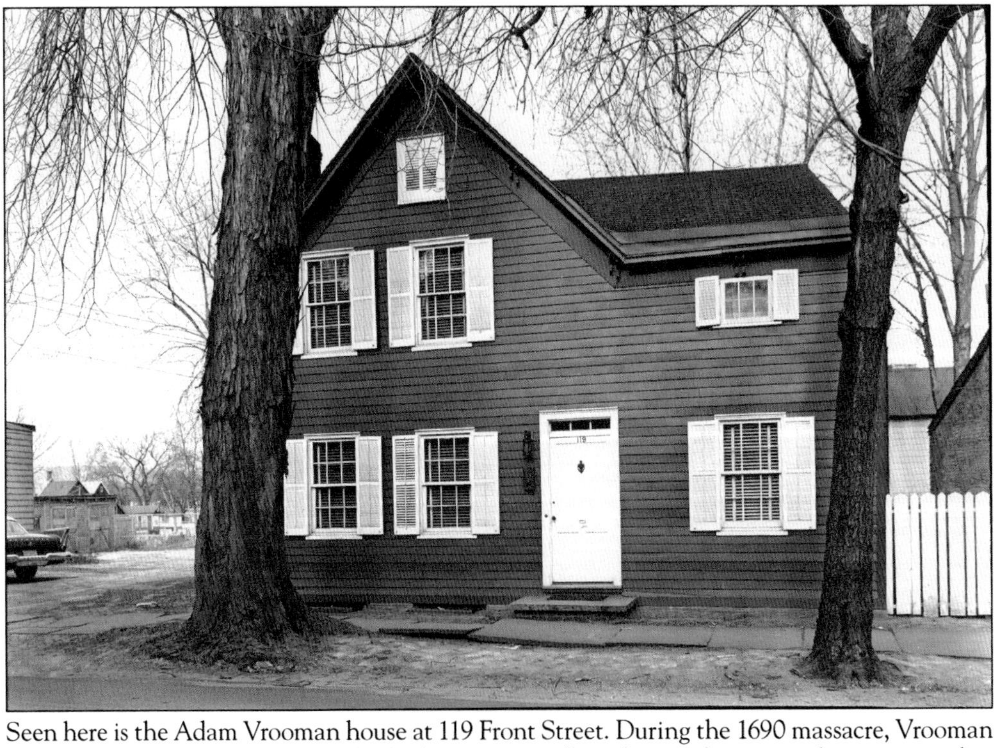

Seen here is the Adam Vrooman house at 119 Front Street. During the 1690 massacre, Vrooman saw his wife killed, his son's head bashed against a wall, and two other sons taken prisoner, but he did not give up and escaped unharmed. He later remarried and moved to this house.

Five

FERRY STREET

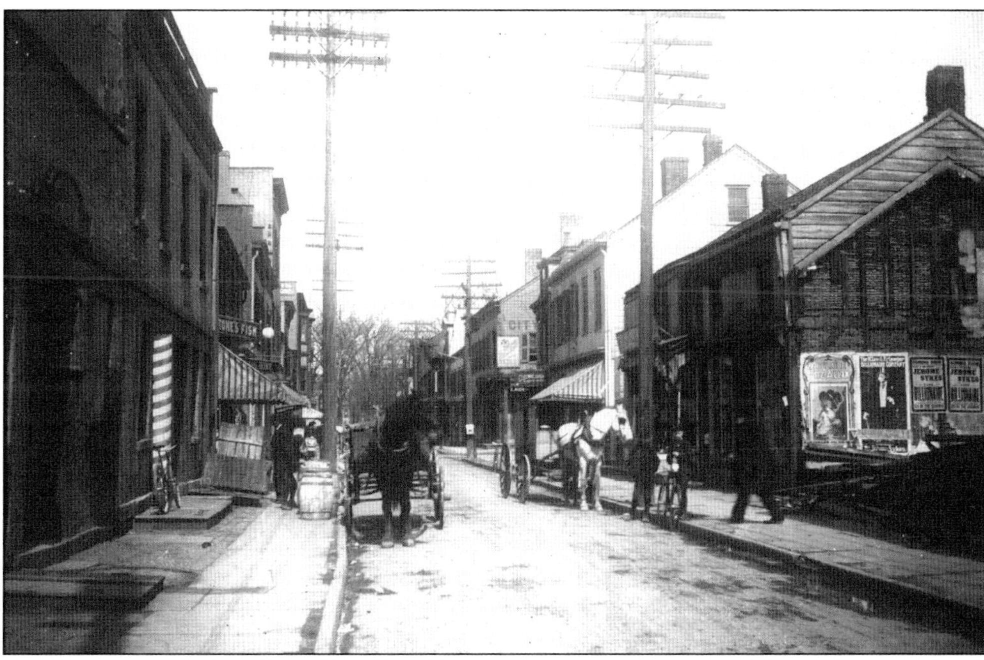

Ferry Street was originally the eastern border of the original stockade and was a *rounwaag* (walkway) for the soldiers to patrol. This view is from State Street looking toward Union Street (City Hotel is on northwest corner of Liberty Street) around 1880. Adelaide Fitz-Allan was playing at the Van Curler Opera House with the Klaw and Erlanger Billionaire Company scheduled for April 14. Notice the barber pole on the left.

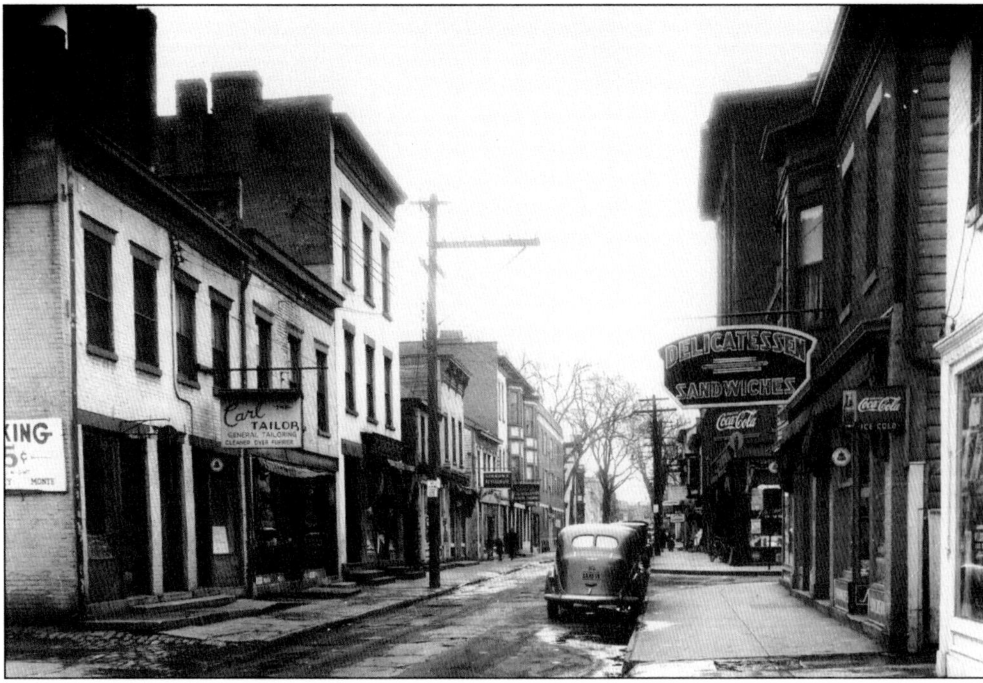

Here is another view of Ferry Street from State Street looking north during the 1940s. Notice that Liberty Street did not continue west as it does today. Many of the earlier wood frame buildings have been replaced by brick structures.

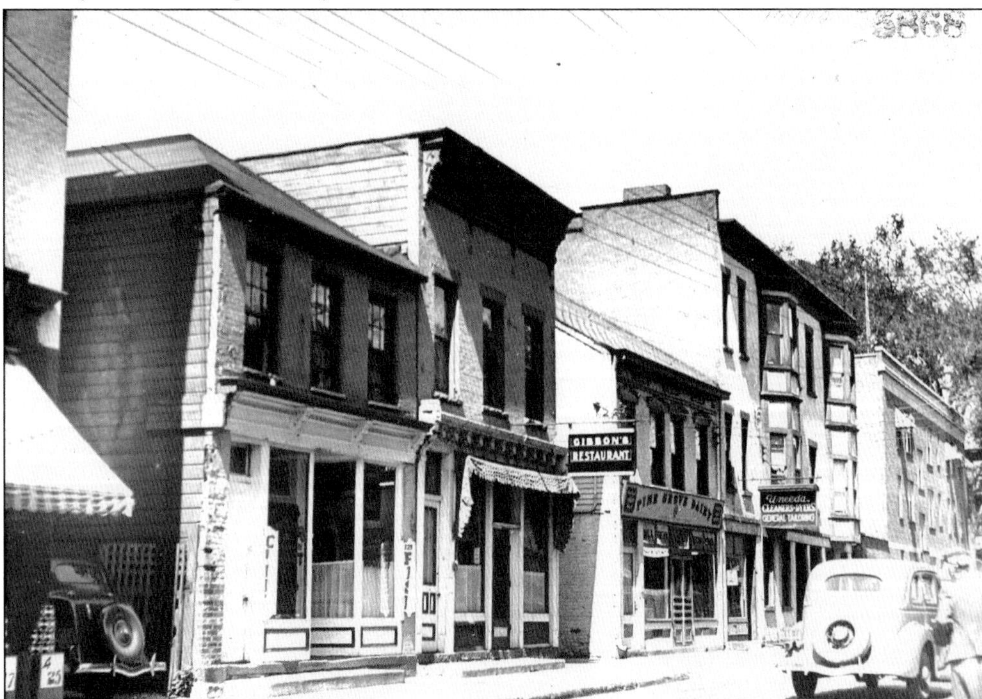

This is a close-up in the 1940s of the west side of Ferry Street (122–128) before Liberty Street was extended. This extension demolished many of these buildings.

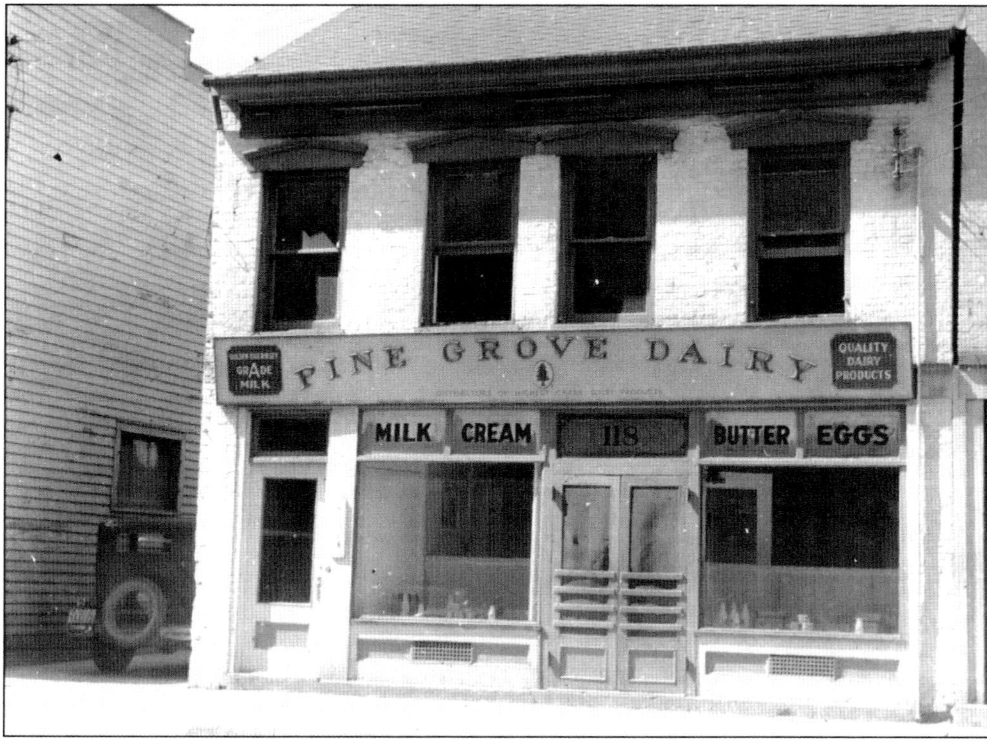

Here is a close-up of the Pine Grove Dairy at 118 Ferry Street before Liberty Street was extended sometime after the 1940s. Everything to the left of it is gone.

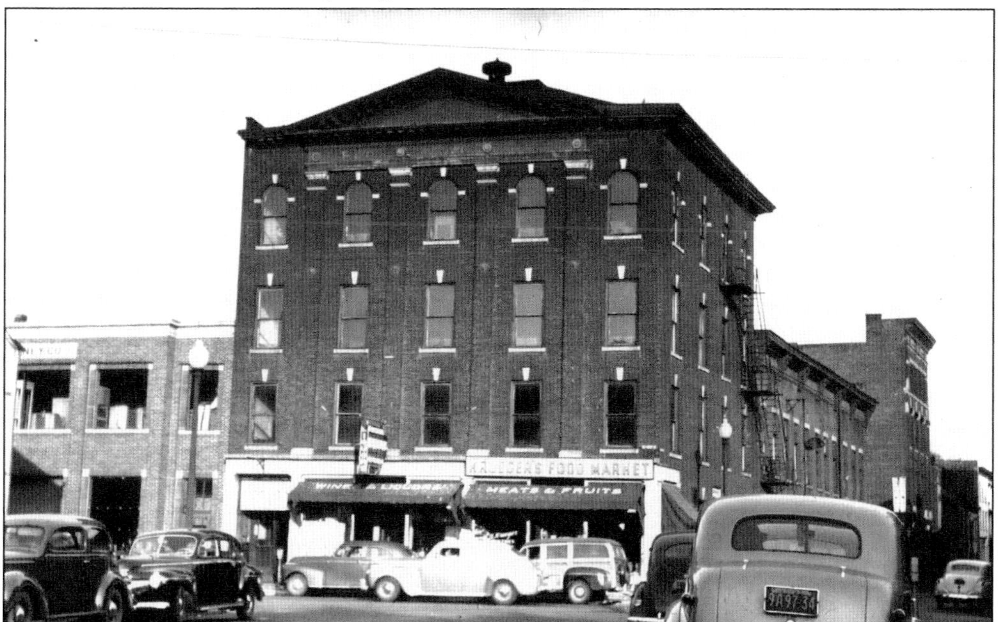

Anthony Hall is on the northeast corner of Ferry and Liberty Streets and has been replaced with apartments. The H. S. Barney warehouse is the tall building behind it on Liberty Street in this 1940s photograph. Notice also Krueger's Market.

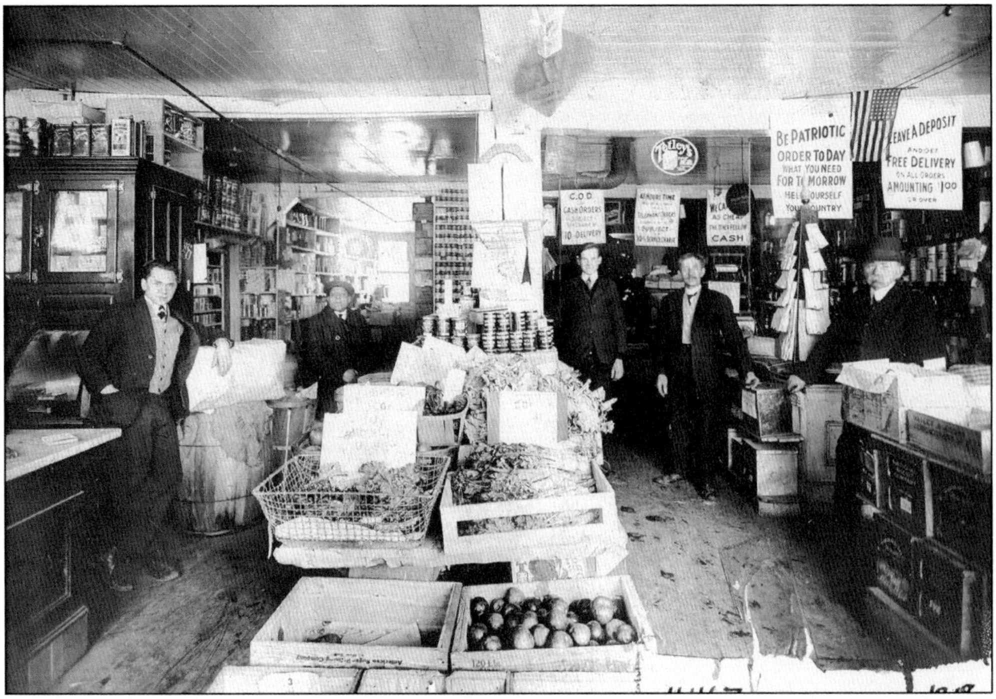

This view is inside Krueger's Market on Ferry Street around 1918. Those were the days when one sold meat wearing a suit and tie. The fellow on the left looks like a young James Cagey.

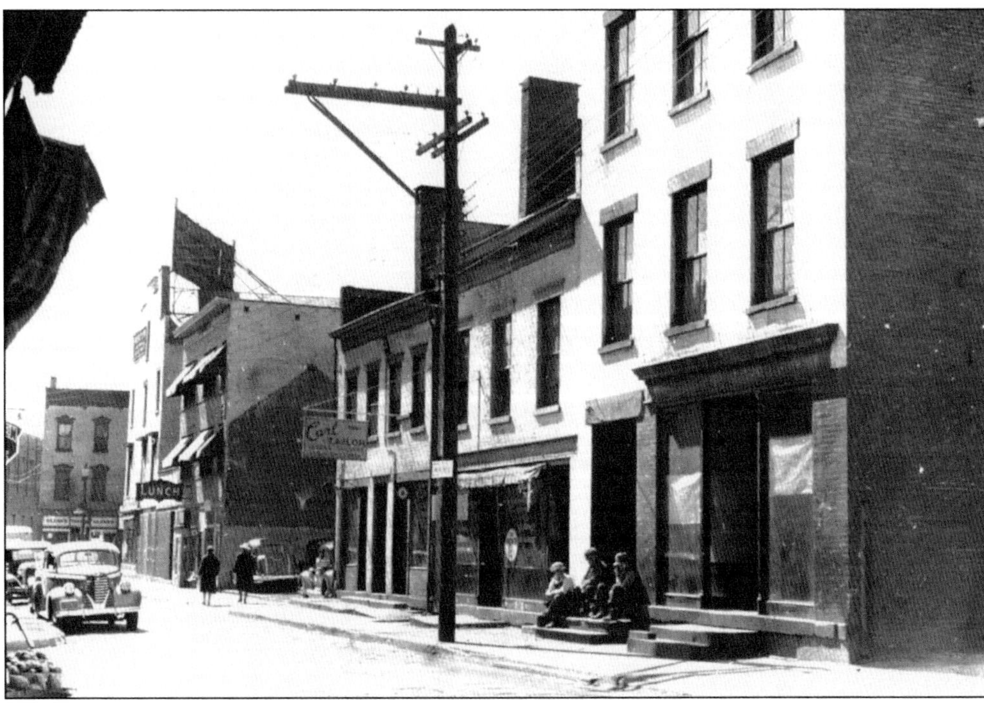

Seen here is a view of 136 South Ferry Street, on the west side of South Ferry Street, looking south towards State Street during the 1940s. All of these buildings are gone.

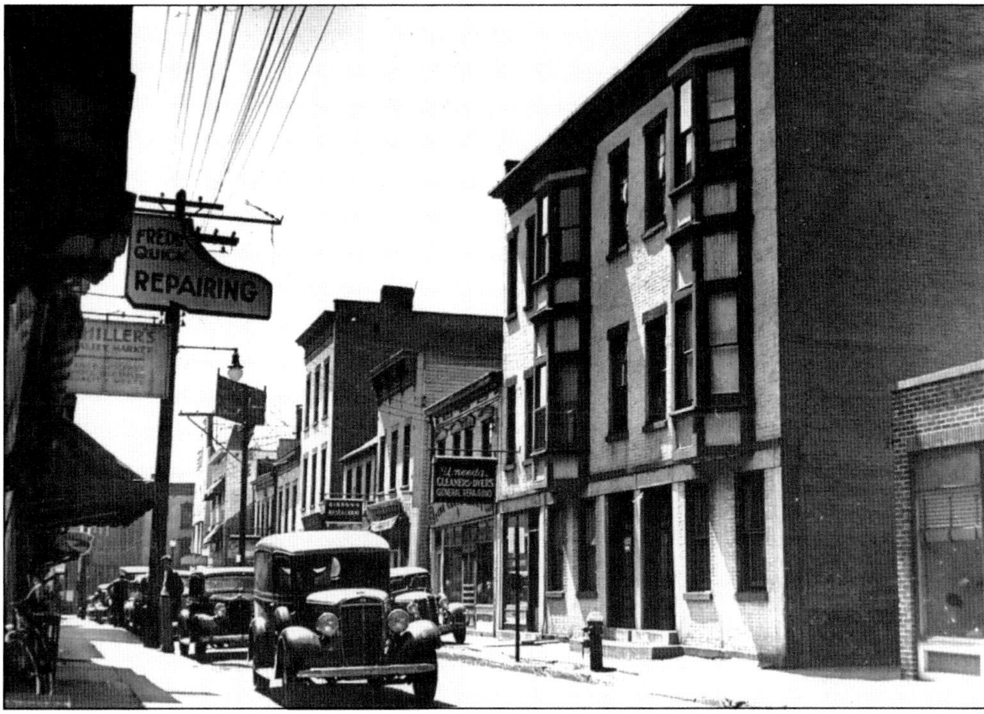

This is the same view as the previous photograph but taken near Union Street and looking towards State Street at 112–120 South Ferry Street.

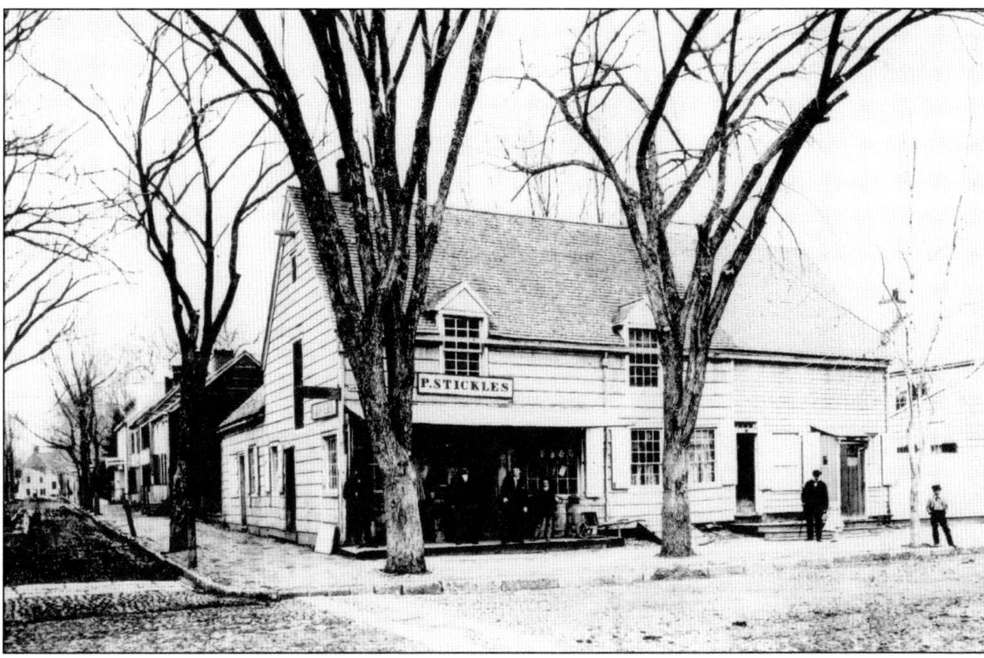

Here is an early view of the northeast corner of Ferry and Union Streets and Pop Stickle's Grocery Store in 1864. Arthur's Market and the park where *Lawrence the Indian* will stand later can be seen down the street. Originally cobblestone, Ferry Street has recently been resurfaced with asphalt.

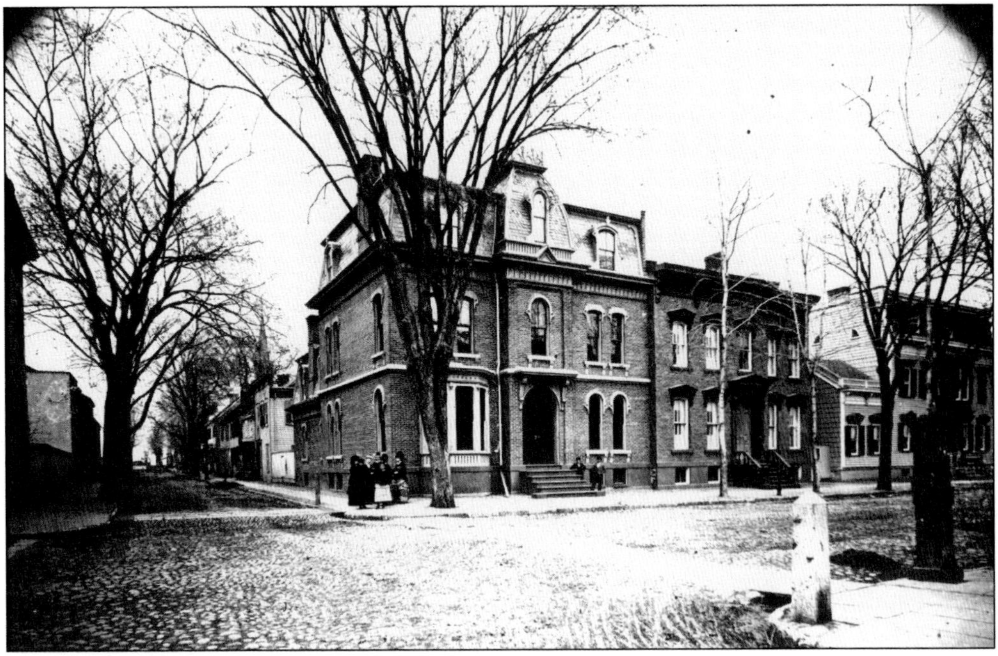

Here is the same view of Ferry Street at the corner of Union Street looking towards Front Street around 1875. There is a gathering of ladies on the corner; notice the horse-head hitching post in front and the corner posts, which prevented wagon drivers from taking short cuts up on the sidewalk. The house was owned then by a Dr. Carmichael.

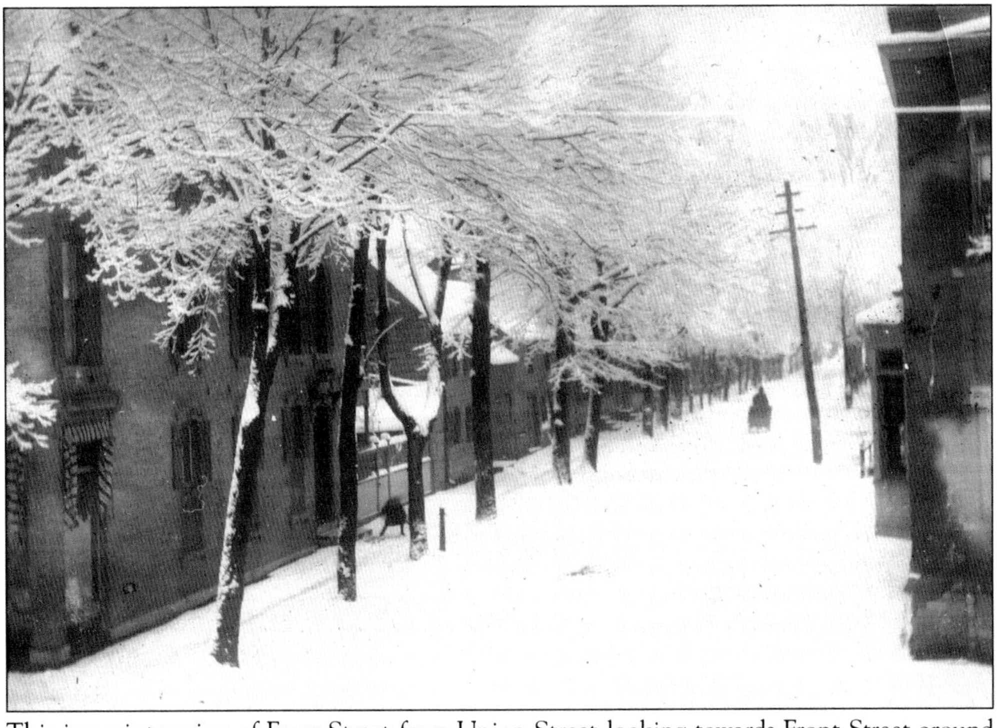

This is a winter view of Ferry Street from Union Street looking towards Front Street around 1900. Notice the solitary sleigh rider and the women to the left shoveling snow.

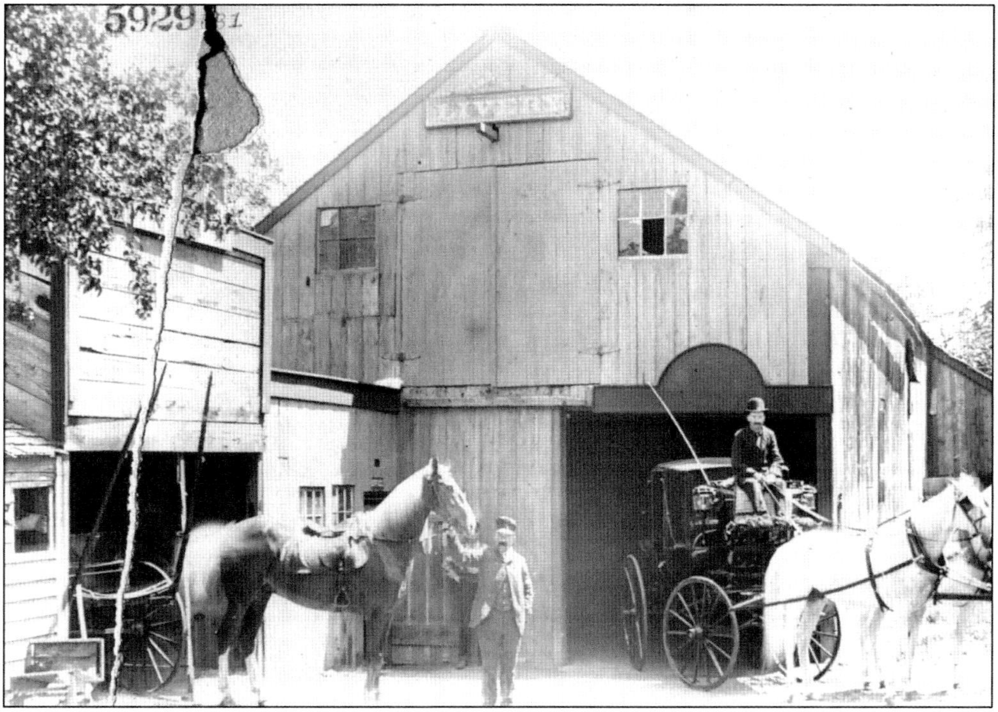

Thomas Simpson had his livery stables and home at 88 Ferry Street at the rear of the northwest corner of Union Street in this 1886 photograph.

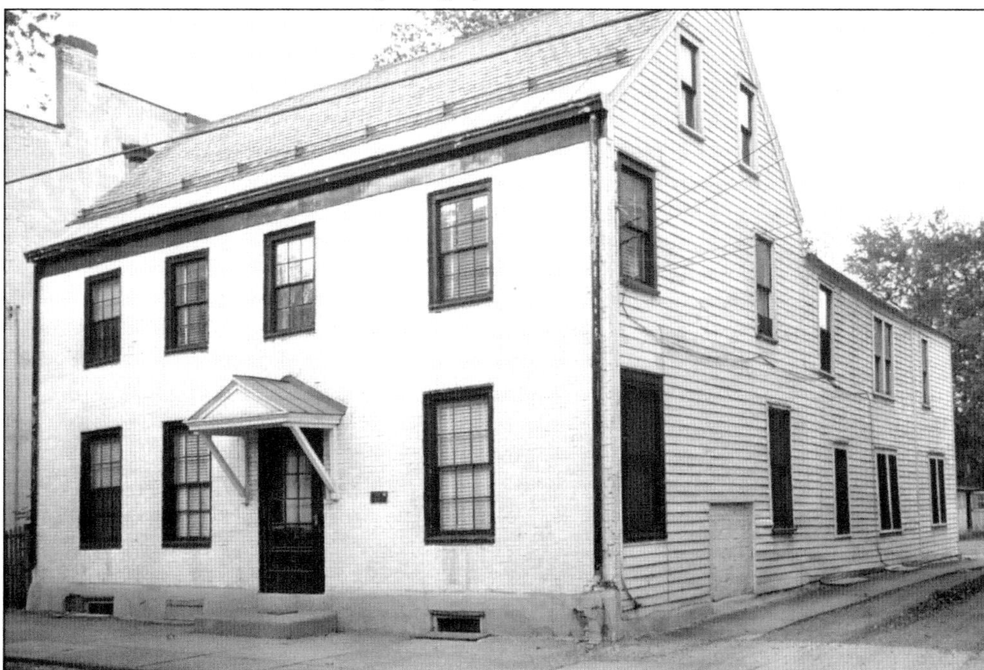

Isaac DeGraaf's home at 14 North Ferry Street was built in 1795 and has Dutch wall ties on the north side (gable end) of the house. There are now wall ties on the front, but these are modern reproductions of Dutch fleur-de-lis wall ties.

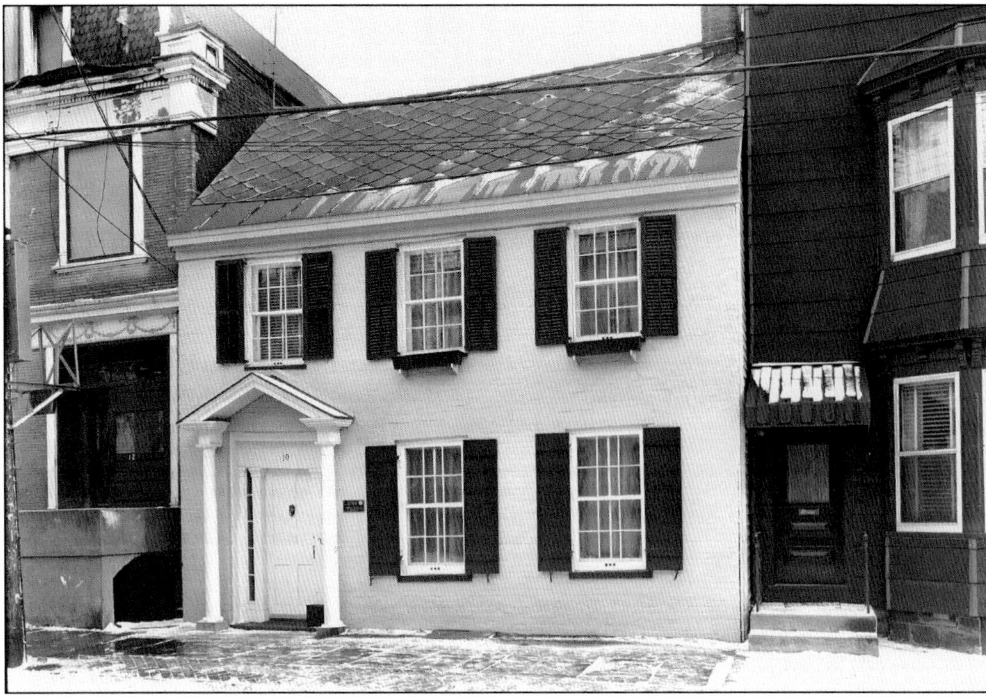

The "Widow Kendall" house at Ferry Street was the home of Anna Hall, who was married to the famous architect Samuel Fuller. She later married butcher George Kendall. The house dates to the mid-18th century.

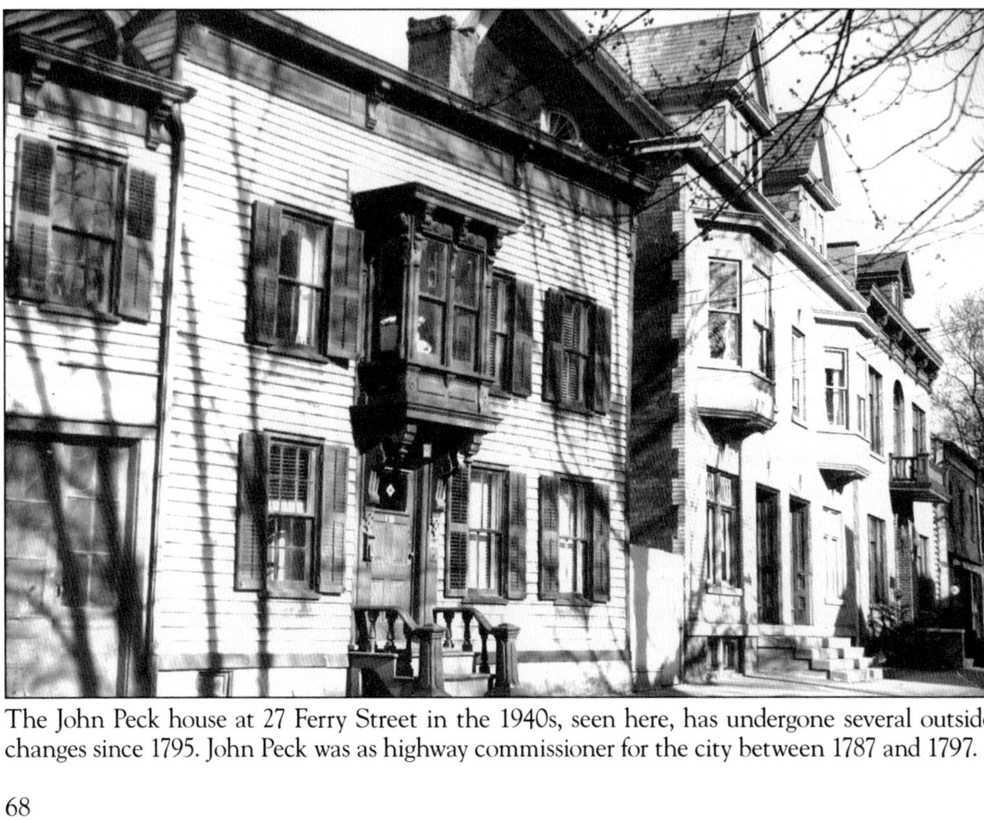

The John Peck house at 27 Ferry Street in the 1940s, seen here, has undergone several outside changes since 1795. John Peck was as highway commissioner for the city between 1787 and 1797.

Here is a view looking west down Ferry Street opposite St. George's Church. This row of 19th-century buildings, 15–13 Ferry Street, occupies a place that originally encompassed three forts: the Dongan Fort, Queen's Fort, and Fort Cosby during the 17th to 18th centuries.

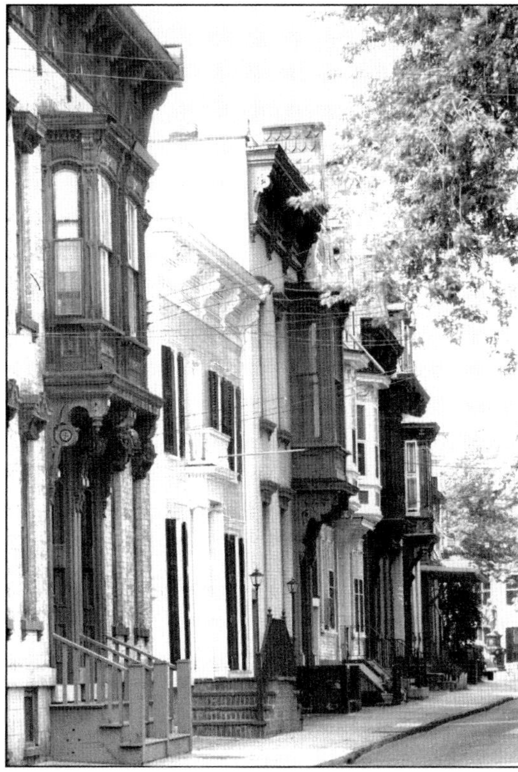

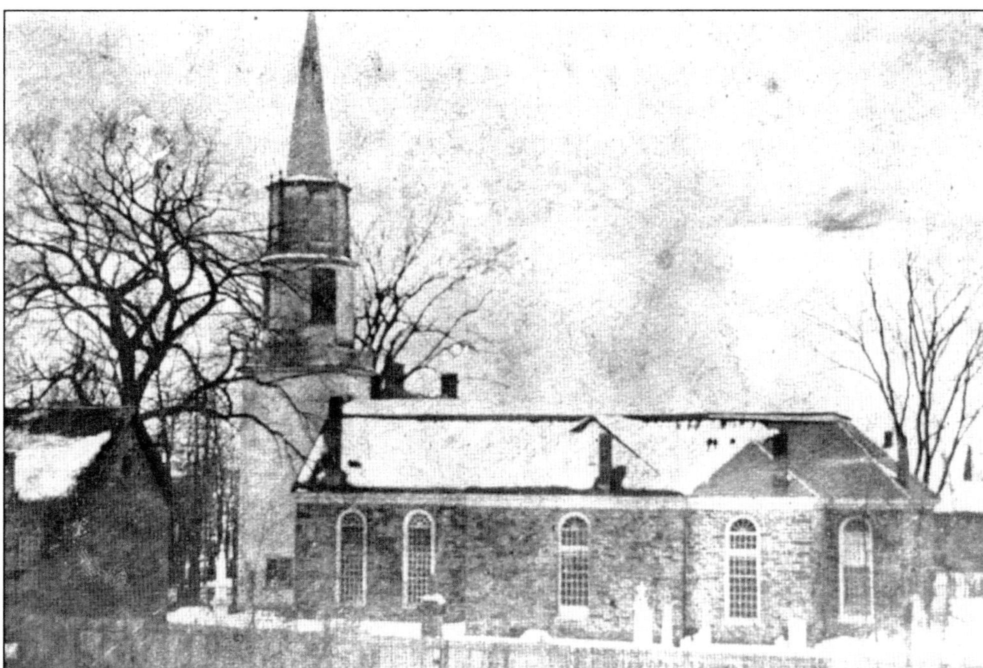

This is a side view looking northwest at St. George's Church in 1900. It was designed by Samuel Fuller, and construction began in 1759 but was not finished until 10 years later. It was the first English church. Sir William Johnson contributed money to make sure it was completed.

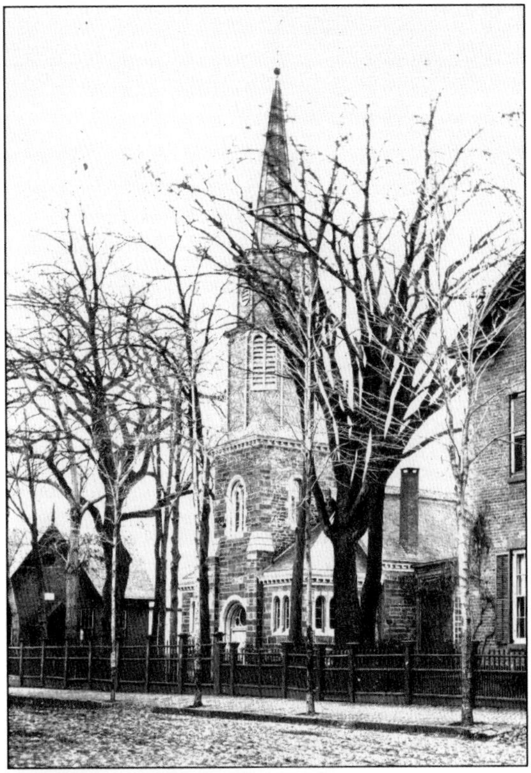

A front view of St George's Church around 1880 also shows their other buildings and original cast- and wrought-iron fence.

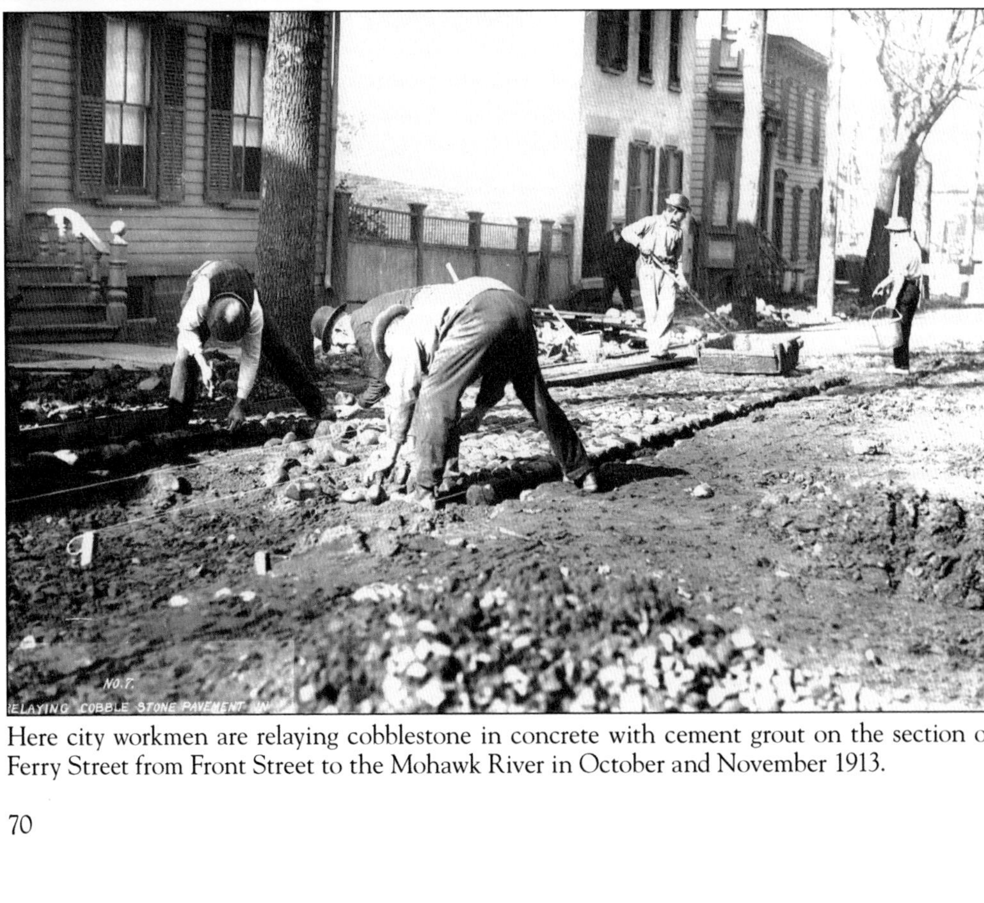

Here city workmen are relaying cobblestone in concrete with cement grout on the section of Ferry Street from Front Street to the Mohawk River in October and November 1913.

Six

UNION STREET

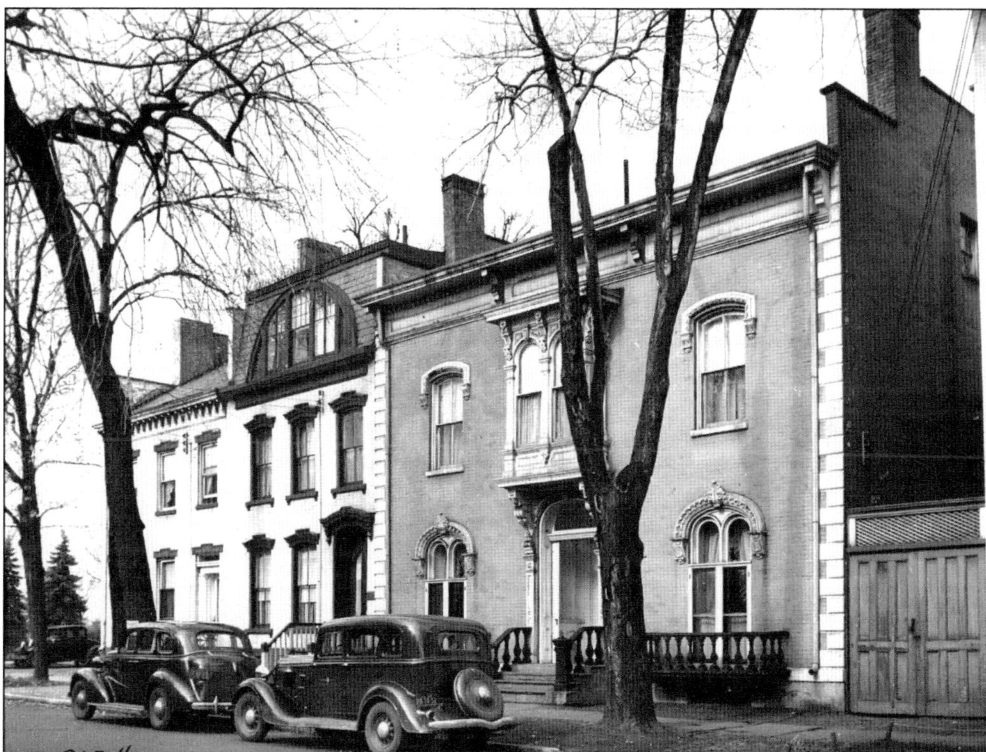

Union Street was the main street of the original stockade along with Church (Cross) Street. Here at the intersection with Church Street, Arendt Van Curler, founder of Schenectady, had his home on the northwest corner. Union Street was a very important street in later years too, as it left the stockade and preceded to Niskayuna and points east after the Revolutionary War. Here, 1–5 Union Street represents the 18th- and 19th-century building styles that replaced the earlier Dutch and English styles.

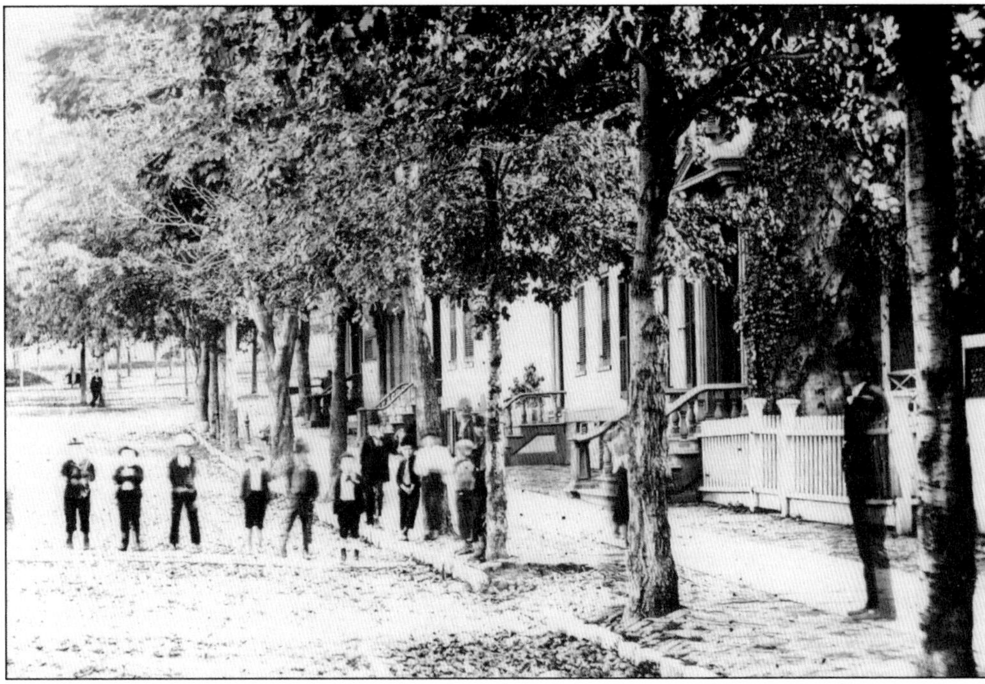

A group of kids pose on the west side of Washington Street at the corner of Union Street looking towards State Street around 1880.

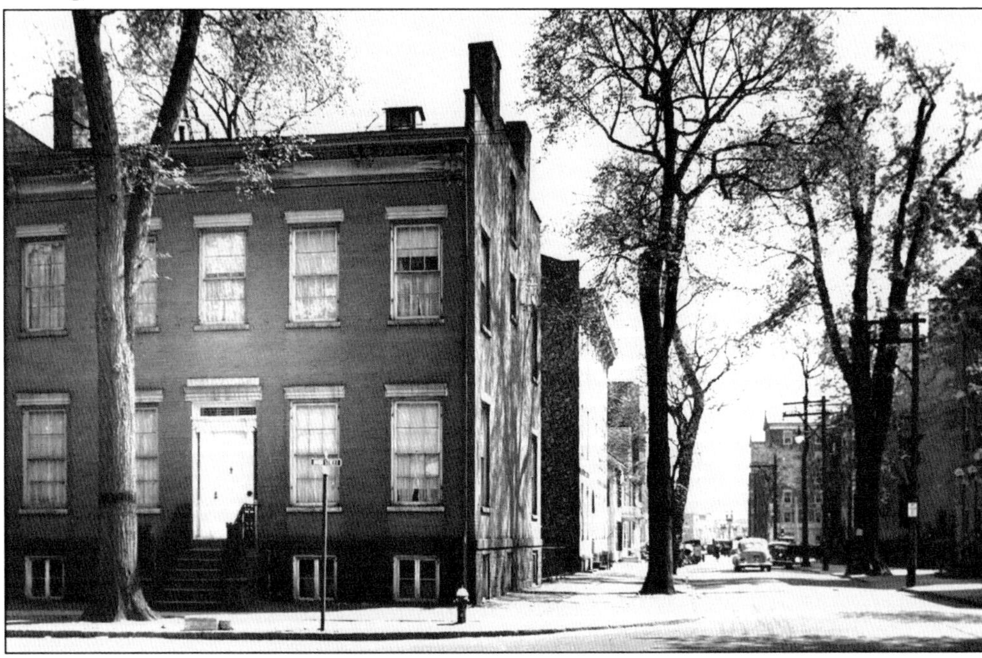

This is the same view as previous but taken years later and showing the east side of Washington Street from Union Street looking towards State Street. The house on the left belonged to Henry Glen. In 1775, he represented Schenectady on the Albany County Committee of Correspondence and served as deputy quartermaster general. He toured the Mohawk Valley in 1783 with George Washington and later was town clerk for Schenectady in 1767.

Here is a view of 7 Union Street in 1938 showing a building of Italianate design. Most architectural styles in America can be seen in the stockade.

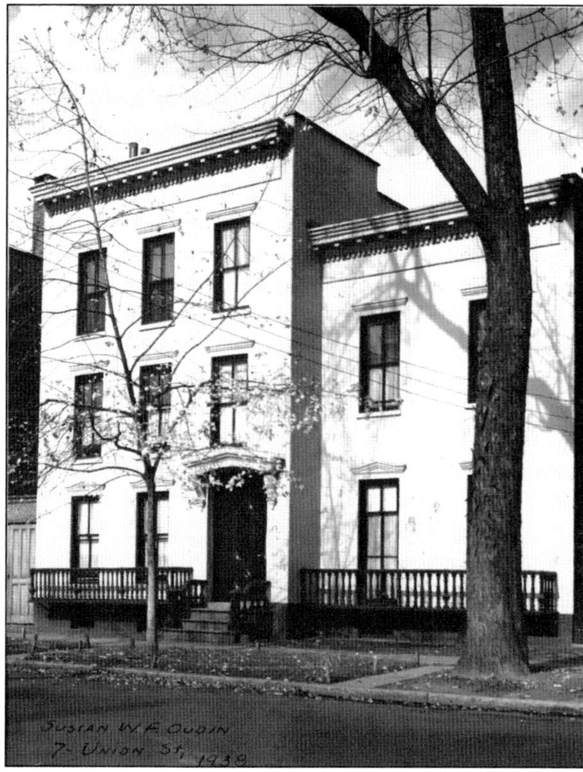

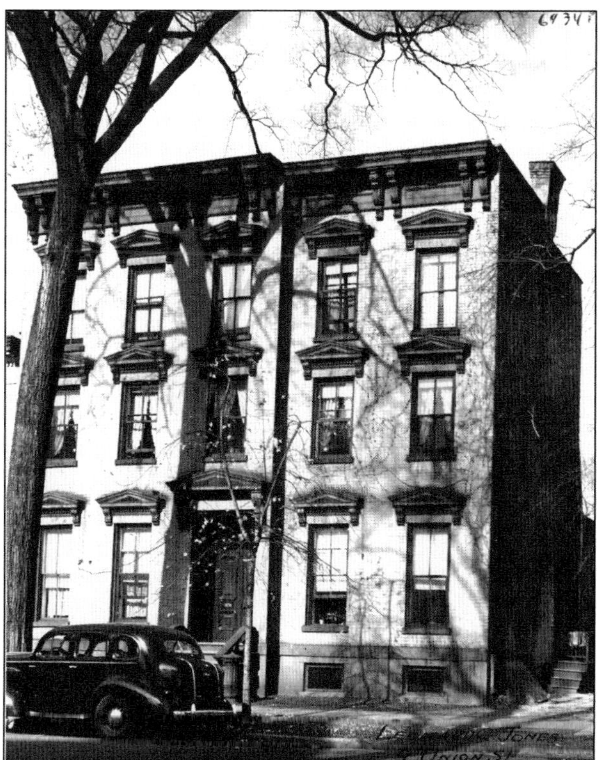

The Jones house at 9 Union Street, seen here in 1938, represents a 19th-century period when homes were larger than the earlier and smaller Dutch homes.

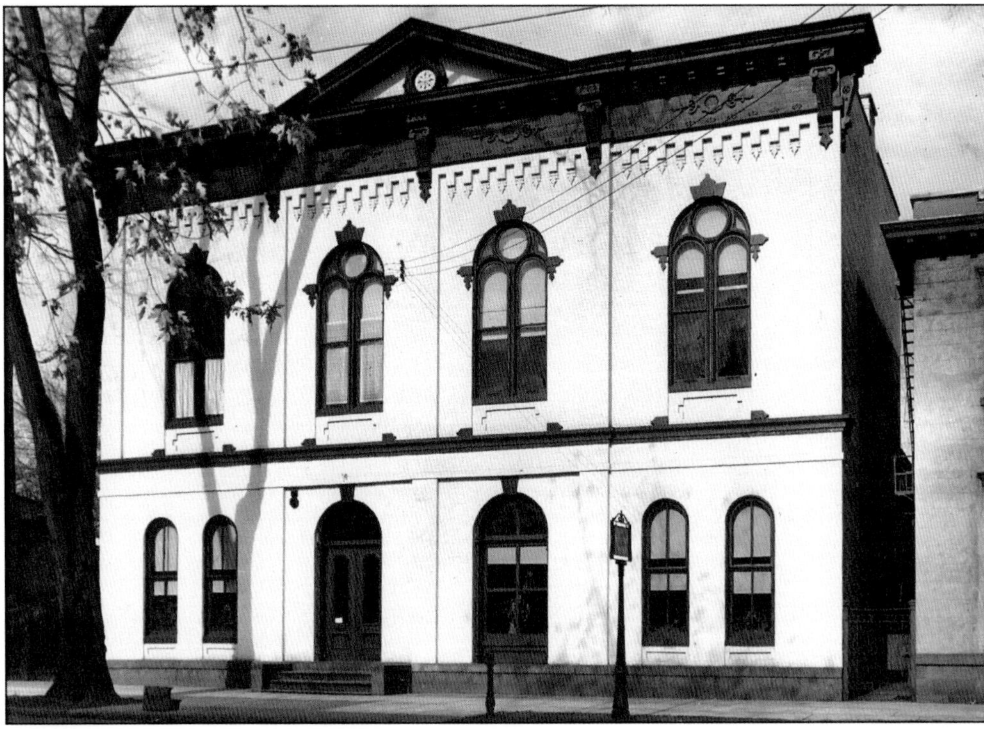

The Schenectady County Clerk's Office at 13 Union Street was built in 1870–1871 by architect Marcus Cummings of Troy. It had several fresco paintings on the ceilings and later was used by the Schenectady County Historical Society (seen here). Notice the stepping stone and hitching post. The building was demolished after 1966 by the Mohawk Club for parking.

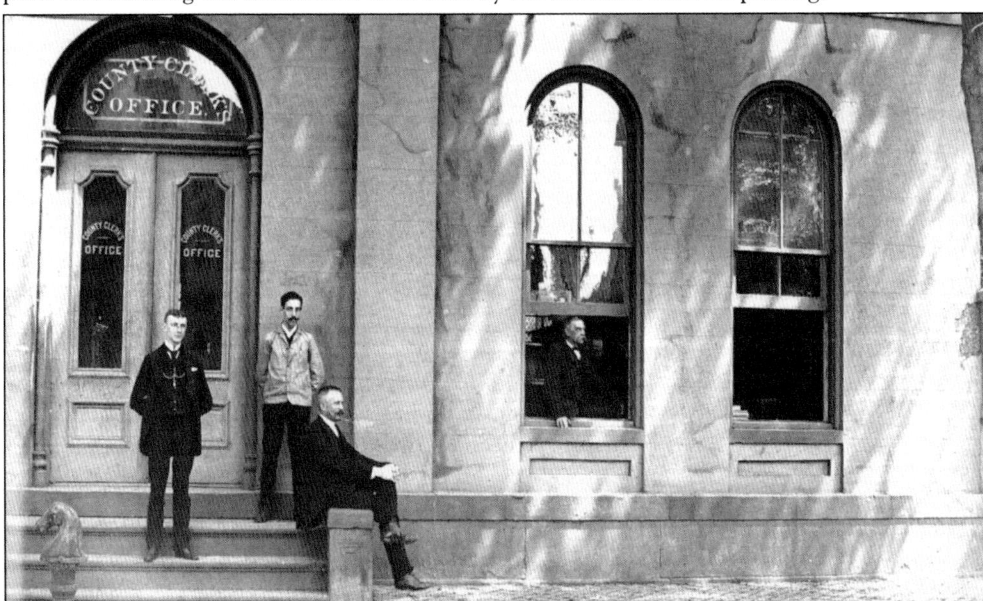

Elmer Milmine (standing on the right) was the county clerk from October 31, 1887, to December 31, 1888. He was appointed by Gov. David Hill. Milmine is standing at his offices at 13 Union Street.

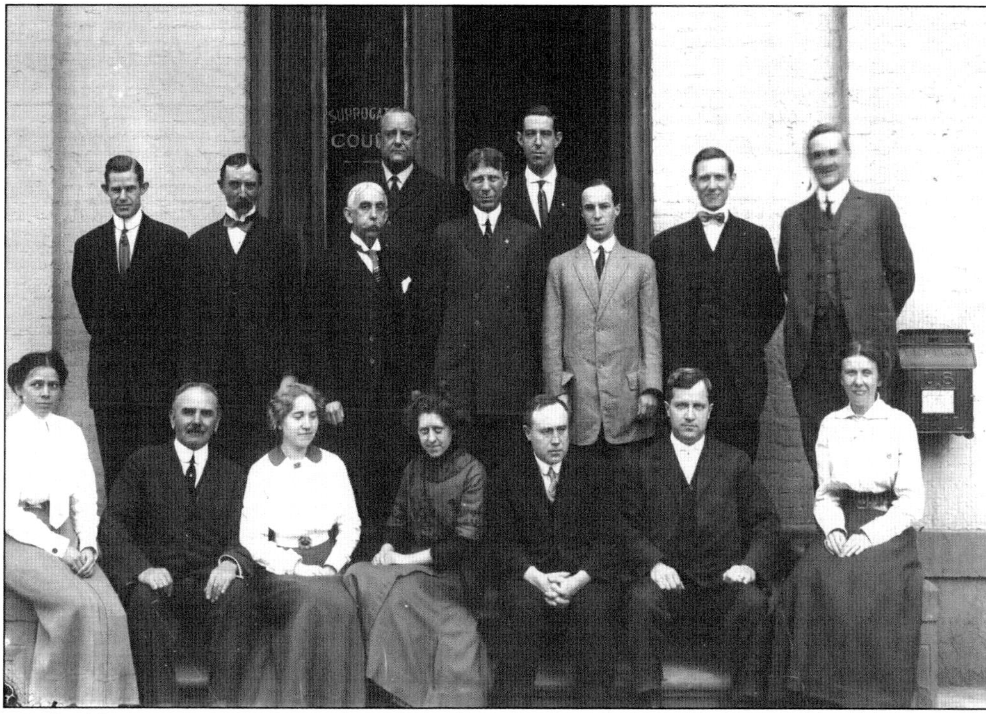

The building at 13 Union Street was also used as the surrogate's court and office, as show in this group shot.

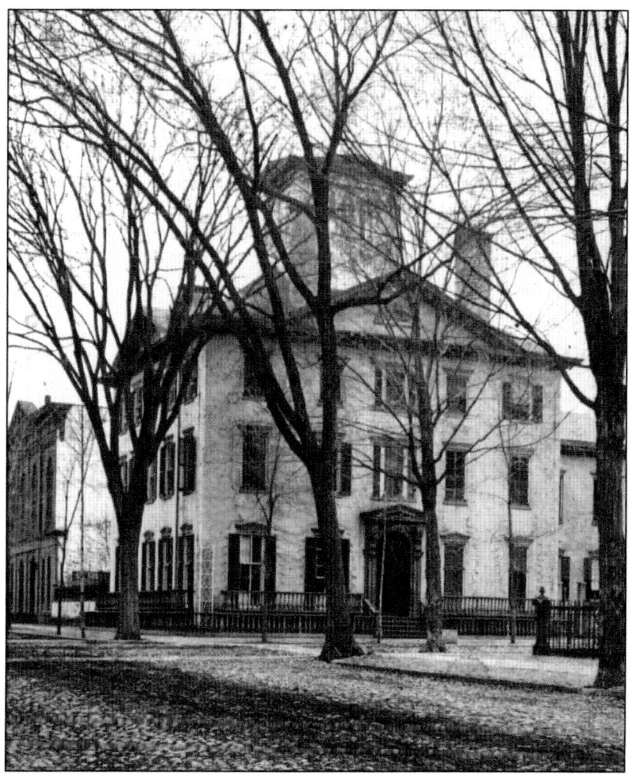

The northwest corner of Church and Union Streets was the home of the Mohawk Bank, Schenectady's first bank. Built in 1816, the entrance was originally on the Union Street side. The current entrance to the building was originally used by David Boyd, the cashier, who lived in the building on the upper floor.

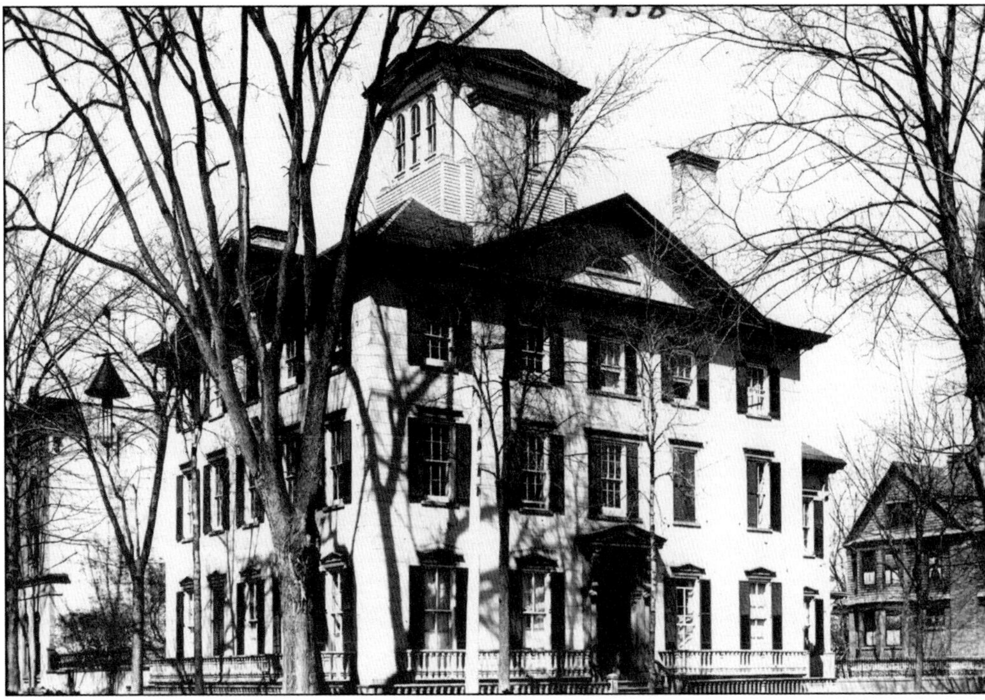

The bank building was purchased by Chauncey Vibbard, one of the organizers of the New York Central Railroad, and converted to a home around 1857. Later it became the home of the New York Temperance Society by Henry Crane and Edward Delavan.

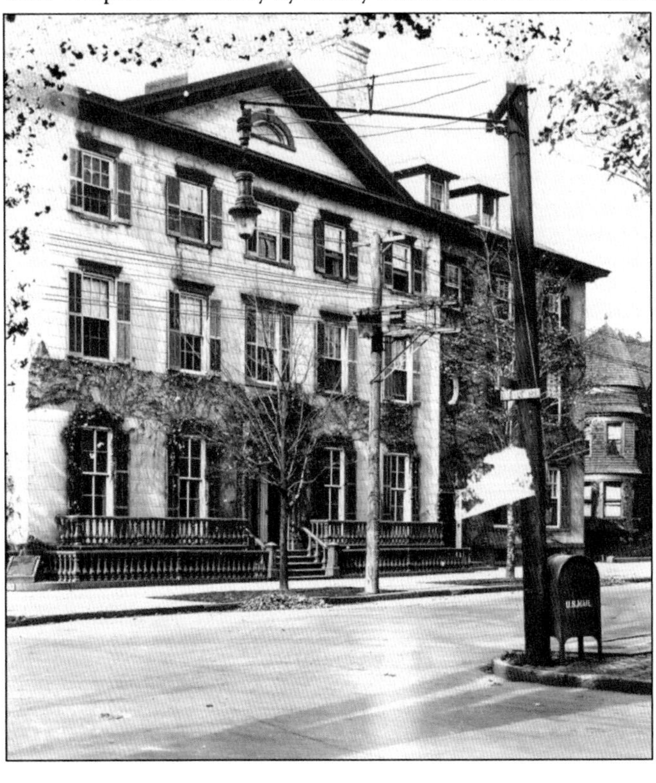

The Mohawk Bank, chartered in 1807, became the Union Classical Institute in 1872, the city's first high school. They added the wing to the right in 1912 after the new high school on Nott Terrace, built in 1903, proved to be insufficient for the growing student population.

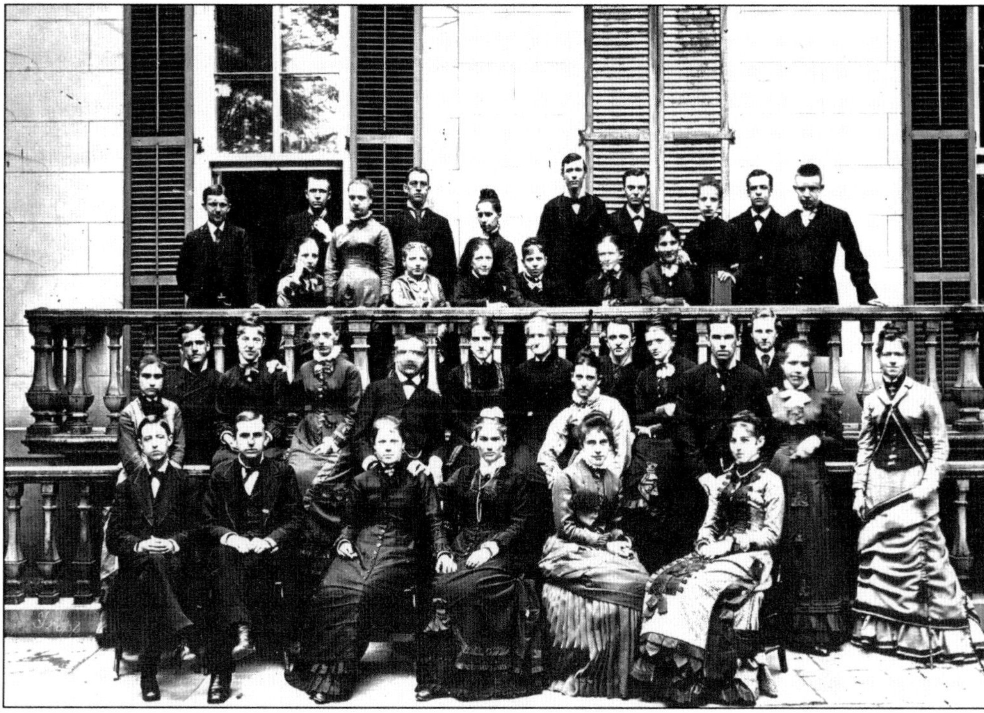

Here is a graduating class of the Union Classical Institute in the 1870s. This appears to have been taken on the north side of the main building near the annex.

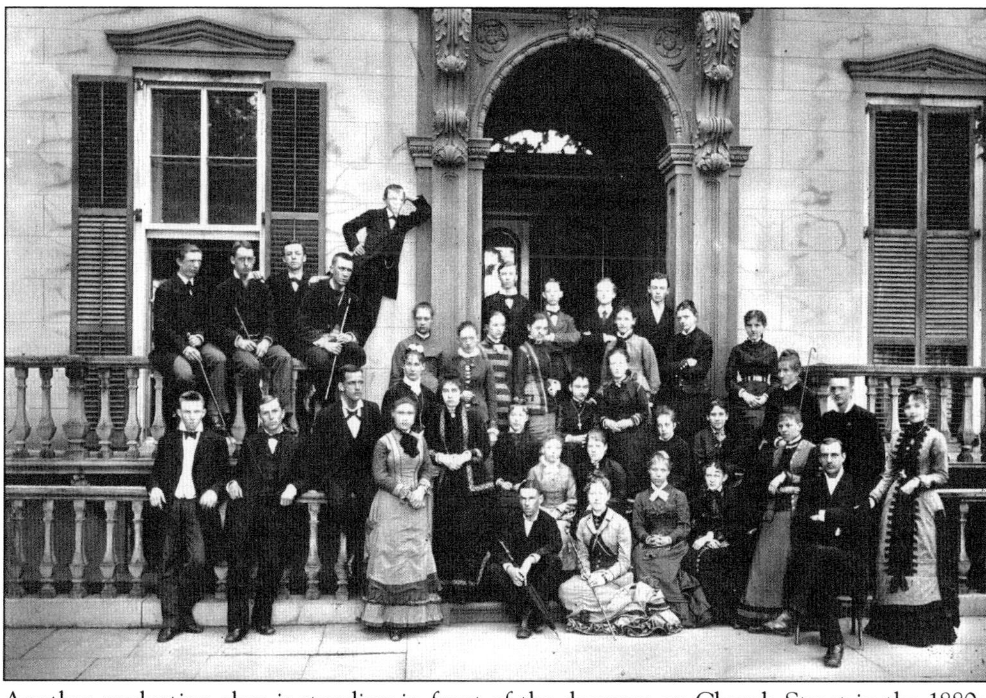

Another graduating class is standing in front of the doorway on Church Street in the 1880s. The building is now called the Stockade Inn and serves as a bed and breakfast, and an excellent dining experience.

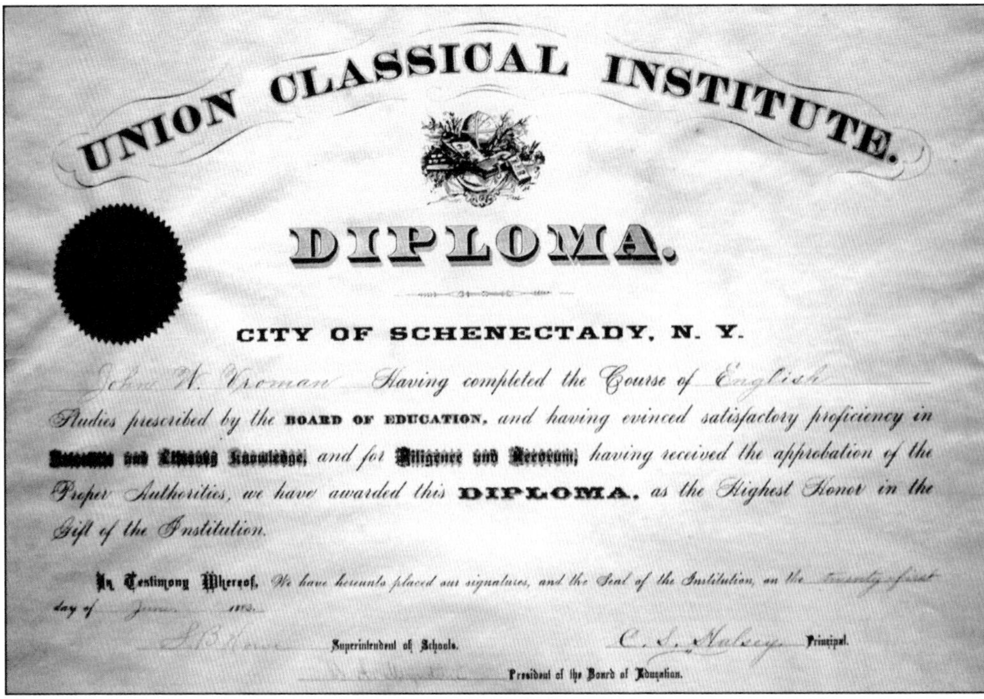
UNION CLASSICAL INSTITUTE.

DIPLOMA.

CITY OF SCHENECTADY, N. Y.

John W. Vrooman Having completed the Course of English Studies prescribed by the BOARD OF EDUCATION, and having evinced satisfactory proficiency in [illegible] and [illegible] Knowledge, and for Diligence and Decorum; having received the approbation of the Proper Authorities, we have awarded this DIPLOMA, as the Highest Honor in the Gift of the Institution.

In Testimony Whereof, We have hereunto placed our signatures, and the Seal of the Institution, on the twenty-first day of June 1883.

Superintendent of Schools.

C. S. Halsey Principal.

President of the Board of Education.

Here one can see the 1883 high school diploma of John W. Vrooman from the Union Classical Institute.

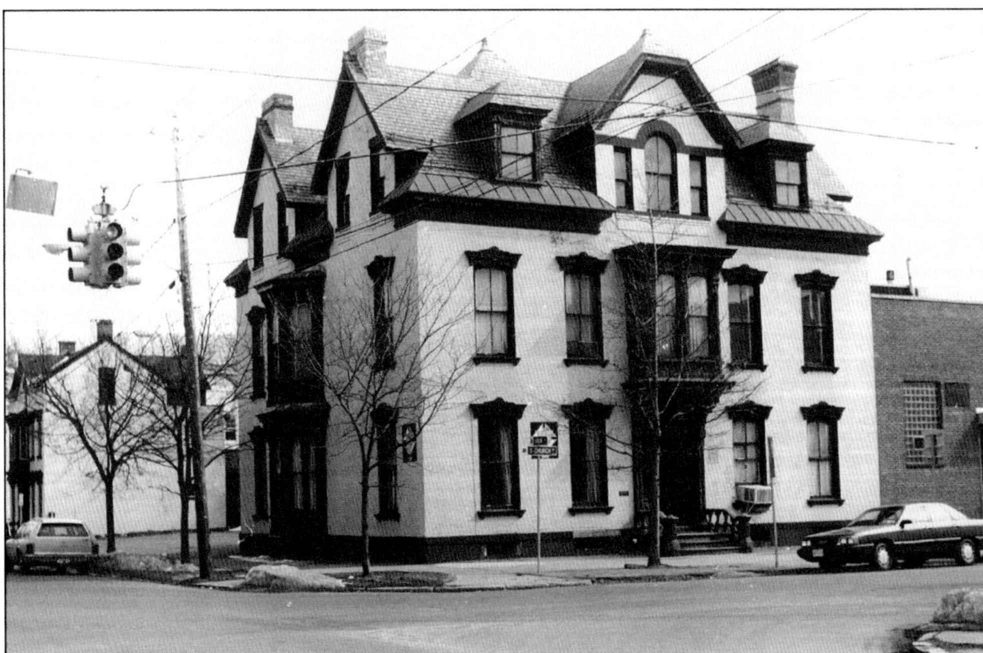

The Dutch architectural styles of the 17th and 18th centuries gradually gave way in the 19th century to larger and stately mansions, as seen here on the southeast corner of Union and Church Streets. As the city and its citizens prospered, so did the visual aspects of the stockade.

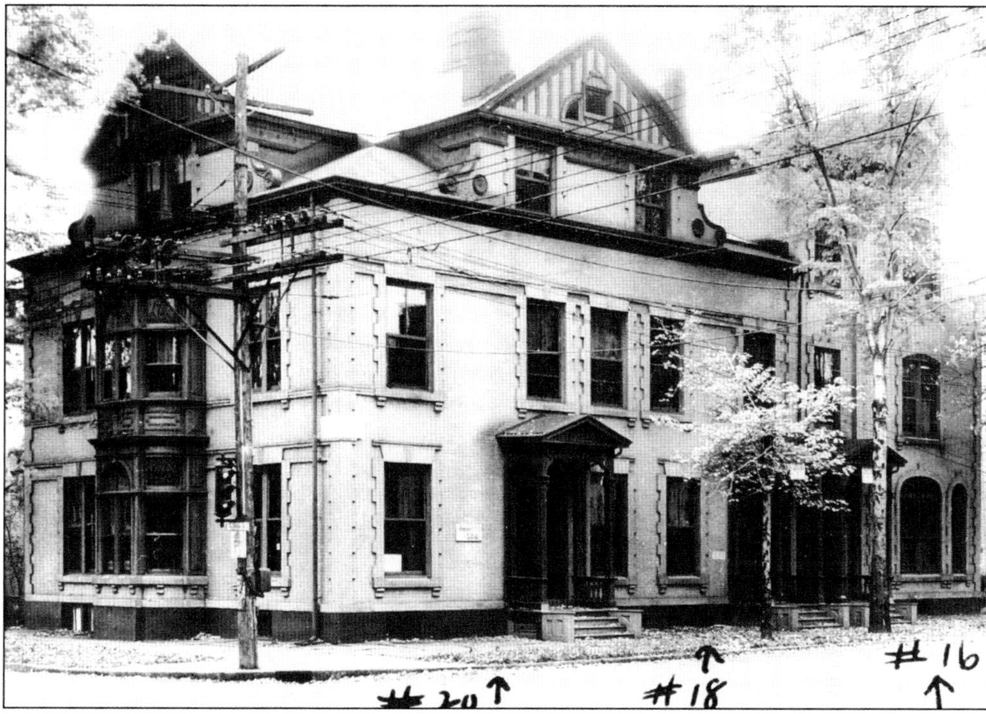

Unfortunately these stately mansions were not always appreciated, as can be seen here on the southwest corner of Union and Church Streets. This elaborate building was torn down for a parking lot for the Mohawk Club.

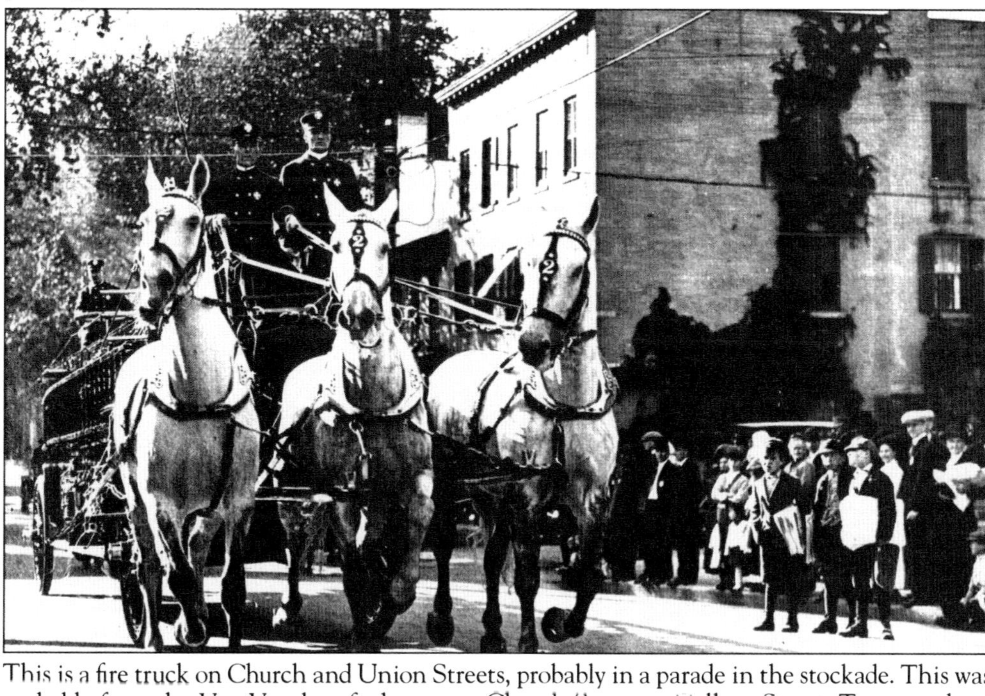
This is a fire truck on Church and Union Streets, probably in a parade in the stockade. This was probably from the Van Vranken firehouse on Church Street or College Street. Two paperboys are hawking their papers on the right.

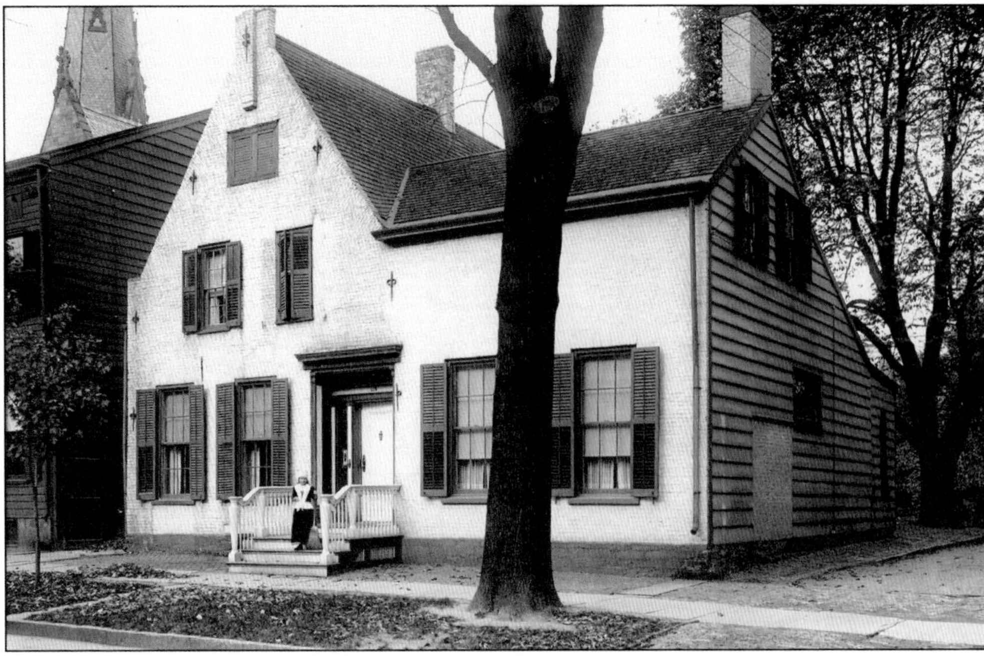

The Abraham Yates house at 109 Union Street was built in 1725 and is one of the oldest Dutch houses in the stockade. For years, this house has become the symbol of the Dutch history of this area. Typical of a Dutch gable with fleur-de-lis wall ties, the addition on the right was built probably in the early 19th century.

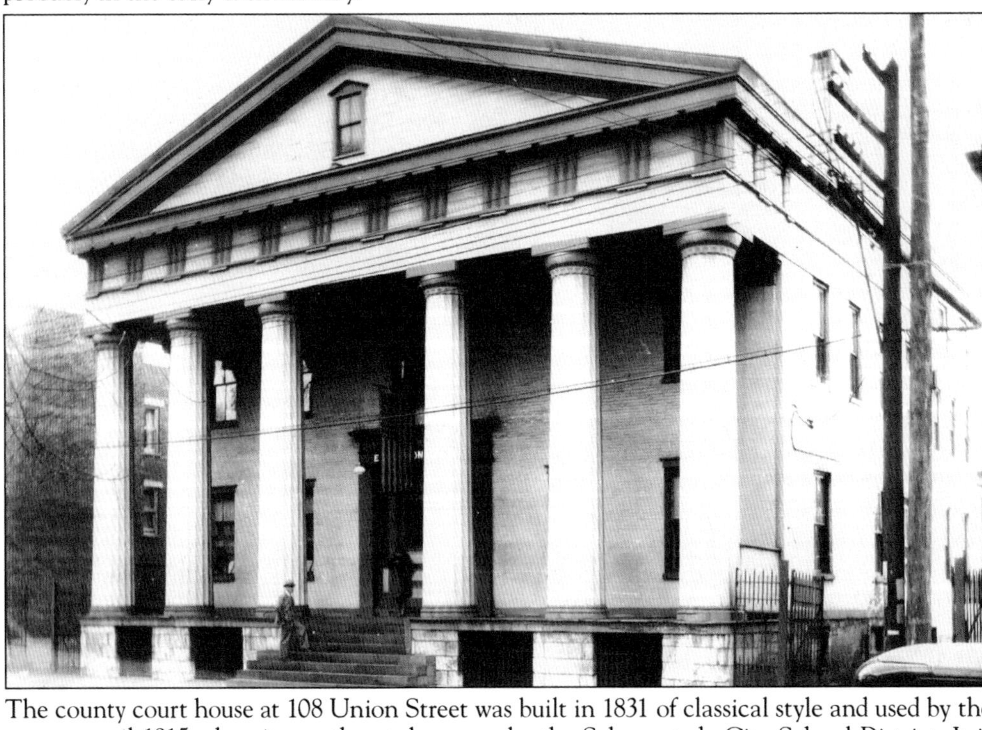

The county court house at 108 Union Street was built in 1831 of classical style and used by the county until 1915 when it was then taken over by the Schenectady City School District. It is privately owned today. It is said that the jail in the basement still has its shackles for prisoners.

Here Sheriff Seth L. Clute poses with kids in 1887 on the steps of the courthouse (and his office).

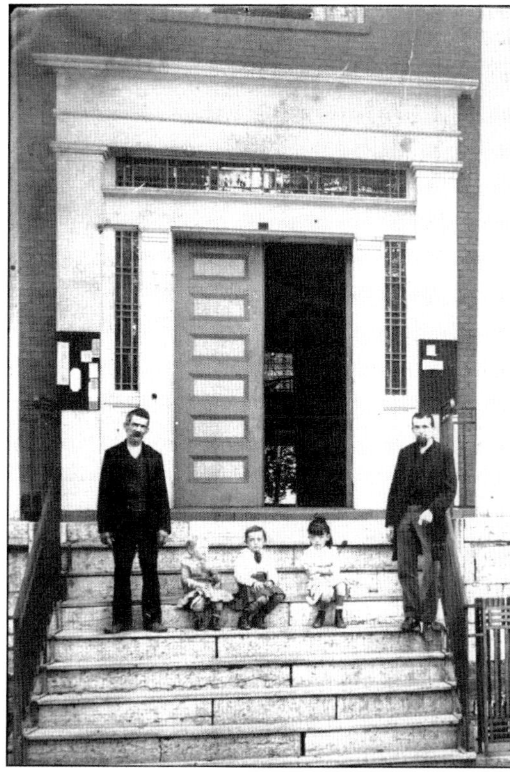

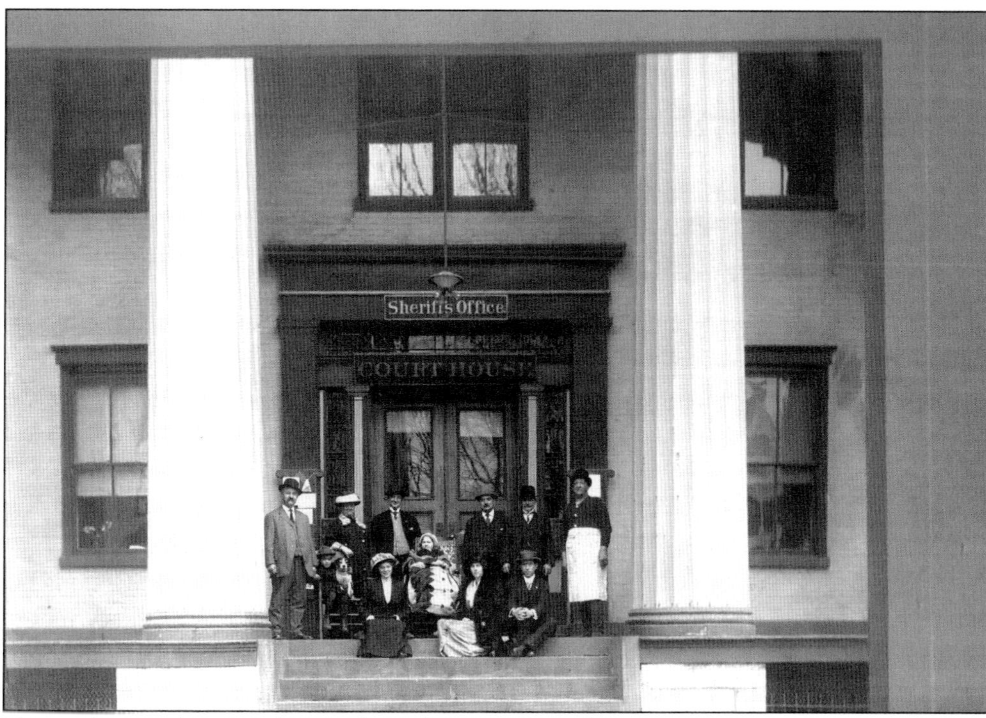

Here is the courthouse with several people posing for a photograph in 1913. The courthouse was taken over by the city board of education in 1913, and this group no doubt represents that.

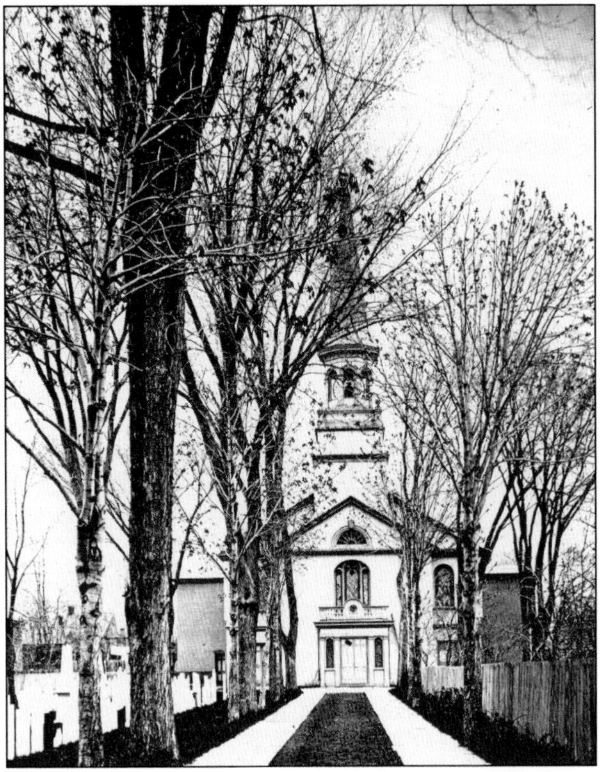

The First Presbyterian Church at 209 Union Street began in 1809 here after the congregation separated from the Episcopal church of St George's on Ferry Street. Additions in 1834, 1839 (or 1859), and 1924, and remodeling over the years has not changed the overall beauty of the church.

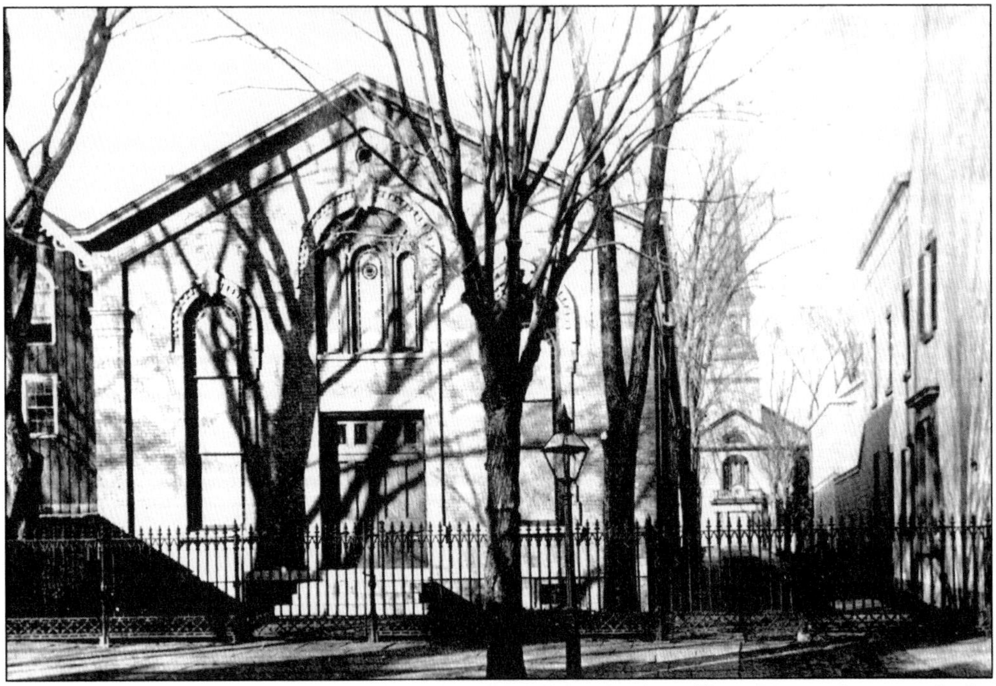

This is a front view of the Presbyterian Church Hall (Mekeek Hall) on Union Street with the church in the background, around 1900. The chapel was built in 1843 but has been modified in 1857 and 1883, and no longer looks like this.

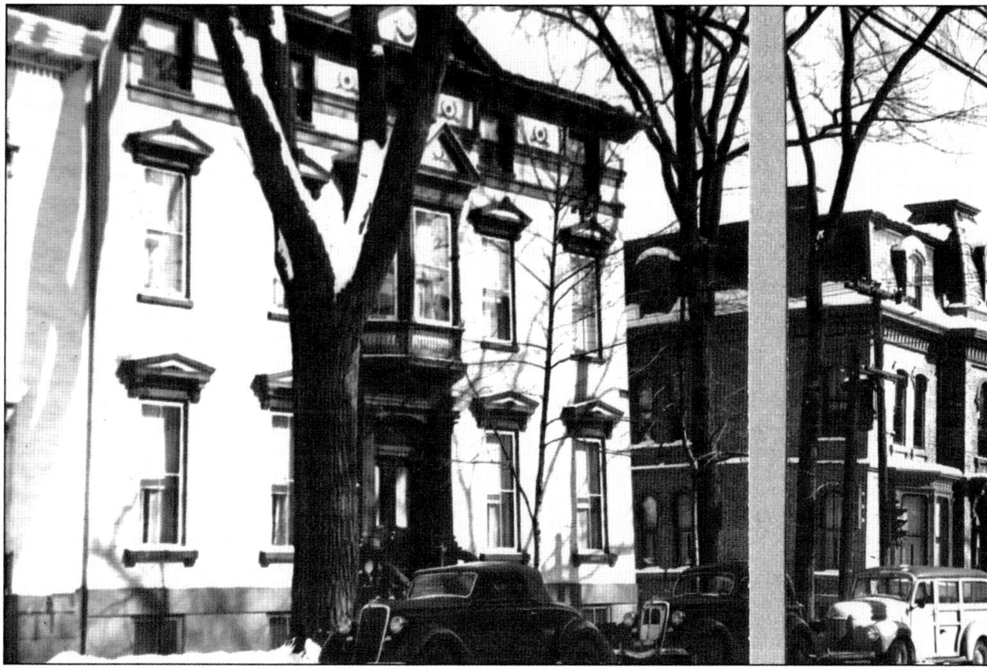

This is the home of H. S. Barney, at 115 Union Street, who created one of the early department stores in the city. The old store now serves as apartment complex. This building was originally built in the late 18th century for the Schenectady Academy, and then served as the Schenectady City Hall before Barney purchased it. It was left to the First Presbyterian Church in 1950 and is now called the Goodrich House.

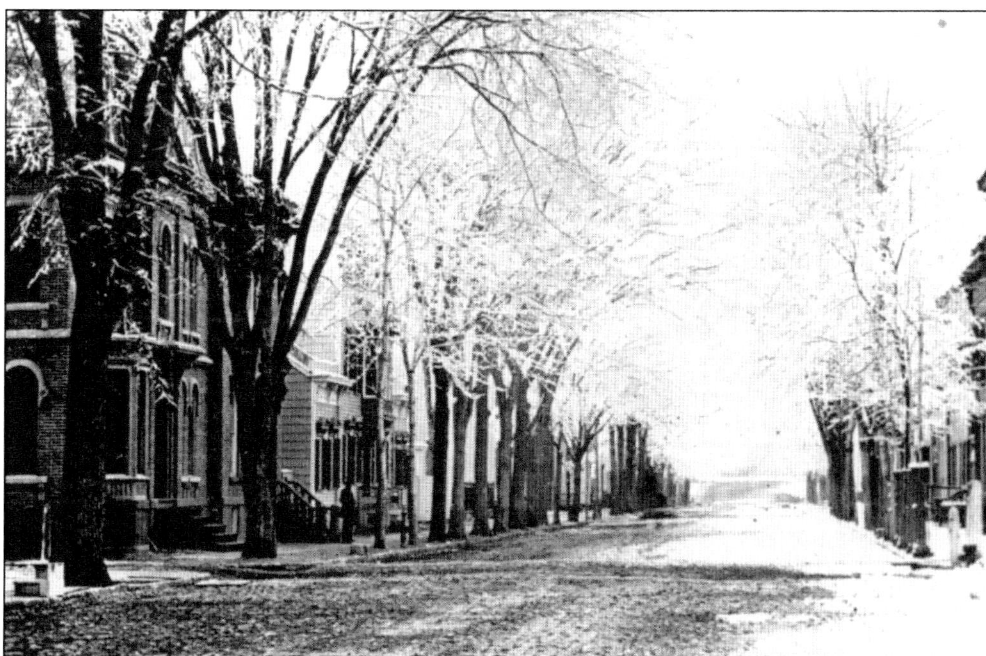

Here is a winter view looking east up Union Street, at the northeast corner of Ferry Street, around 1880. The Carmichael residence is on the left.

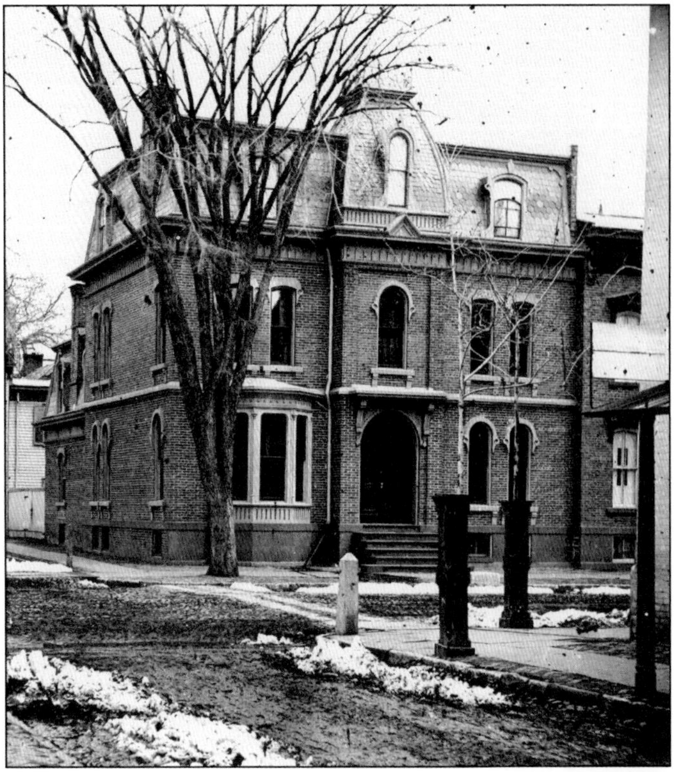

Seen here is an 1880s winter close-up of the northeast corner of Union and Ferry Street. Built between 1864 and 1875, 201 Union Street was the home of Dr. Carmichael. Notice the herringbone brick pattern in the sidewalk, and the cobblestones street. The white pillar prevented wagons from taking shortcuts up on the curb.

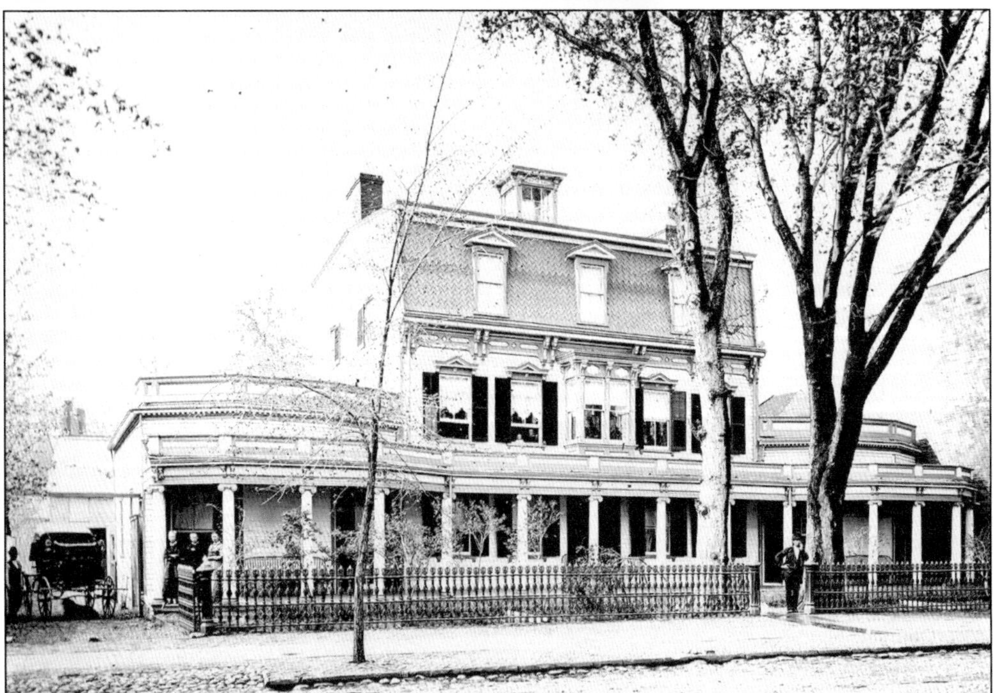

Known as the Romyen and Duane residence, it was replaced by a three-story brick building that is near the Ellis mansions (of Edward and Charles Ellis) on Union Street.

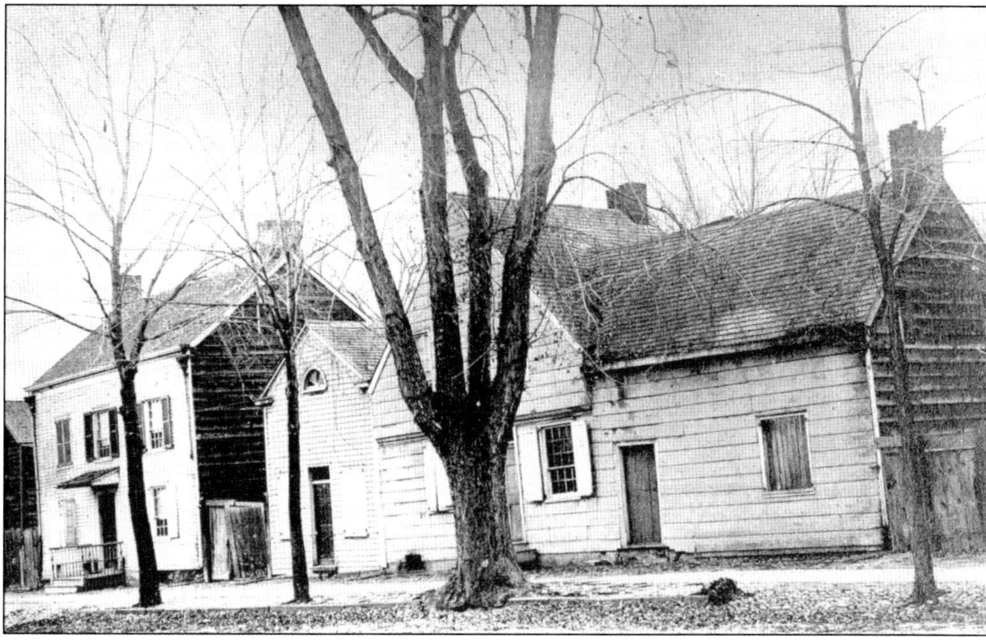

The 1850 Peek residence was torn down to make way for the two Ellis mansions at 215 and 217 Union Street.

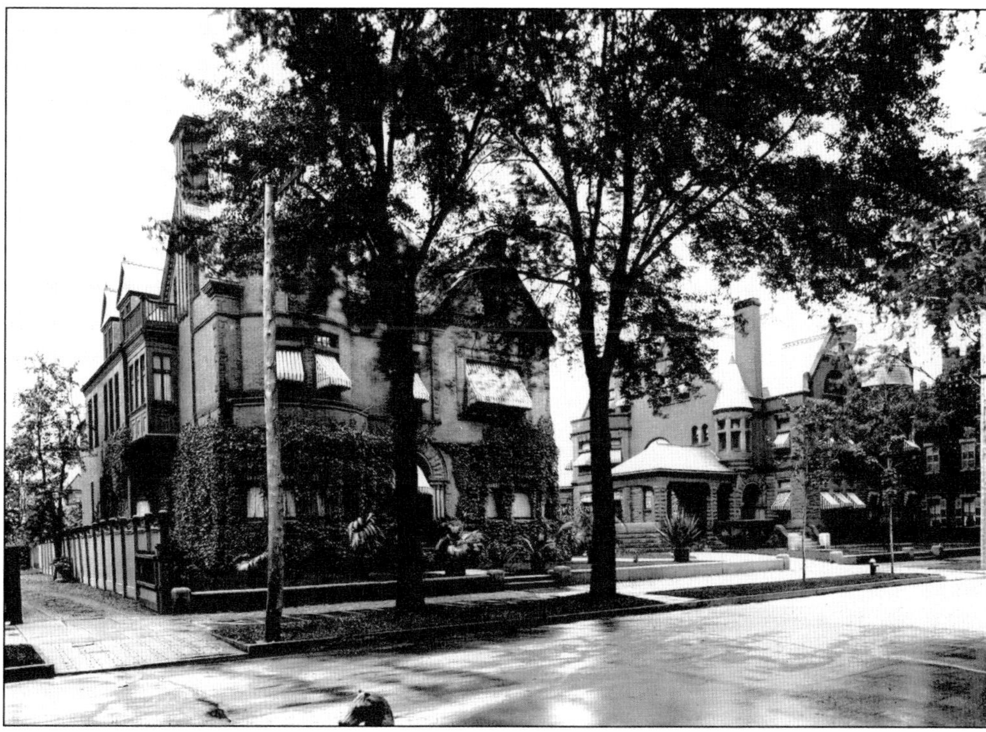

Edward and Charles Ellis were the sons of John Ellis, founder of the Schenectady Locomotive Works. Both headed the Schenectady Locomotive Works after the death of their father (John took over first, then Charles, followed by Edward). Ellis Hospital is named in honor of John Sr. Interestingly, all three mansions still survive.

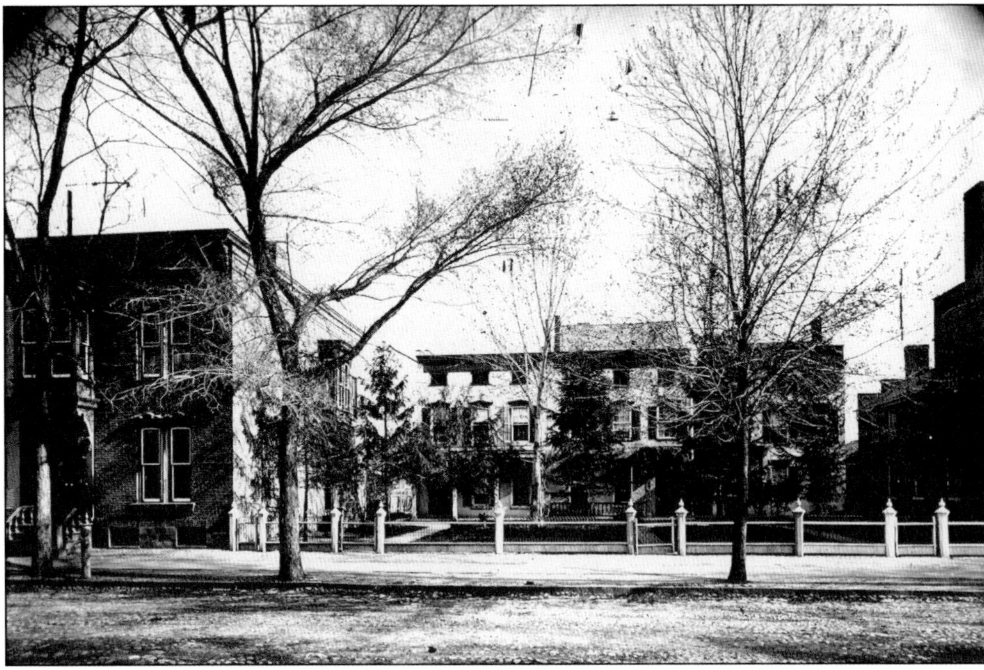

This is a row of 19th-century buildings in upper Union Street near College Avenue along the cobblestone street. These homes are setback from the street allowing a larger front yard that is not common in the stockade area.

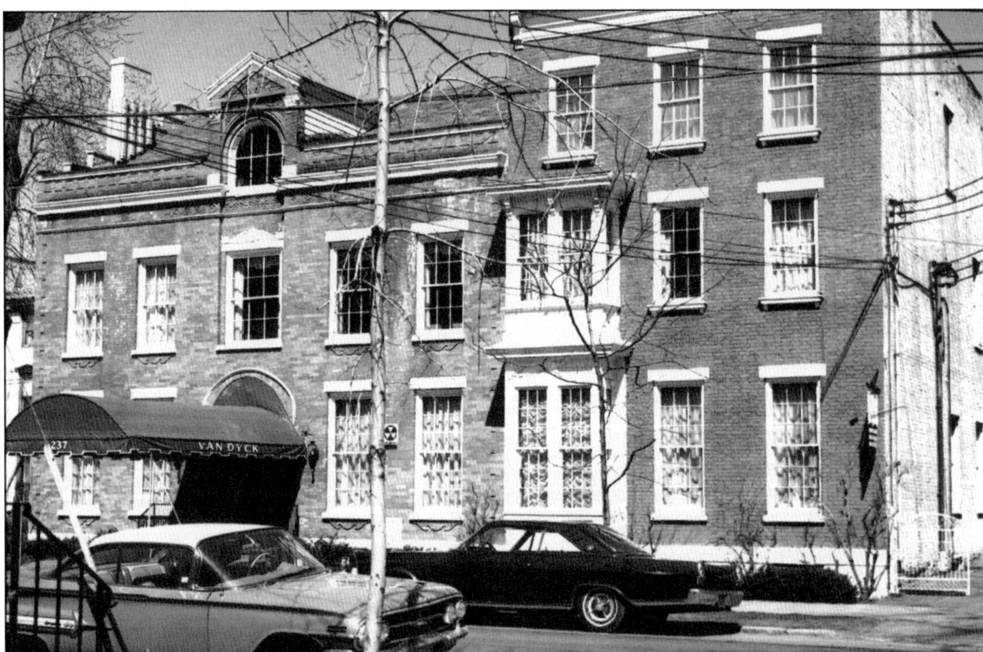

The Van Dyke Restaurant and Jazz Club at 237 Union Street is seen here in the 1960s. Since 1947, these two buildings have for more than 50 years been the centerpiece for jazz entertainment in the city, including performances by Dizzy Gillespie, Earl Hines, and Coleman Hawkins. It has been closed for a few years, but will probably reopen.

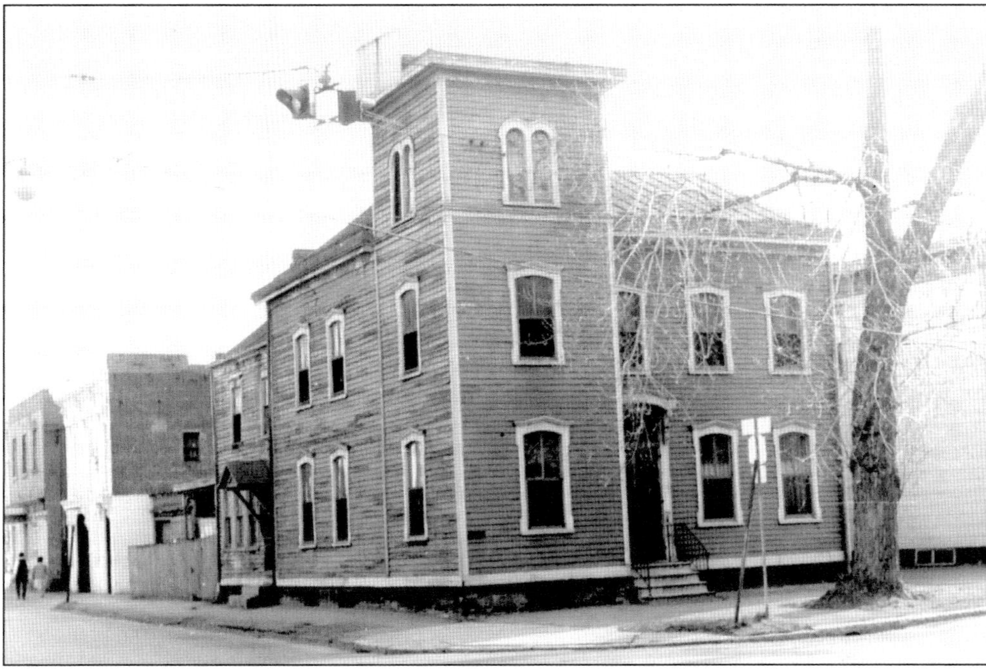

Dr. Elizabeth Gillette's (1876–1965) offices and home at 254 Union Street are being renovated for offices and a museum today. Gillette was the first female surgeon in Schenectady County in 1901, and the first upstate women elected to the New York State legislature in 1919.

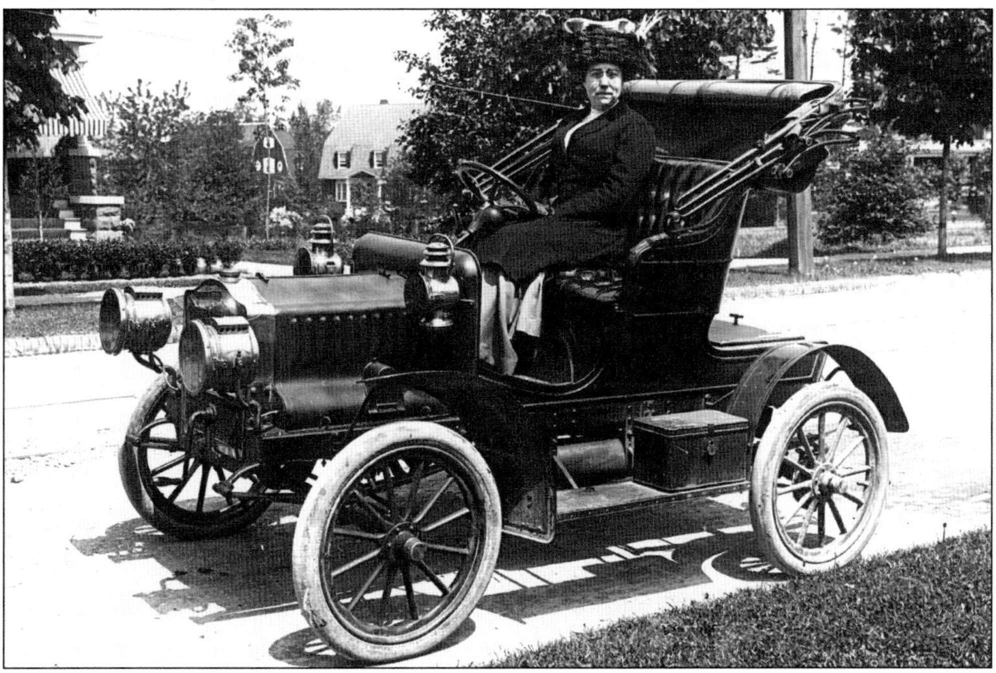

Here is Gillette in her automobile getting ready to make a house call. Before owning a car, she took the trolley, or wagon, or walked to her patients. As the first upstate woman elected to the New York State legislature in 1919, she could write laws but could not vote until women won the right in 1920.

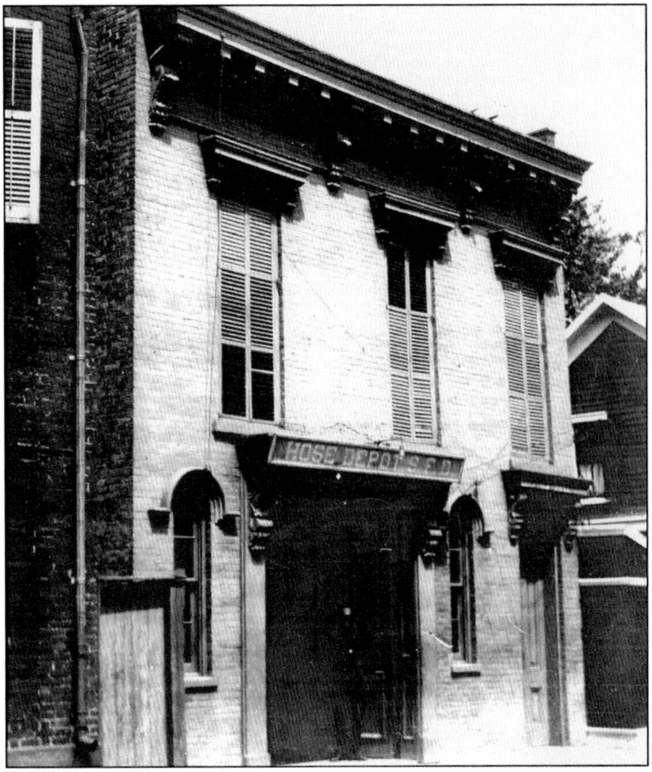

This little firehouse could protect part of the stockade. This is the Hose Depot at College Avenue (then Elbow Street) next to the Erie Canal.

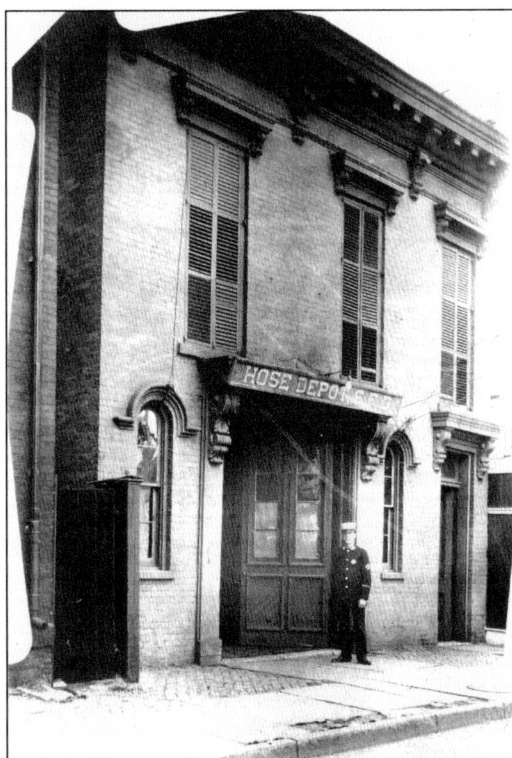

This is a closer view of the Hose Depot with Capt. Sanford Alberts. This building was recently torn down for a parking lot.

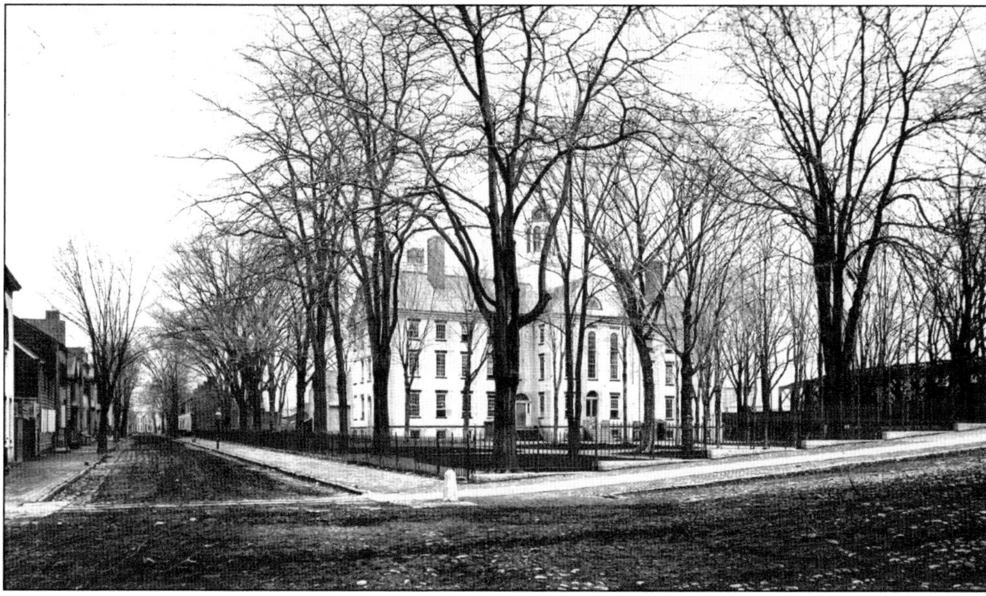

West College (also known as Union College), founded in 1795, was the first nondenominational college in the country and the first chartered college in New York State. This building for West College was built in 1804 at the corner of College Avenue, Union Street, and the Erie Canal. This building became Schenectady City Hall from 1814 until 1857. From 1854 to 1857, though, it shared the building with the city's public school system, Union School.

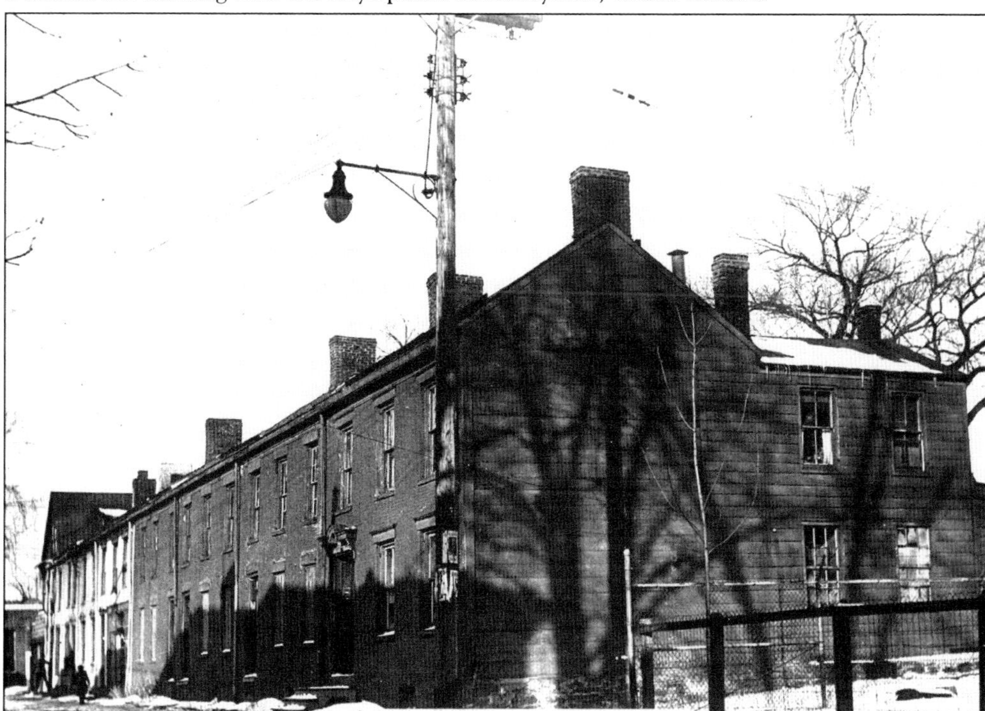

These were the dorms for the students at West College and are located a few hundred feet north of the former college on North College Street. They are now used as residences.

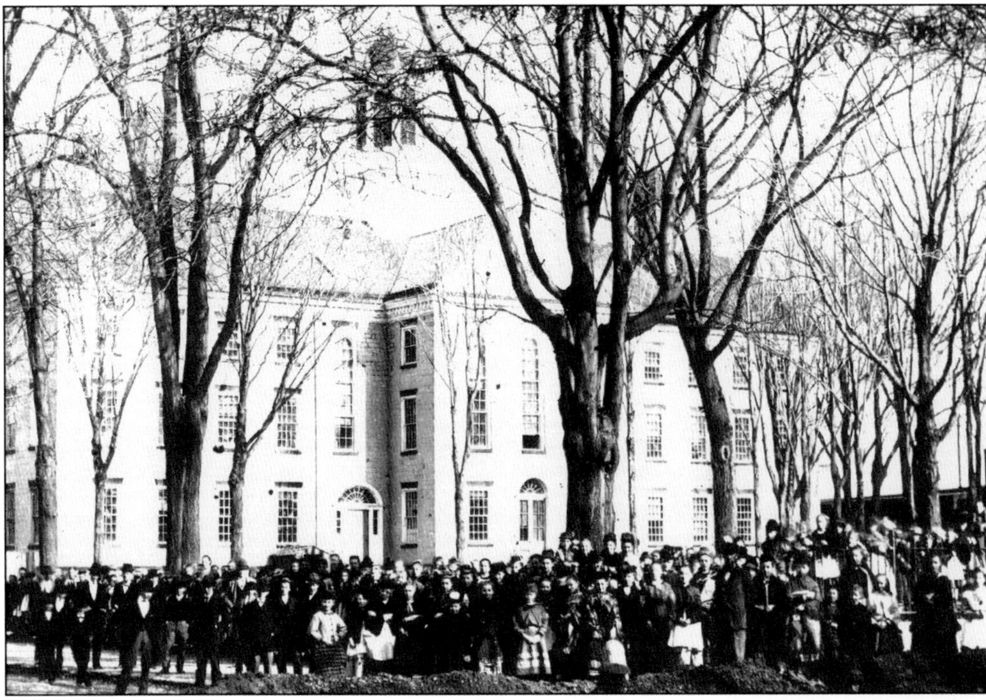

Here is a view of the students at Union School, when the West College building was used by the city school district from 1854 to 1890.

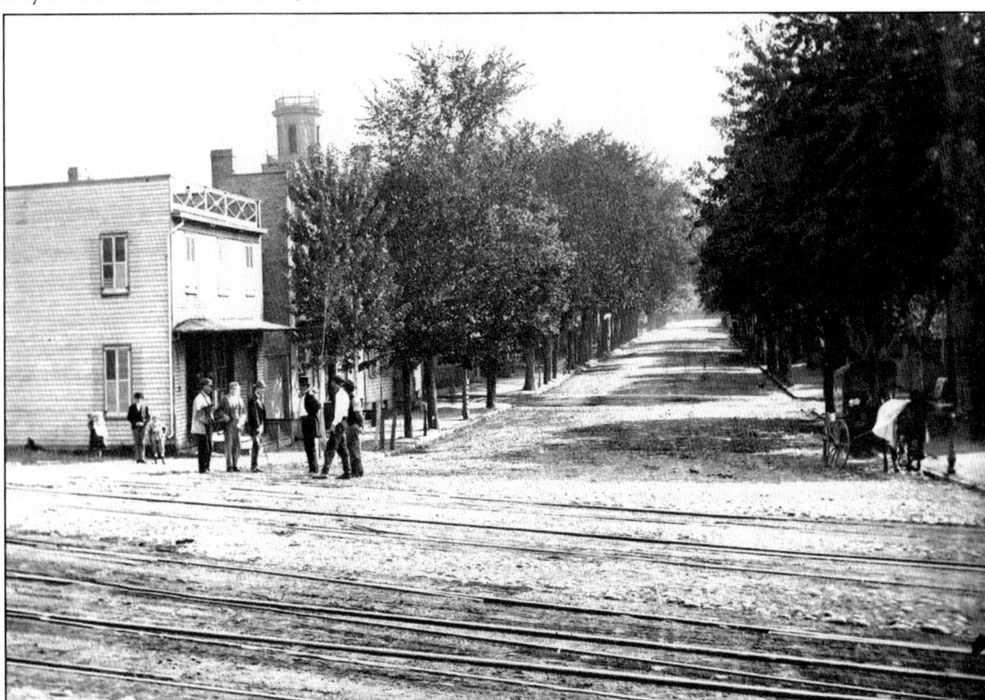

This is a view of Union Street at the railroad tracks, just past the Erie Canal, looking west around 1870. This is before the elevated tracks were built.

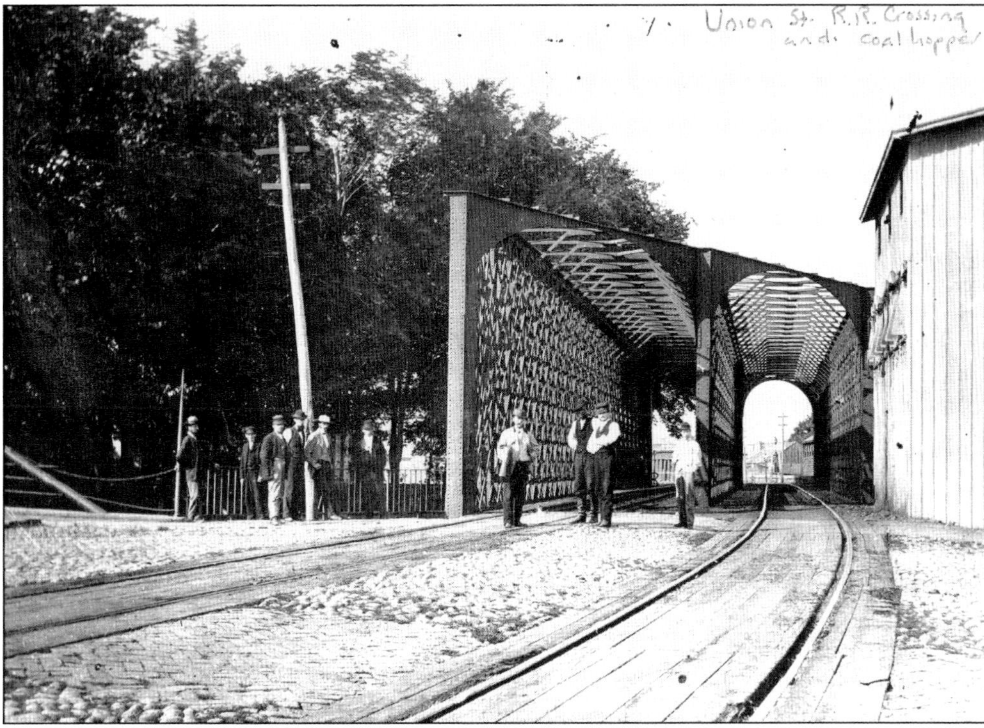

The original Union Street bridge (and coal hopper) went over the Erie Canal, as seen here along with the Union Street pedestrian bridge on the left.

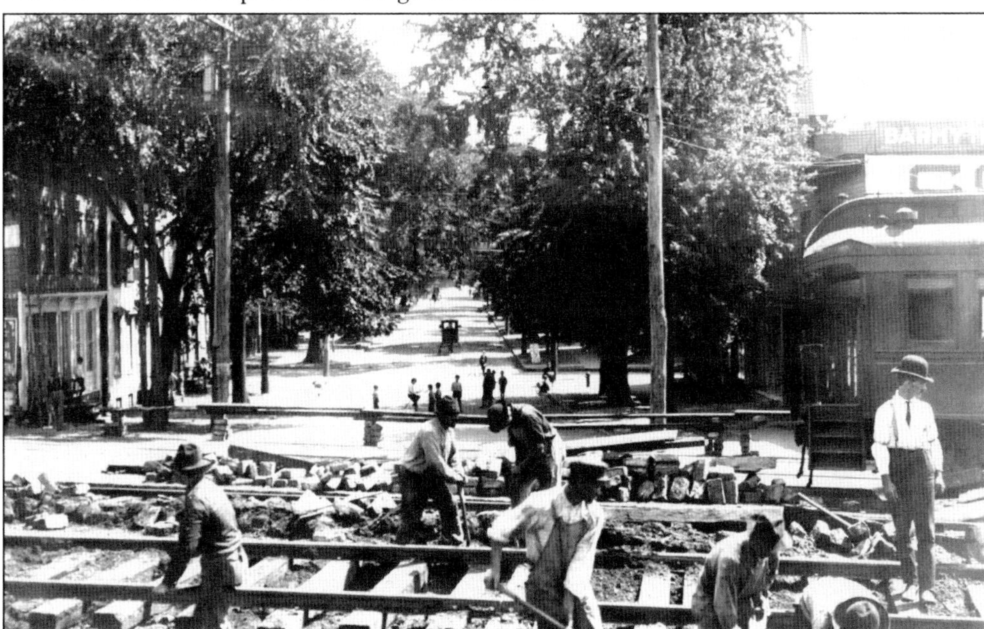

There were several tracks through the city, and after a number of people being killed by the fast moving trains, the railroad was ordered to elevate the tracks, which is what is in the city today. Here workers can be seen beginning to elevate the tracks; this began in 1900 and lasted until 1908.

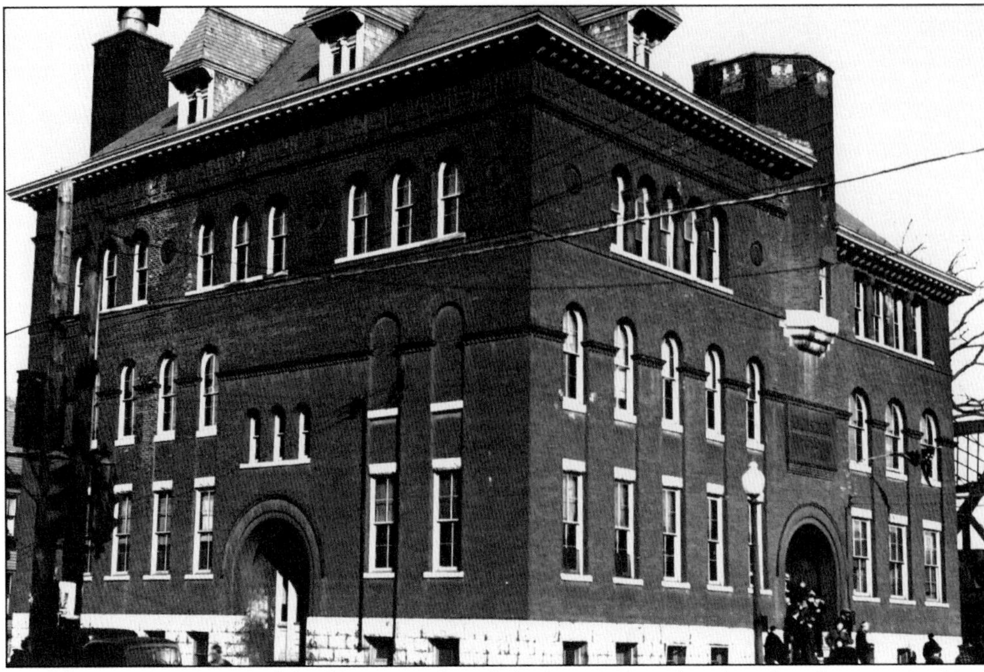

The West College/city hall building was demolished in 1890 and replaced with a new building called Union School, seen here in 1935. This was the high school and then was used for apartments. It was raised in 1960 and serves today as a parking lot for the Van Dyke Restaurant and Jazz Club.

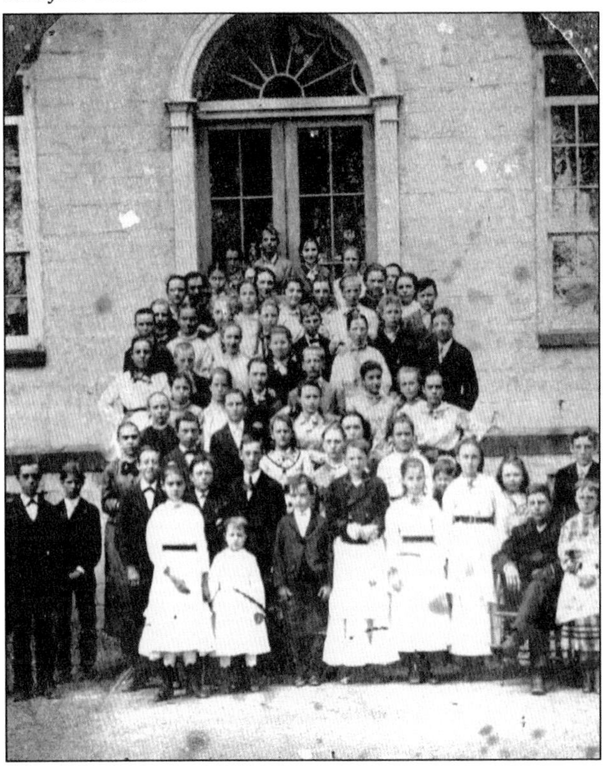

Here a graduating class of Union School can be seen on June 21, 1875.

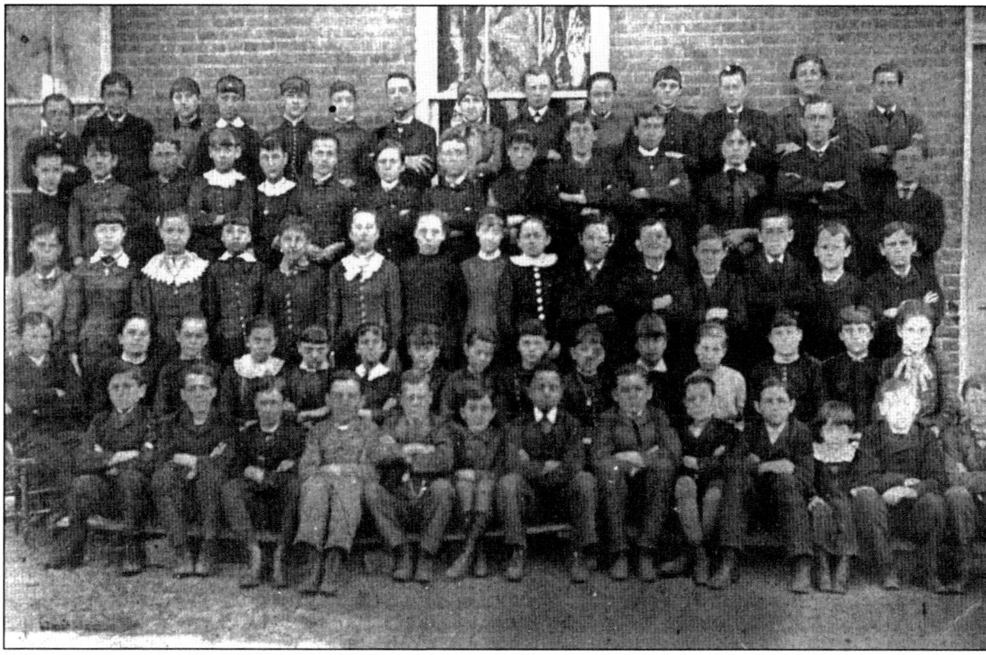

This is another graduating class of Union School in the 1880s.

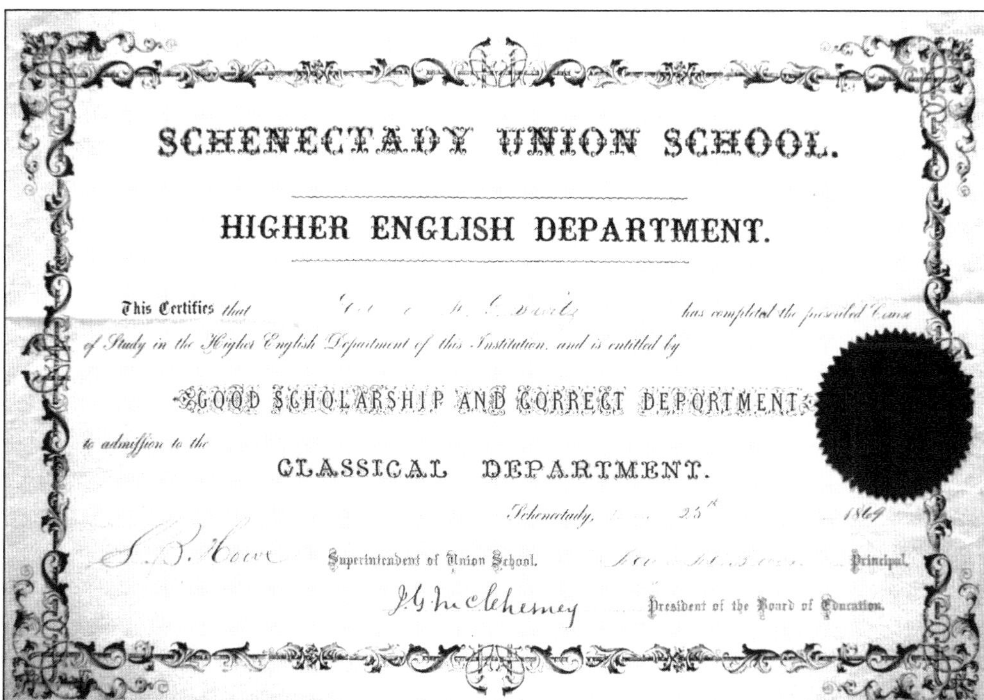

SCHENECTADY UNION SCHOOL.

HIGHER ENGLISH DEPARTMENT.

This Certifies that [illegible] has completed the prescribed Course of Study in the Higher English Department of this Institution, and is entitled by

GOOD SCHOLARSHIP AND CORRECT DEPORTMENT

to admission to the

CLASSICAL DEPARTMENT.

Schenectady, [illegible] 25th 1869

S. B. Howe Superintendent of Union School. [illegible] Principal.

J. G. McChesney President of the Board of Education.

Here is the Union School diploma belonging to Celene Savitz, who graduated on June 25, 1869.

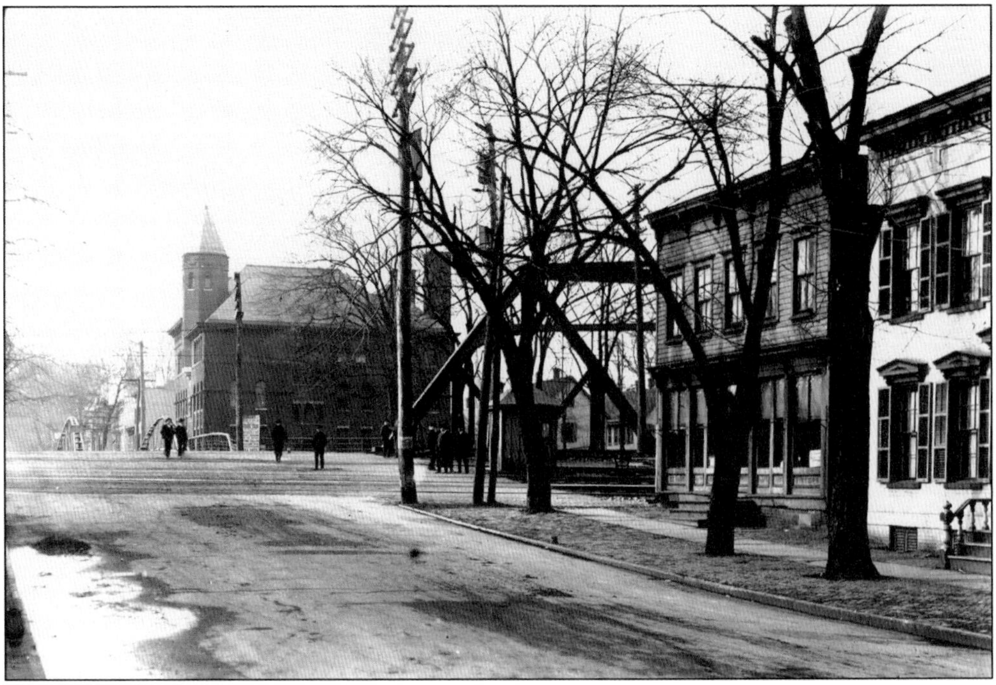

Seen here is a view looking west from Union Street on the other side of the tracks, before they were elevated. One can see the Union School and the two bridges that crossed the Erie Canal in this c. 1910 photograph.

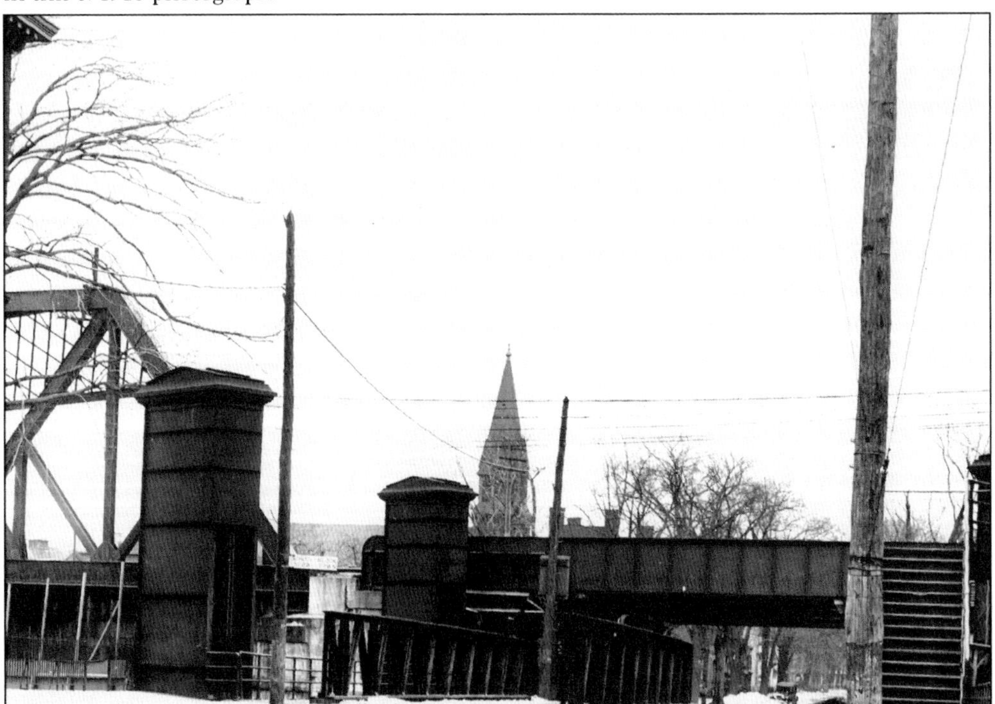

This is a view of Union Street and the Erie Canal hydraulic lift bridge. Notice that the sign that says "school block slow down." This was for the nearby Union School, barely seen on the left.

Seven

Church Street

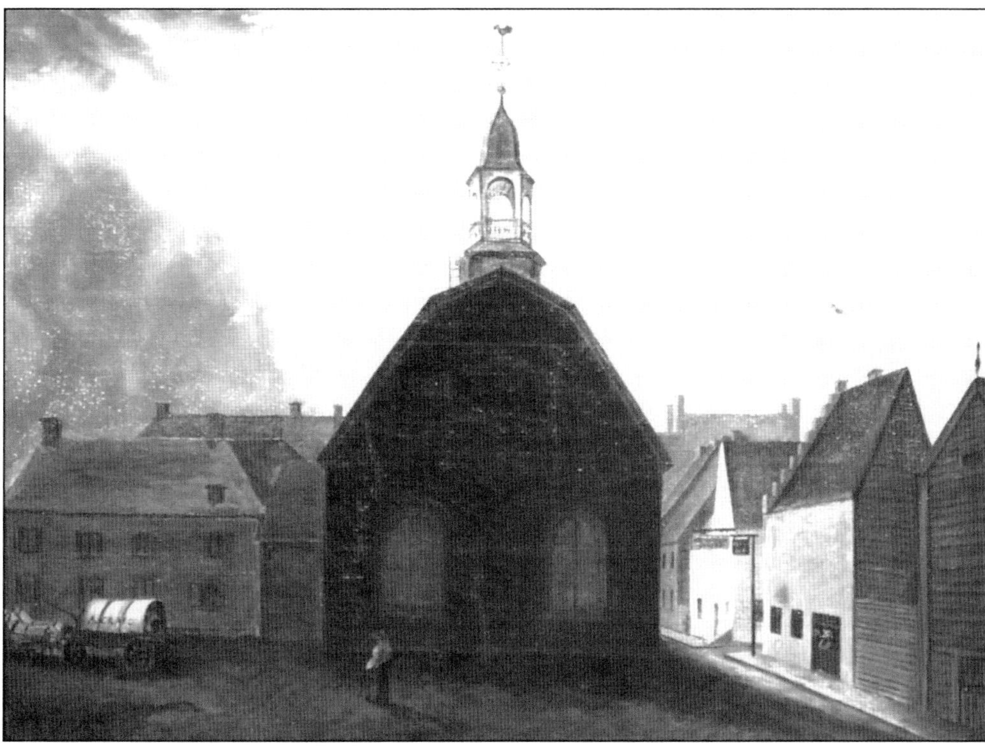

This is a painting of the Dutch Reformed church as it sat in the intersection of Church and Union Streets during the 18th century. The Dutch Reformed church played a prominent role in the lives of early stockade settlers. It is here that several townspeople erected a liberty flag and pole prior to the Revolutionary War.

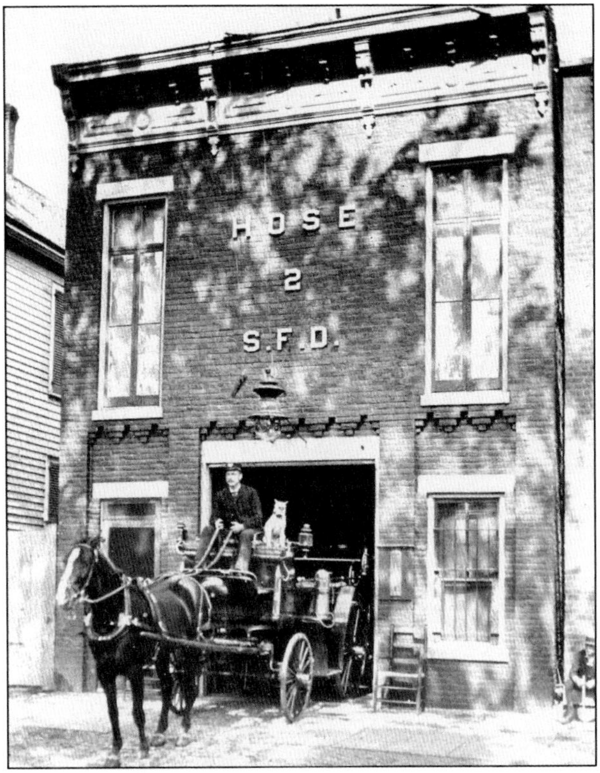

The Van Vranken Hose No. 2, located at 107 South Church Street, also protected the stockade residents. Here S. Van Vranken and mascot dog Mike pose in this 1890s-era photograph.

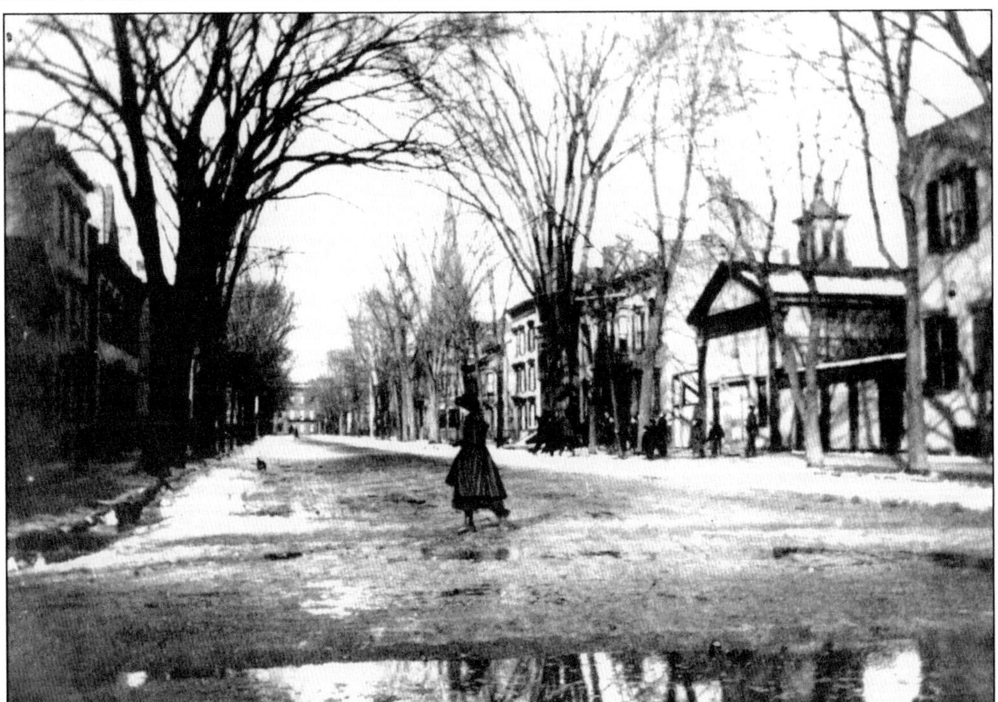

Here is a lonely woman walking across Church Street at the intersection of State Street around 1890 in the wintertime. This is the location of the stockade's south gate.

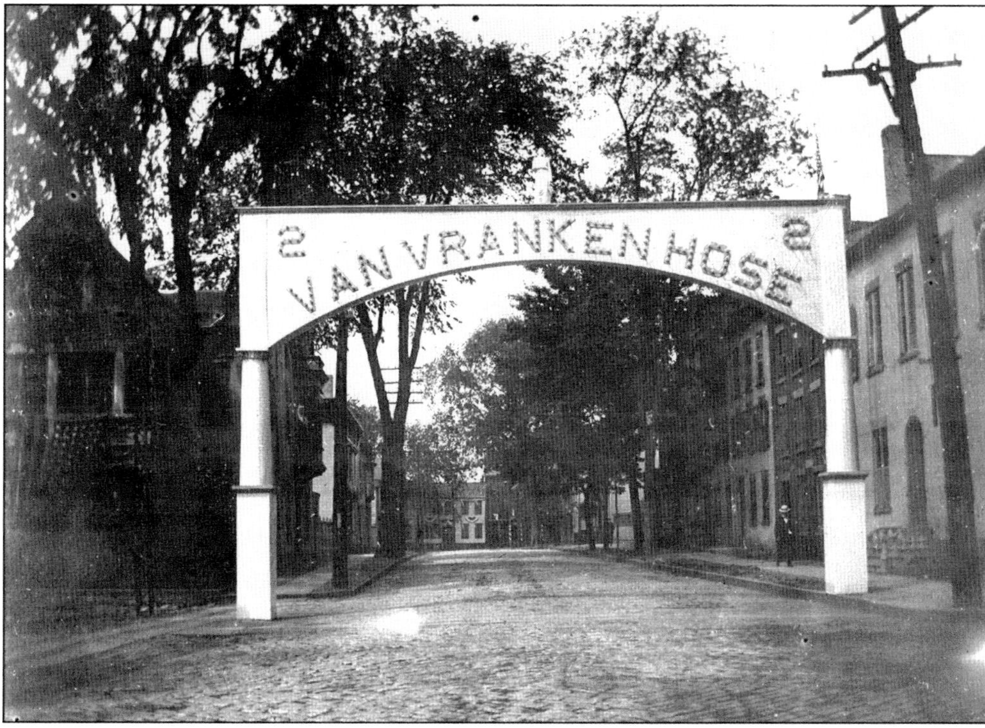

Van Vranken Hose No. 2 is obviously celebrating one of its anniversaries with a sign at the intersection of State and Church Streets (the original south gate of the stockade) in 1897.

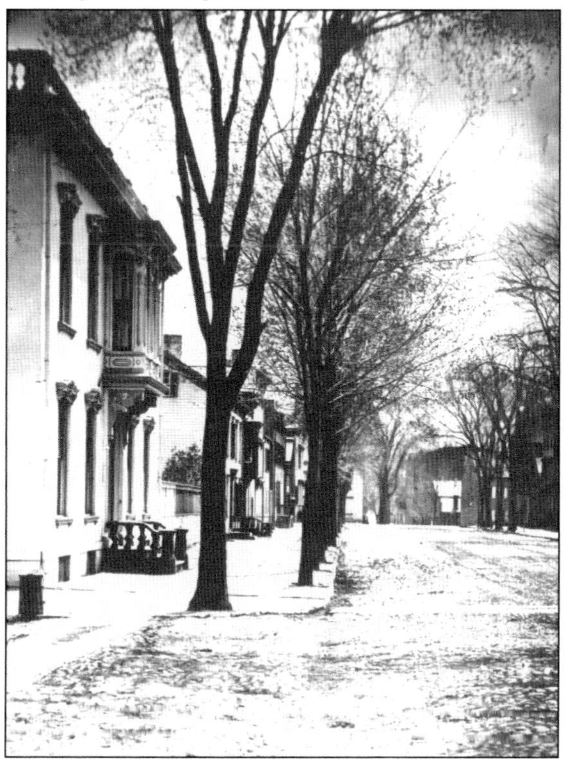

Here is a view of the southeast corner of Church and Union Streets showing the cobblestone street around 1900.

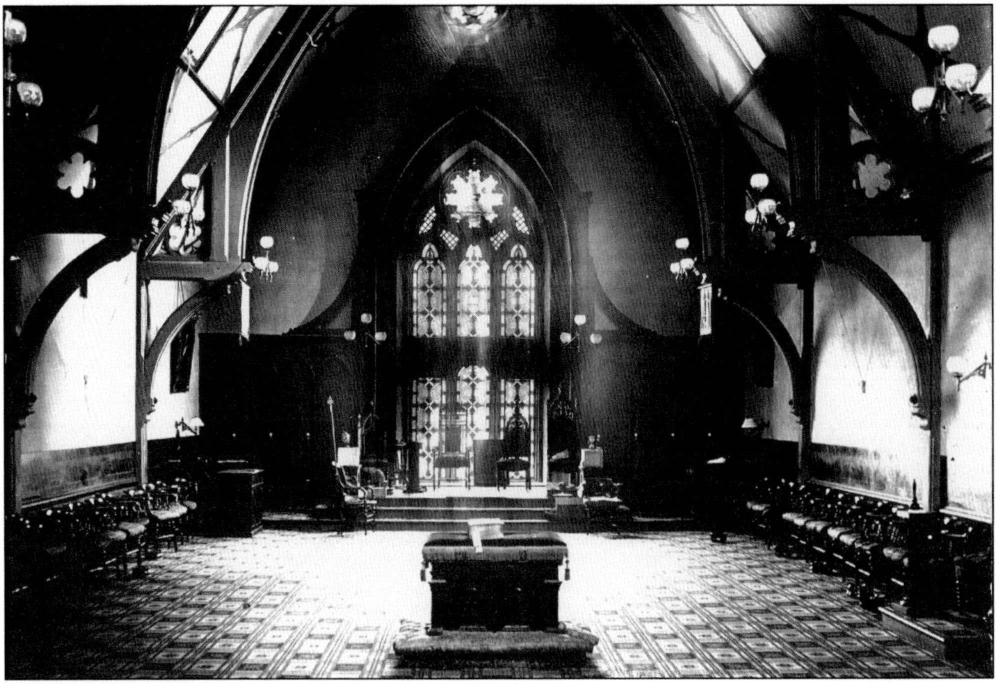

Here is a rare view of the interior of the Masonic temple at 12 South Church Street, now the Civic Players performing arts center. The Civic Players have been in this building since 1928. The Masons organized in Schenectady as early as 1774.

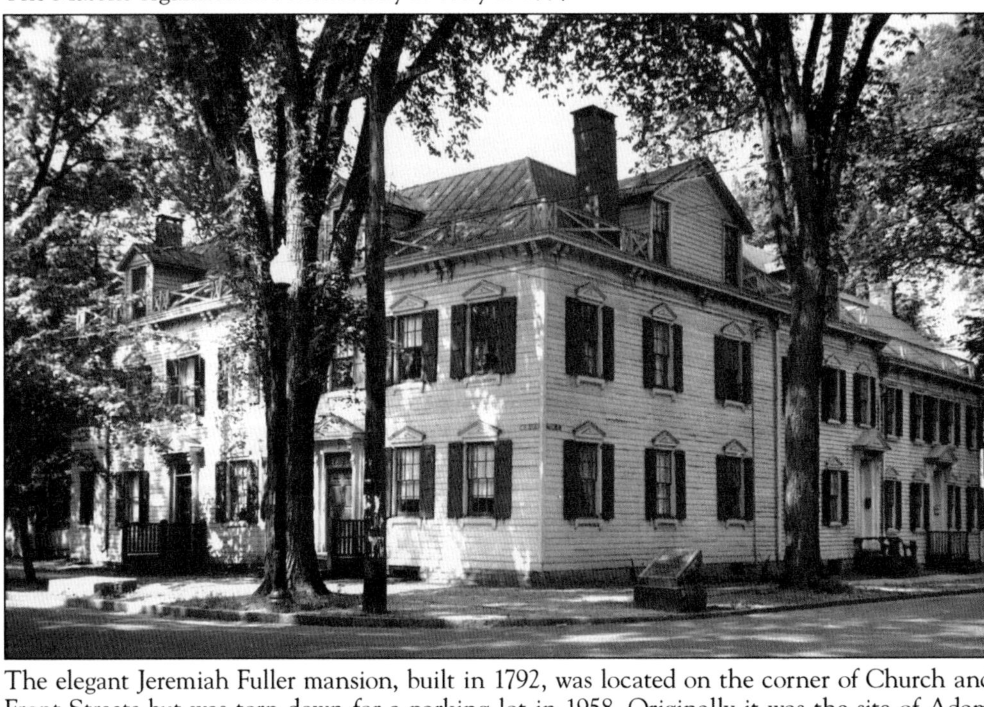

The elegant Jeremiah Fuller mansion, built in 1792, was located on the corner of Church and Front Streets but was torn down for a parking lot in 1958. Originally it was the site of Adam Vrooman's home and where he took the stance against the French and Native Americans in 1690. Unfortunately this is before preservation of the stockade was considered an alternative.

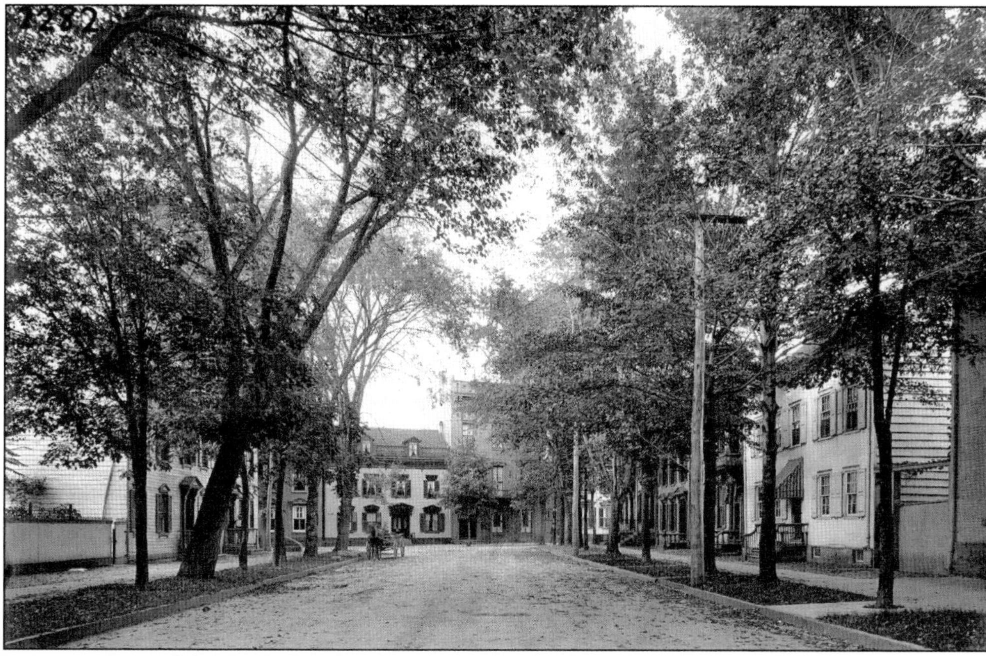

Here is a beautiful view from Church Street looking towards Front Street in 1890. The Fuller mansion can be seen on the left and the Brouwer-Rosa house on the right. At the end of this street stood the north gate where Symon Schemerhorn rode his famous ride to Albany during the massacre of 1690.

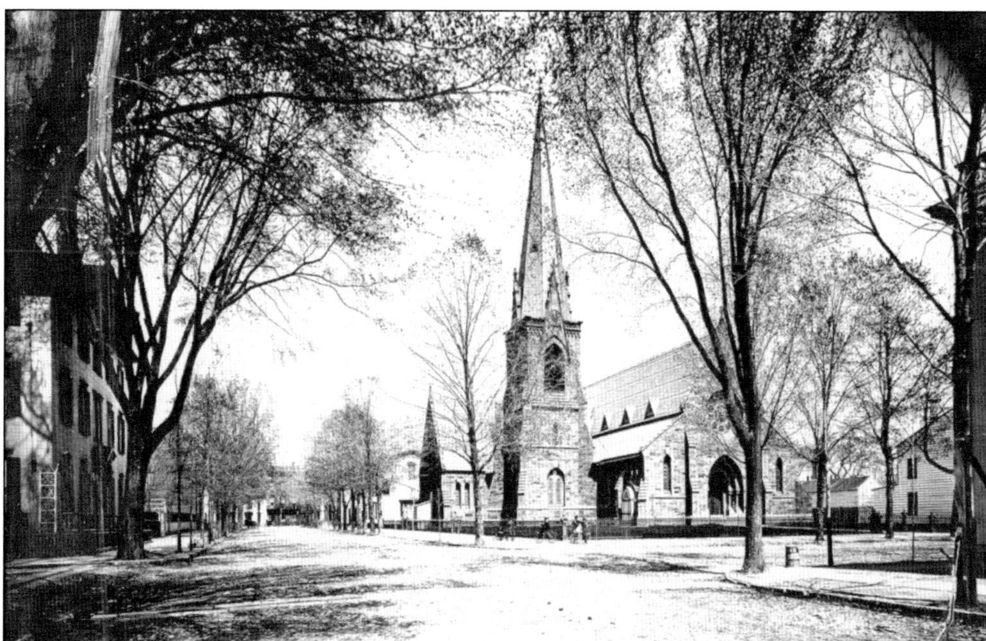

Here is a view of the fourth Dutch Reformed church on the intersection of Church and Union Streets in 1870. The Mohawk Bank (now Stockade Inn) is on the left. This church burned in 1948 and was restored to the present structure. The third version of the church stood in the middle of this intersection.

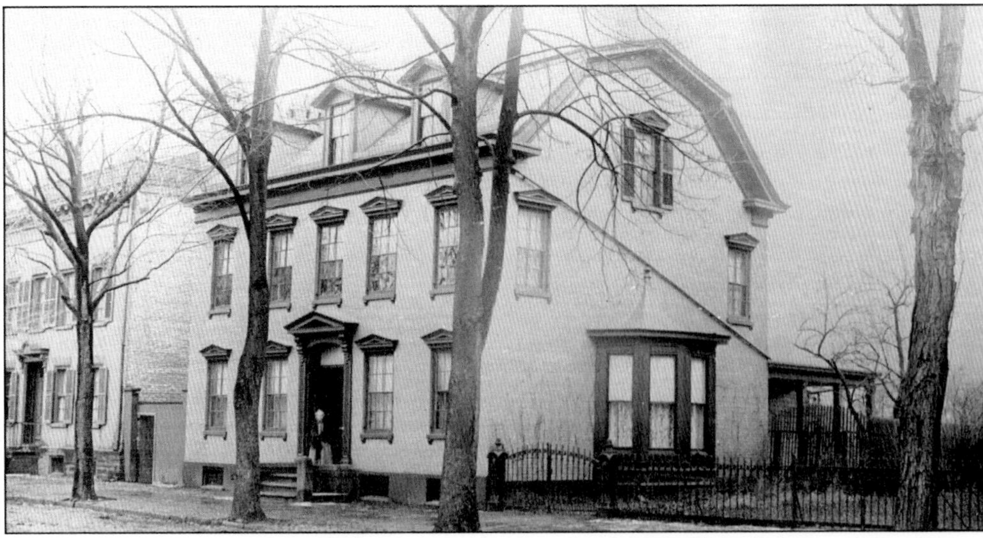

This is the original site of the Mohawk Bank at 10 and 13 North Church Street, shown here in 1887. The home was used by the bank from 1808 to about 1818. The bank built a newer building on the northwest corner of Church and Union Streets between 1816 and 1829, which is now the Stockade Inn.

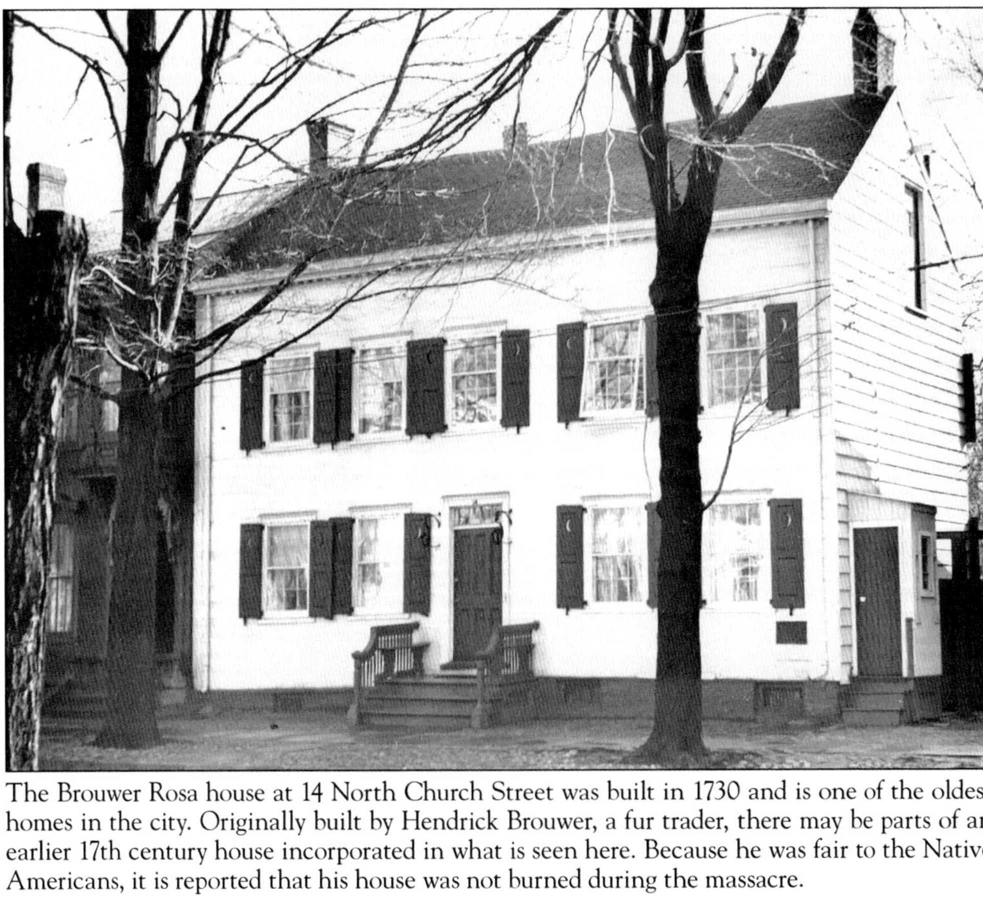

The Brouwer Rosa house at 14 North Church Street was built in 1730 and is one of the oldest homes in the city. Originally built by Hendrick Brouwer, a fur trader, there may be parts of an earlier 17th century house incorporated in what is seen here. Because he was fair to the Native Americans, it is reported that his house was not burned during the massacre.

Eight

The Mohawk River

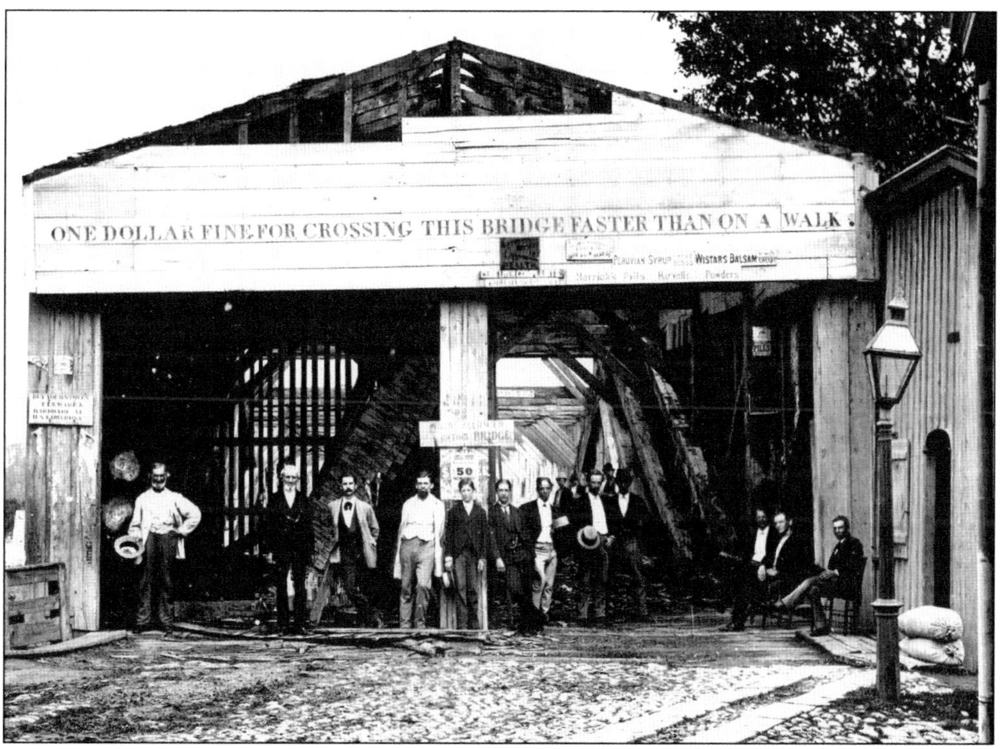

One of the first bridges across the Mohawk River was built in 1808 and was wooden and designed by Theodore Burr, cousin of Aaron Burr. It was 900 feet long with cables made of large pine planks bolted to each other. This toll bridge opened on December 6, 1808. In 1873, it was purchased by the Town of Glenville and used until 1874 when it was demolished, only to be replaced with a steel bridge on the same stone piers. This picture of the bridge in 1874 shows workers ready to take it down.

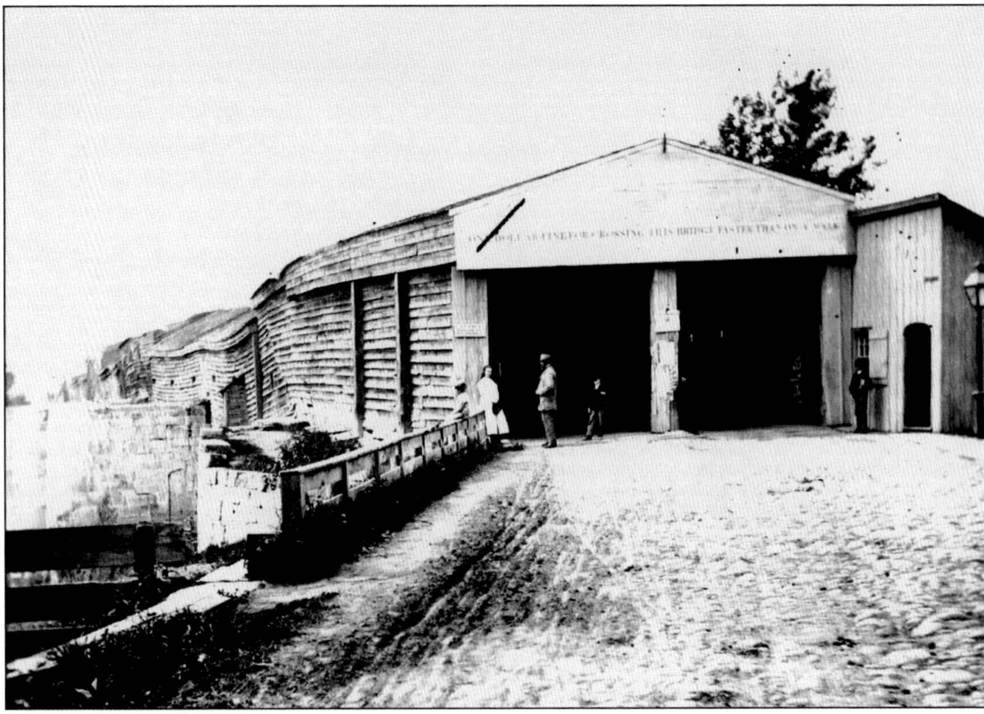

The wooden bridge was covered after four new piers were added to the original three. This gave the appearance of several barns attached to each other. It also gave haven to birds and bats at night. The tollbooth on the right was moved later to the left side.

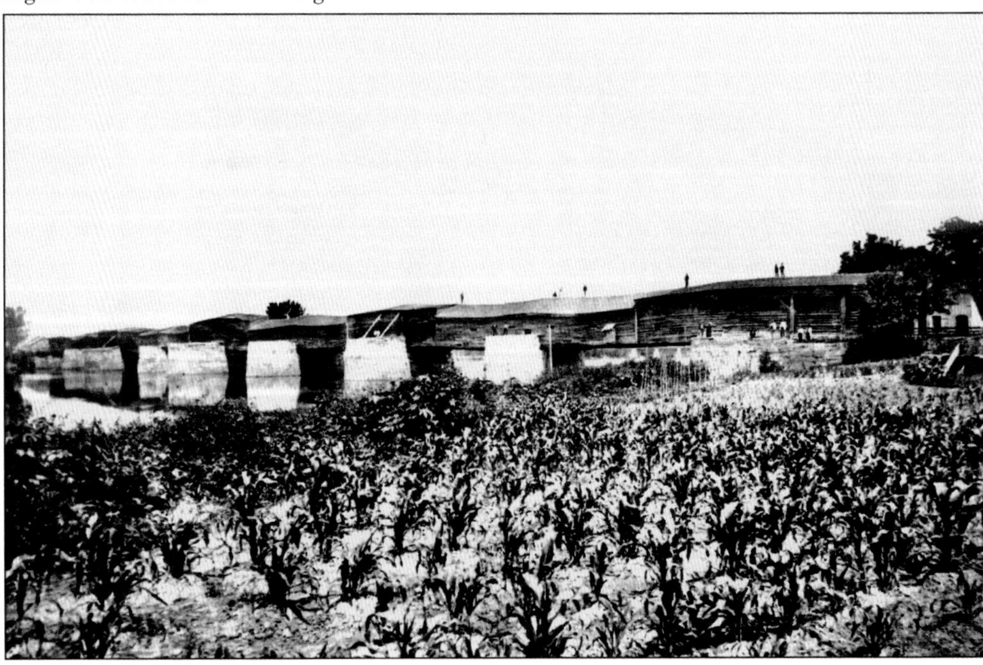

This view of the south side of the bridge in 1874 shows workers beginning to take it apart, but notice the fields of broomcorn growing in the foreground. Schenectady was famous for making brooms during this period of the 19th century.

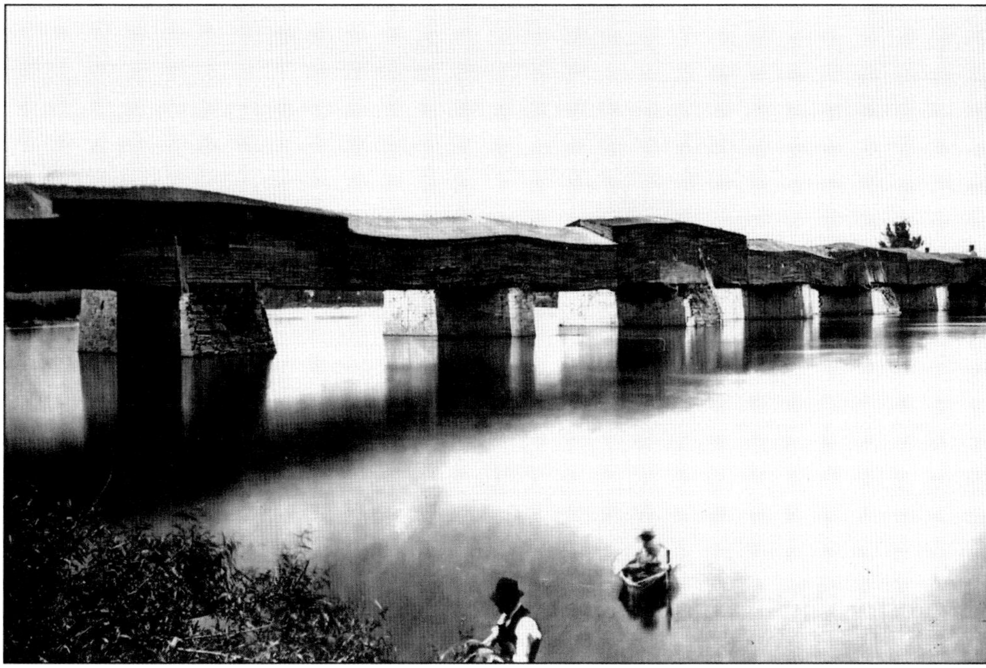

Seen here is another view of the bridge with two canoeists in the foreground, looking towards Schenectady.

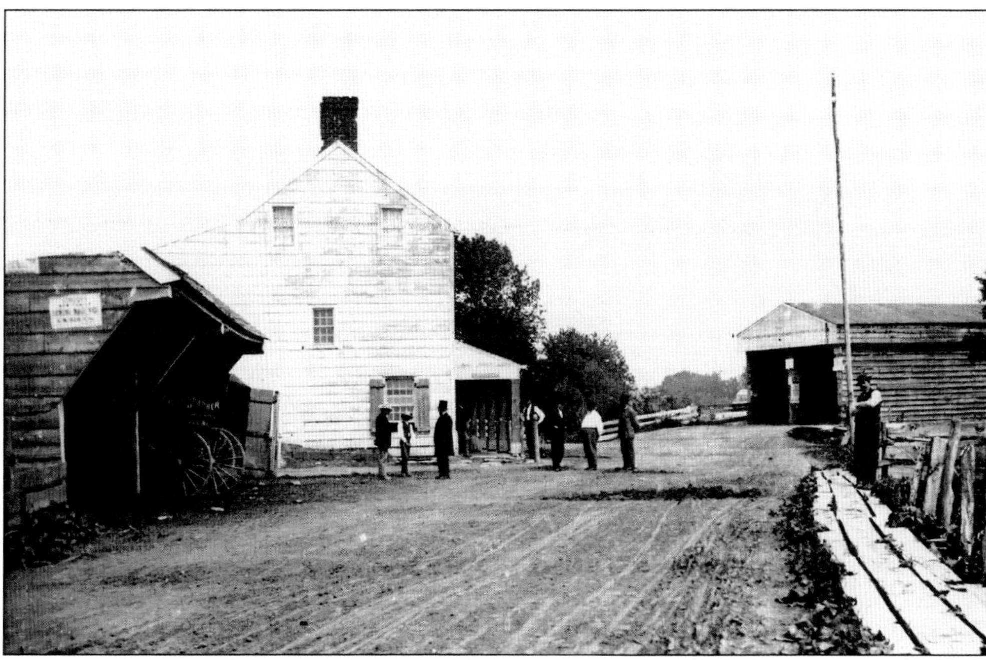

On the Scotia side of the bridge, the Mohawk Turnpike began (actually the bridge was owned by the Mohawk Turnpike and Bridge Company as well) with this "dyke" road, today called Schonowe Avenue. The building on the left was Meyer's Tavern in this 1870s photograph.

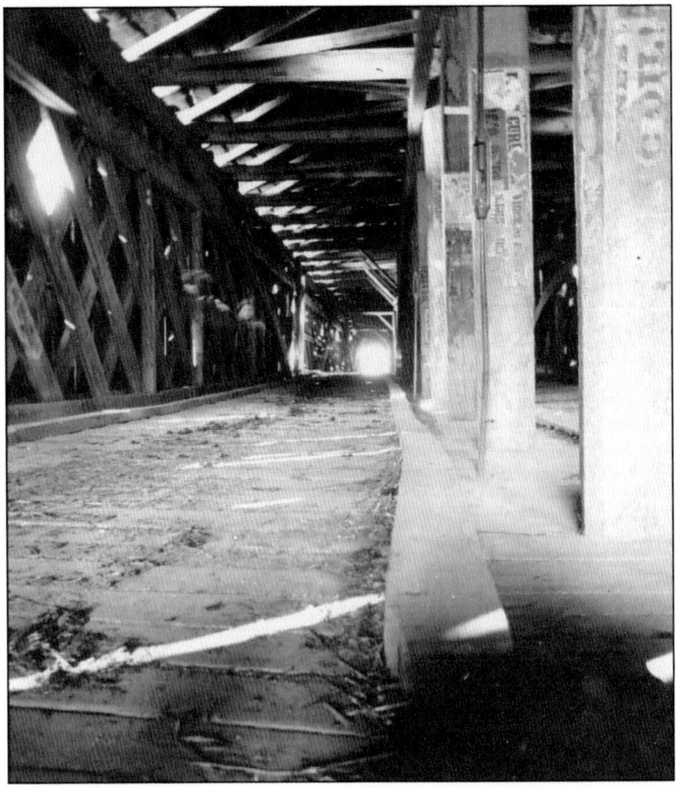

Inside the bridge, light was let in through cracks and at an opening three-feet square on each pier. At night, a total of four oil lamps dimly lit the view. Two lanes were separated by wooden vertical planks, keeping both directions divided.

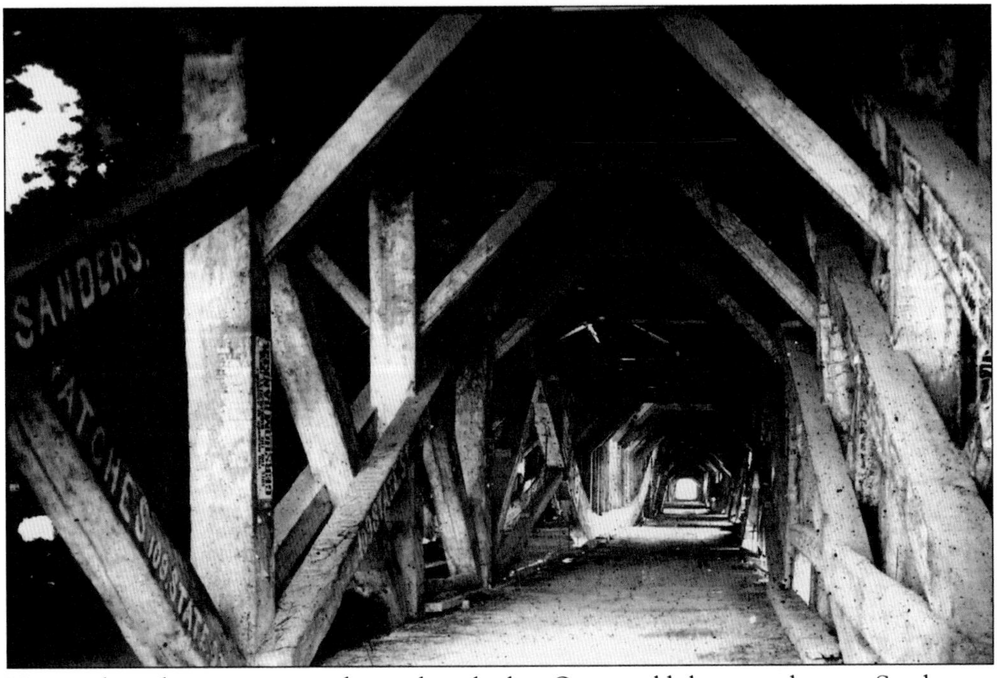

Notice the advertising painted on the planks. One could buy watches at Sanders at 108 State Street.

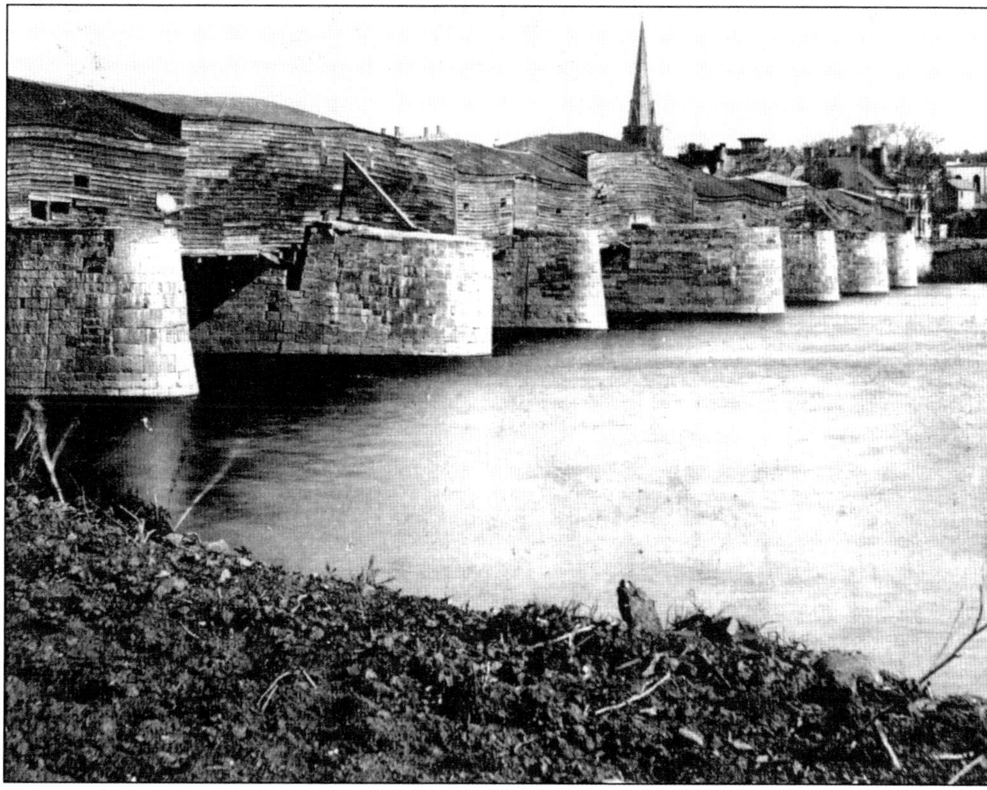
Here the bridge can be seen starting to buckle and wave and deteriorate.

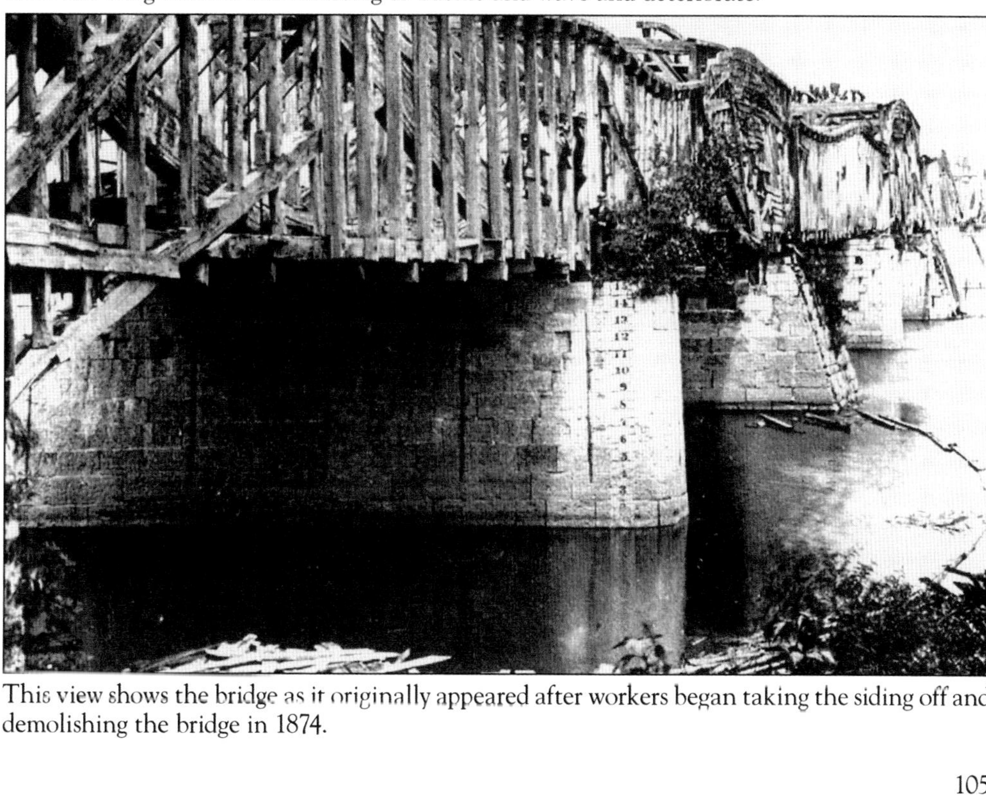
This view shows the bridge as it originally appeared after workers began taking the siding off and demolishing the bridge in 1874.

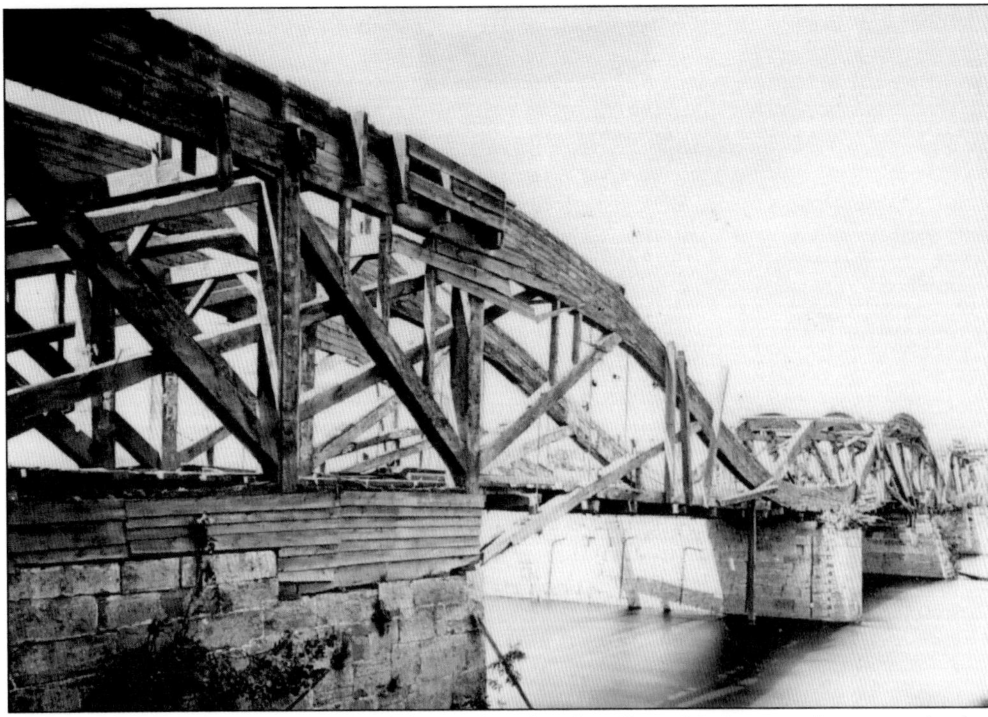

This view shows the original arched design by Theodore Burr. Unfortunately, it was the last time—and for most, the first time—as this 1874 photograph is of its demolition.

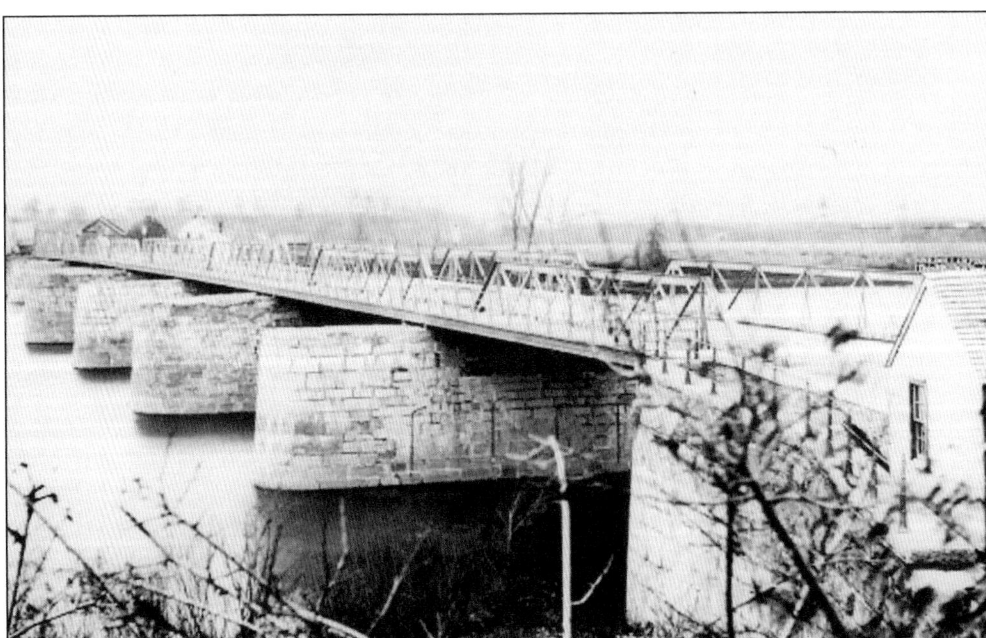

Here the new steel bridge can be seen that replaced the Burr bridge in 1874. They used the existing stone piers of the old wooden bridge.

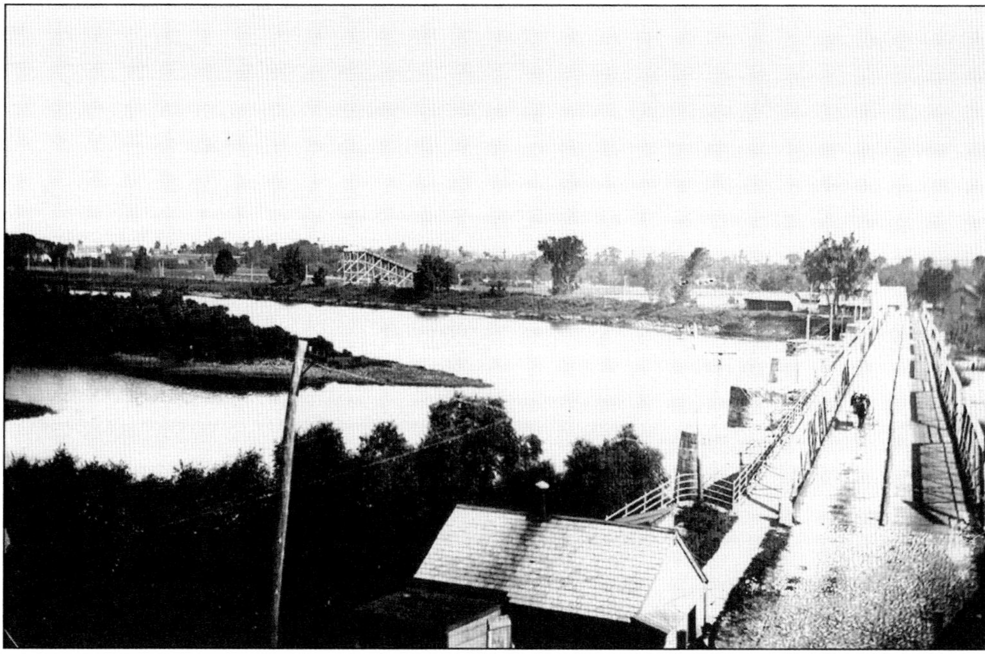

With the new steel bridge, the tollhouse was moved to the left, and Washington Street was cobbled. Here a great aerial view can be seen of a lone wagon going to Scotia on the steel bridge. The toboggan slide on the Scotia side and Meyer's tavern at the western end of the bridge can also be seen.

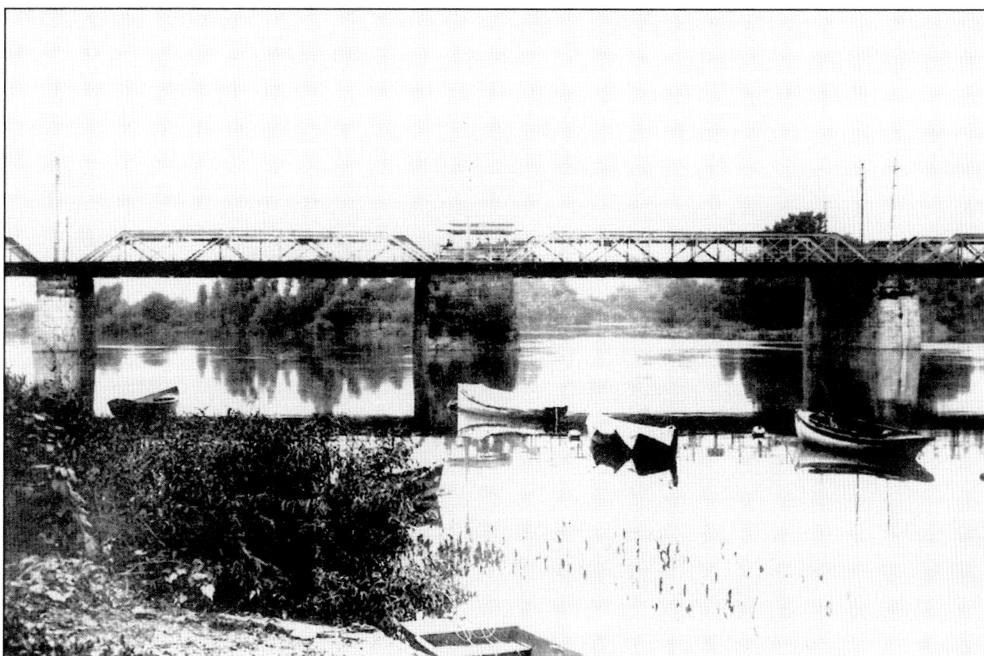

The bridge became the trolley bridge in April 1902 when the Schenectady Railway used it, along with the Fonda, Johnstown and Gloversville Railroad (FJ&G), to bring interurban trolleys to Amsterdam. The photograph is from 1902.

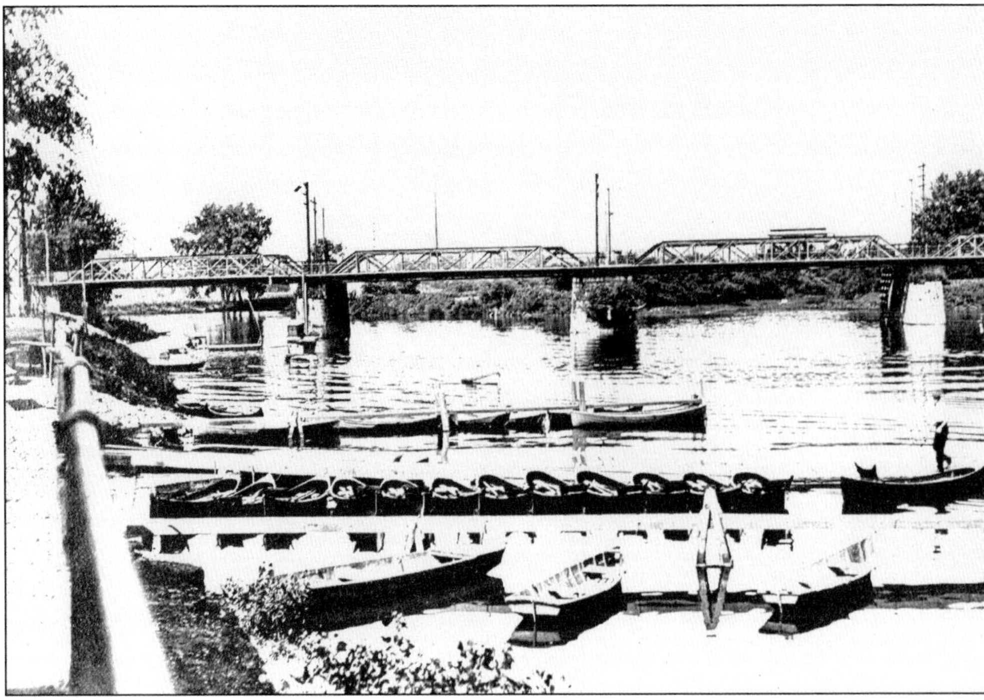

Here is another view of an open-air trolley going over the bridge. Notice the number of docks and canoes on the riverbank.

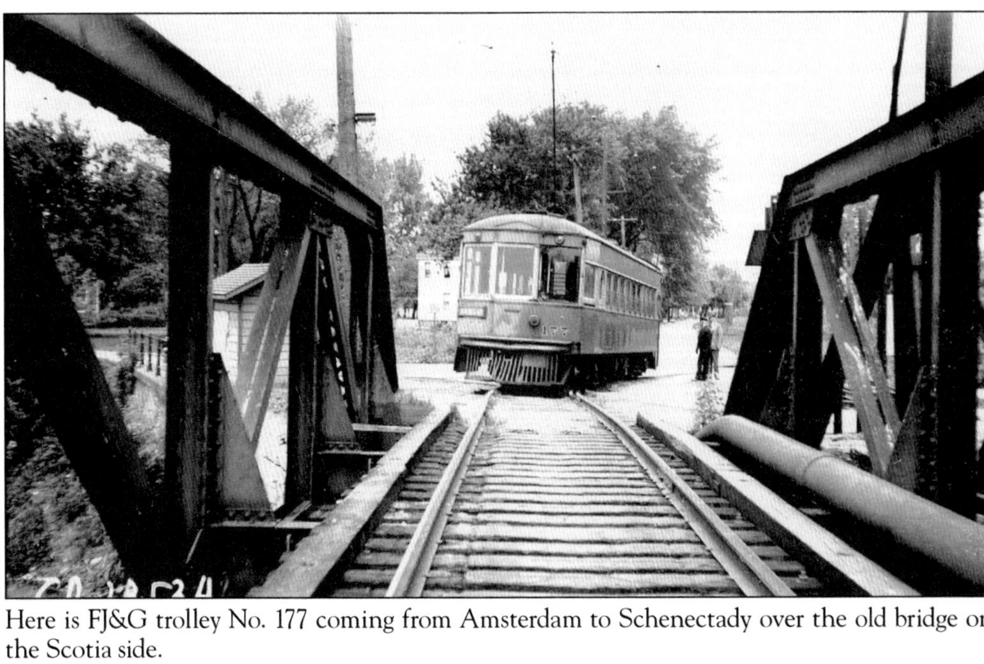

Here is FJ&G trolley No. 177 coming from Amsterdam to Schenectady over the old bridge on the Scotia side.

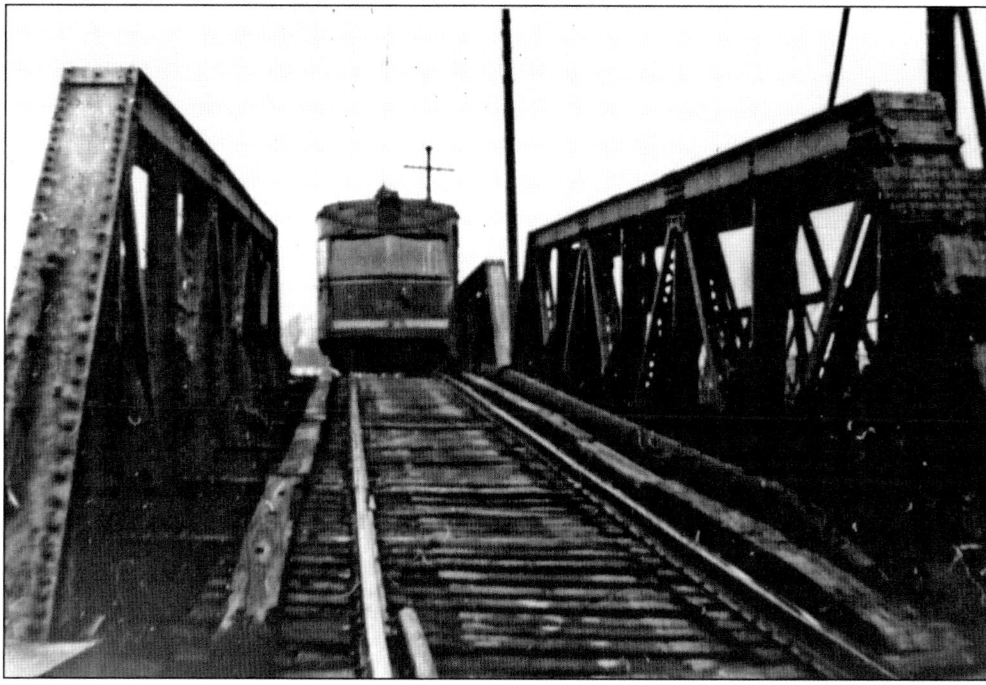

This is a bullet train coming over the Scotia Bridge to Schenectady. These started running in January 1933 but stopped in 1938 when the bridge was condemned. They needed a loop to run since they could not run backwards like the old trolleys.

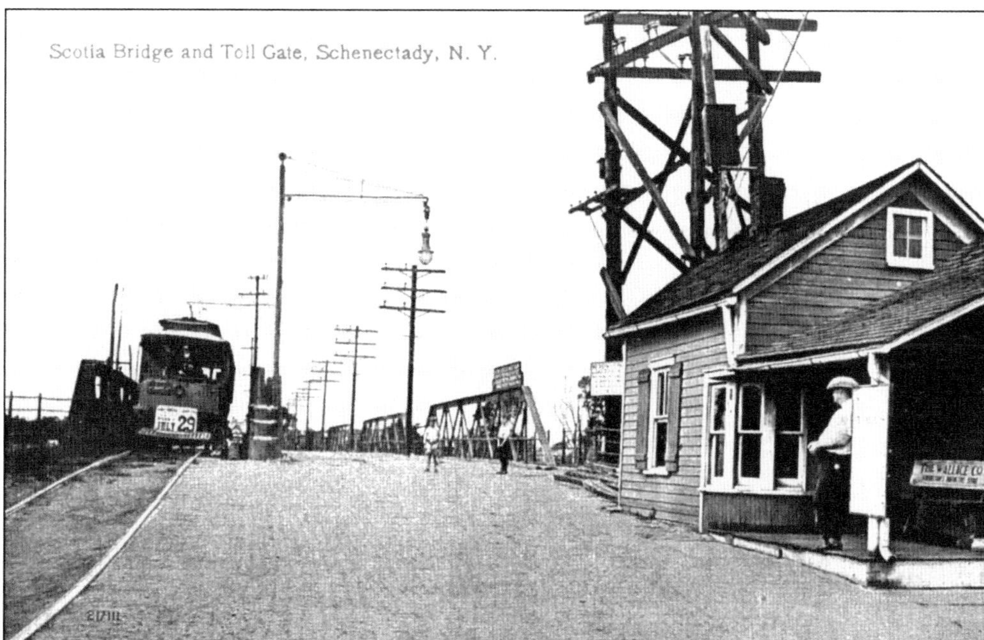

Here is a postcard showing the old bridge, trolley, and tollbooth. The tollbooth was moved back to the right side. Notice the right side of the bridge was used by pedestrians, wagons, and automobiles.

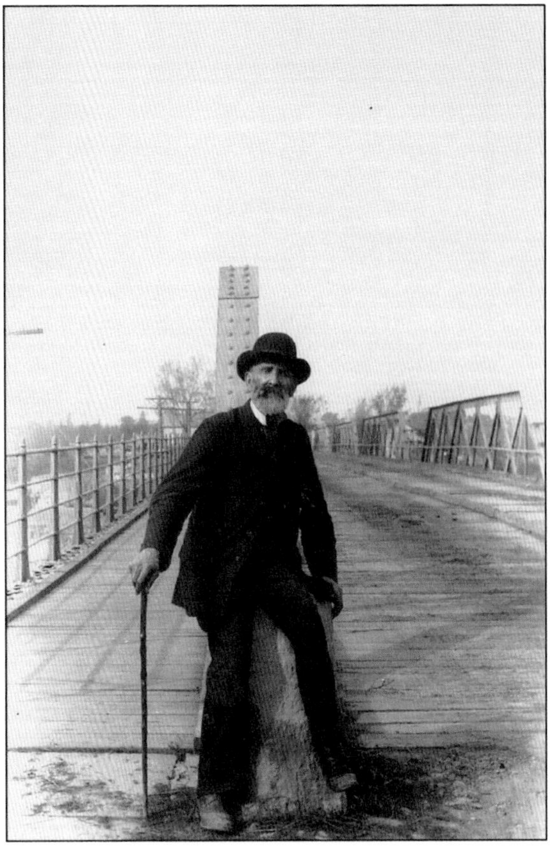

This is toll collector John Collard on October 1, 1892.

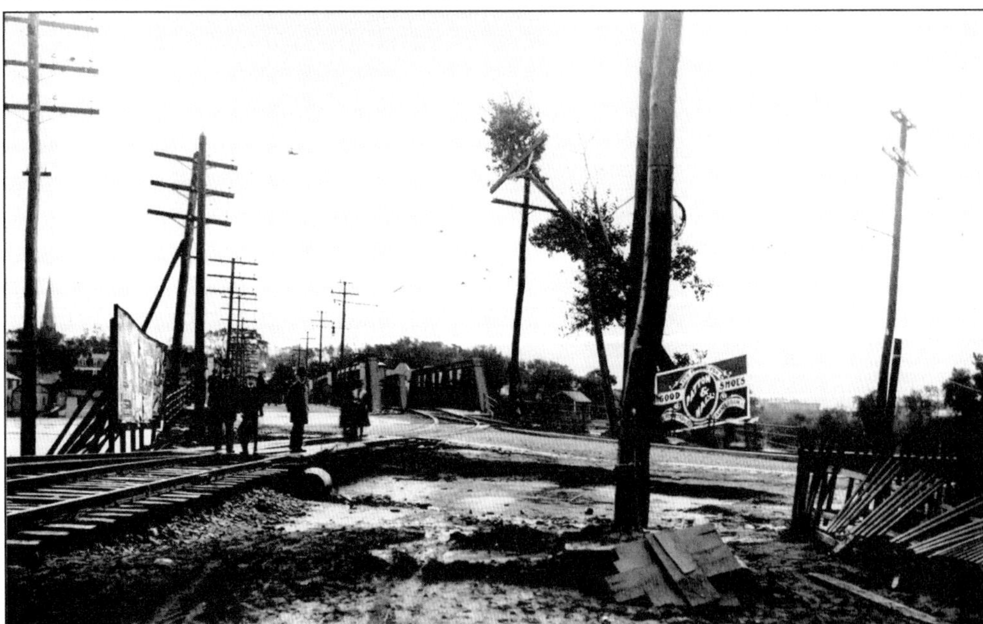

Here is a view of the bridge from the Scotia side in 1903. The billboard reads "Patton & Hall. It's for Good shoes, Schenectady and Amsterdam."

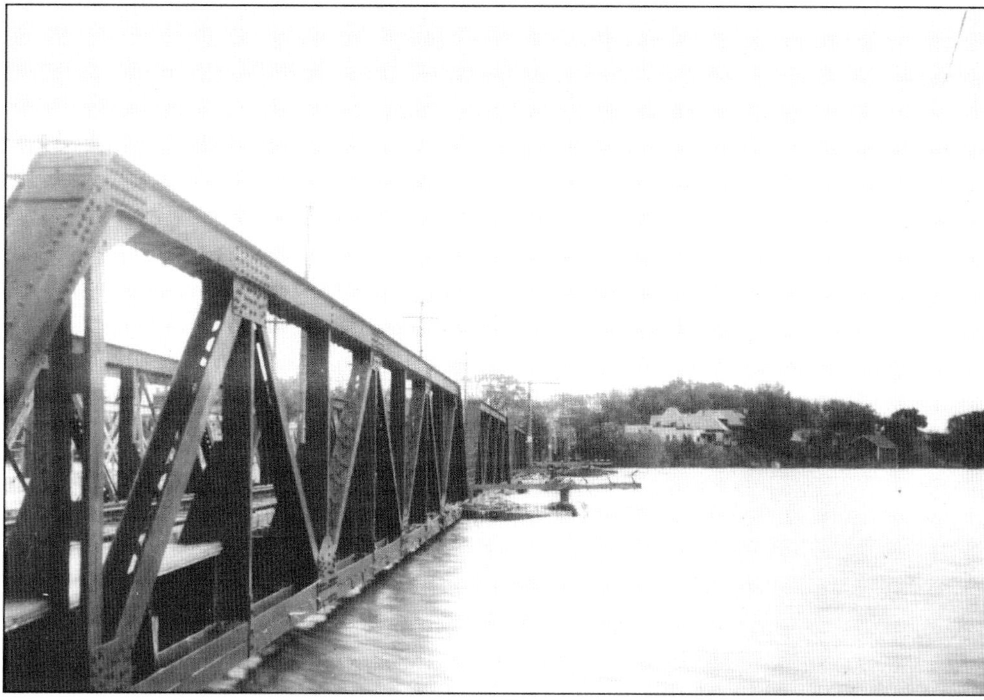

Constant flooding from the Mohawk River threatened the bridge and other bridges, not to mention the businesses and homes closer to the river. Here the flood of 1903 comes right up to the bridge floor as one looks to the city.

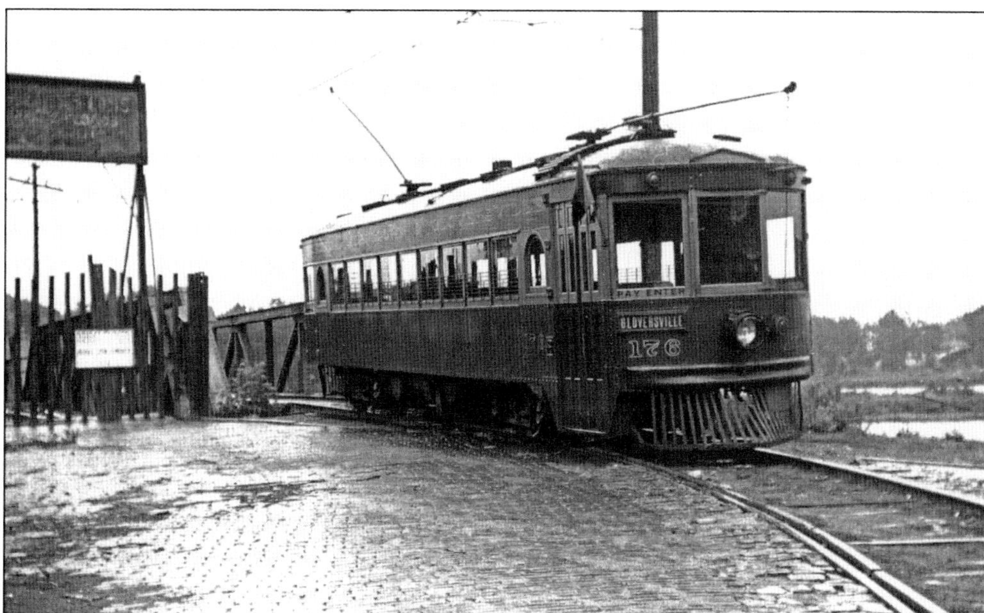

Here is the end of the bridge days. The pedestrian side is closed and this FJ&G trolley No. 176 may be making its last entrance to Schenectady on June 26, 1938. The following year, the bridge was closed completely and taken down.

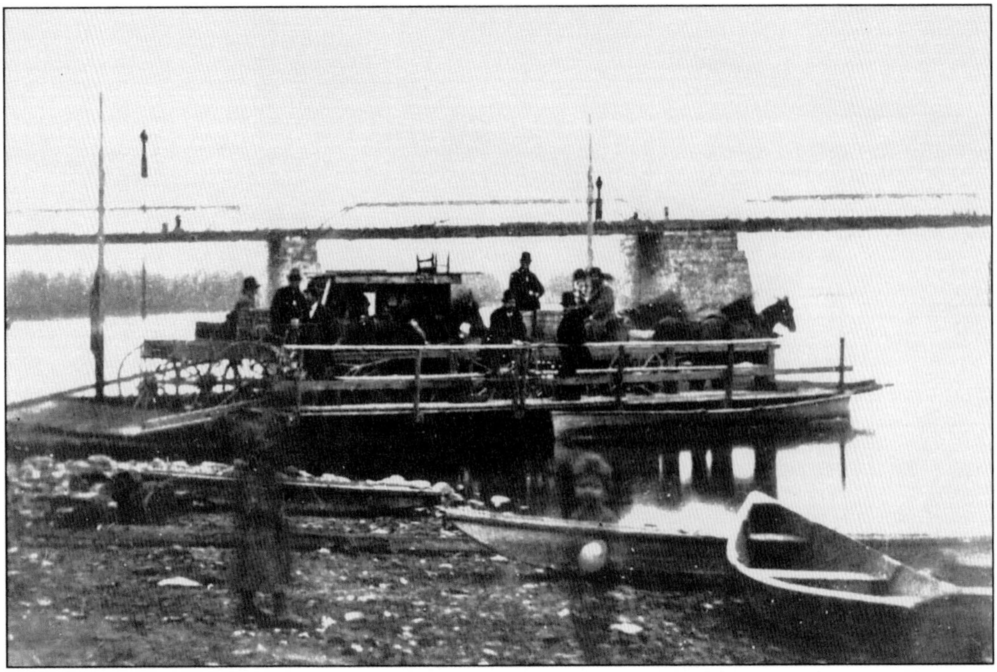

When they were building the steel bridge, a ferry was resurrected to take people across the river at the foot of Governors Lane. Before the Burr Bridge was built, a ferry was the only way to get across at the end of Ferry Street to Glenville or further up at Hoffman's Ferry.

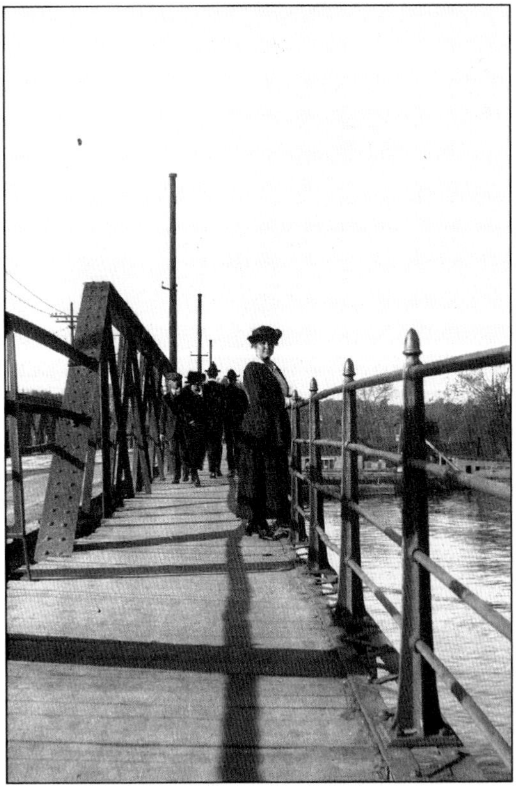

Seen here is a young woman posing for a photograph on the bridge around 1900.

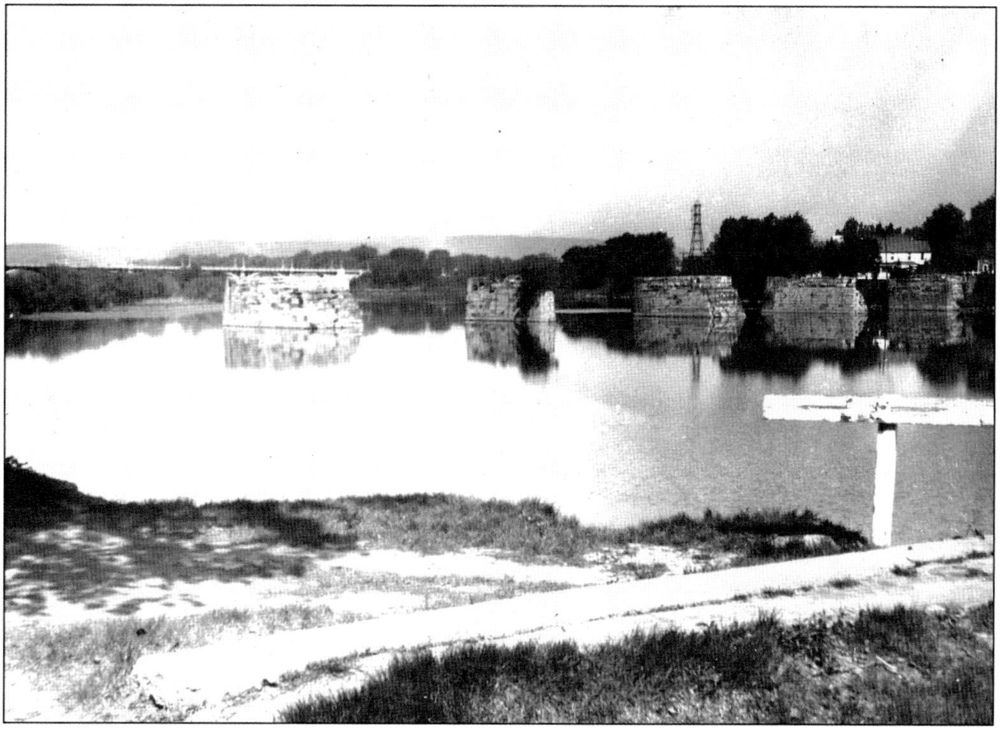

After the bridge was taken down, all that remained were the piers from the original Burr Bridge. Soon after, these piers were taken out of the river and all that remains today is the piers at each end of the original span. Freeman's Bridge, erected in 1855, and the Great Western Gateway Bridge in 1925 put an end to the importance of this first bridge across the Mohawk River at Schenectady.

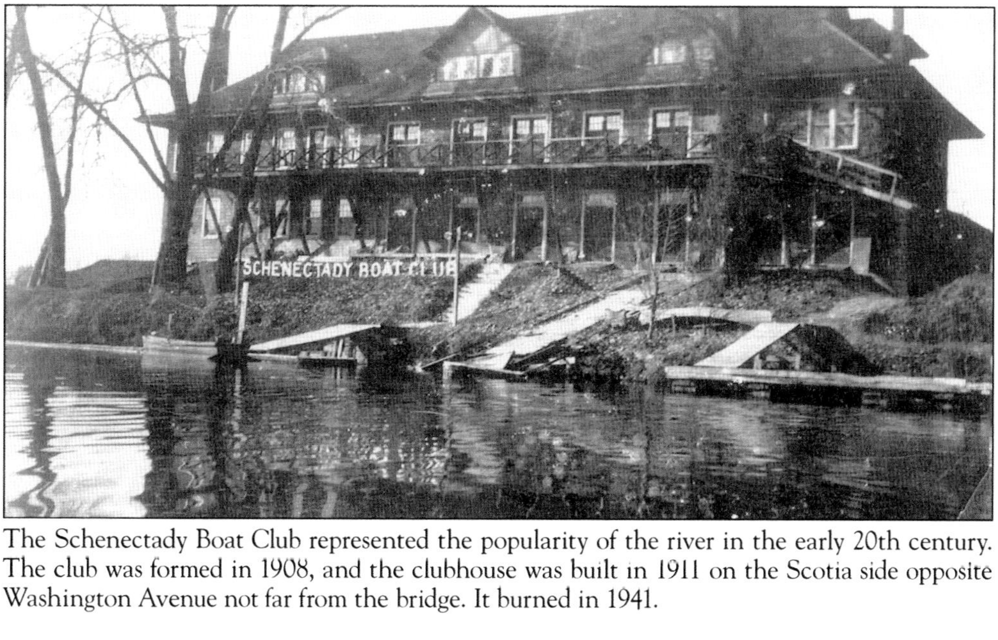

The Schenectady Boat Club represented the popularity of the river in the early 20th century. The club was formed in 1908, and the clubhouse was built in 1911 on the Scotia side opposite Washington Avenue not far from the bridge. It burned in 1941.

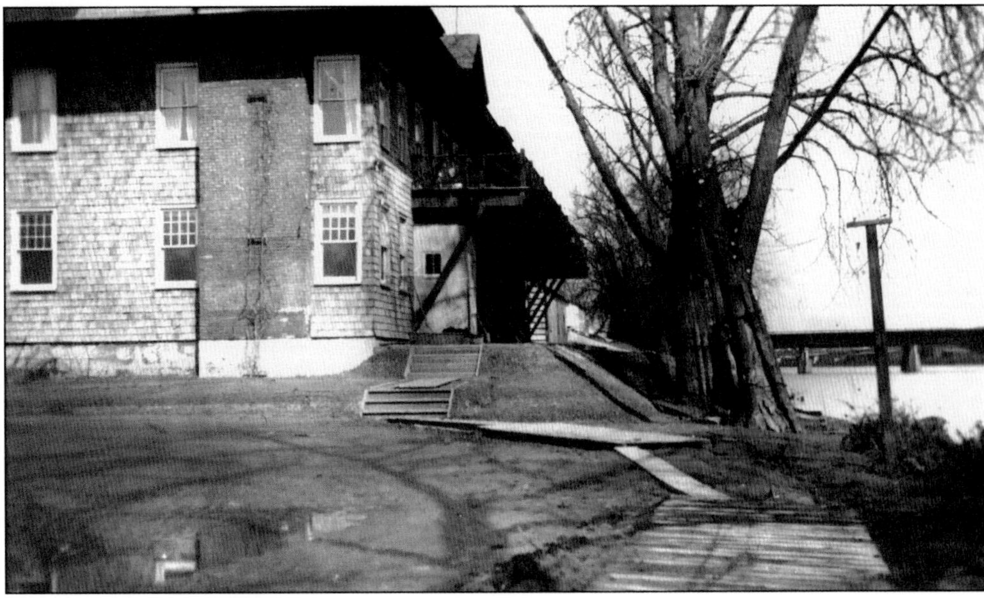

Here is the Schenectady Boat Club with the railroad bridge in the background in 1921.

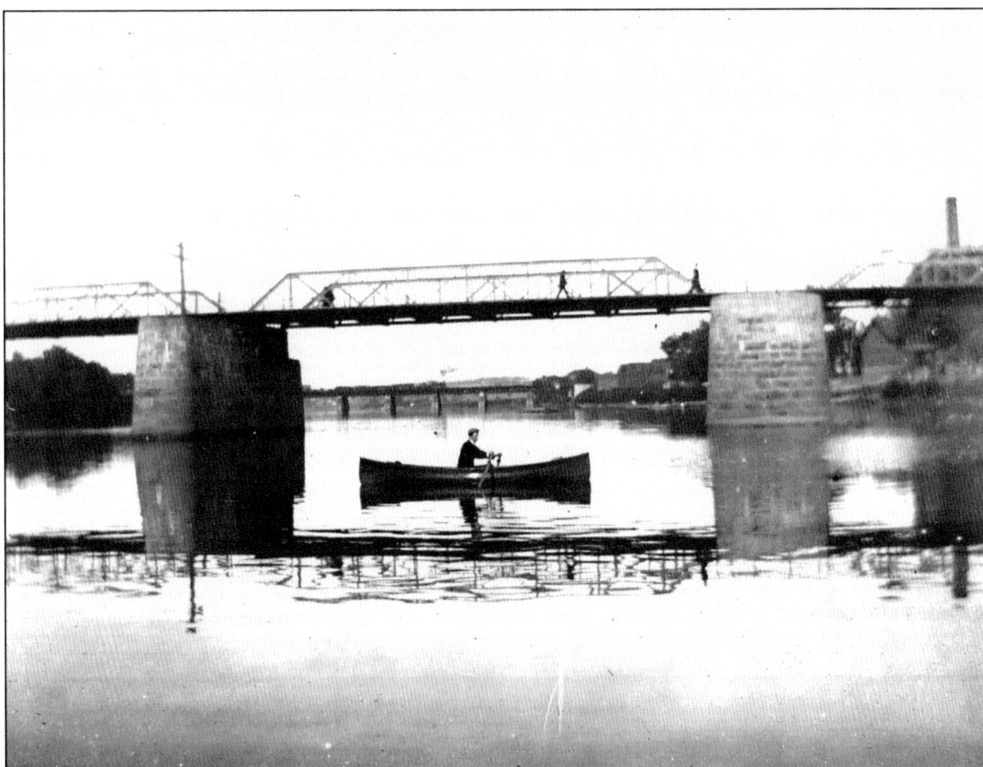

This is a view looking north at the Scotia steel bridge, with a lonely canoeist paddling to shore and people walking across the bridge. The smokestack of the Ferry Street pumping station can be seen on the right and the railroad bridge further north with a steam locomotive crossing on its way to the Schenectady station.

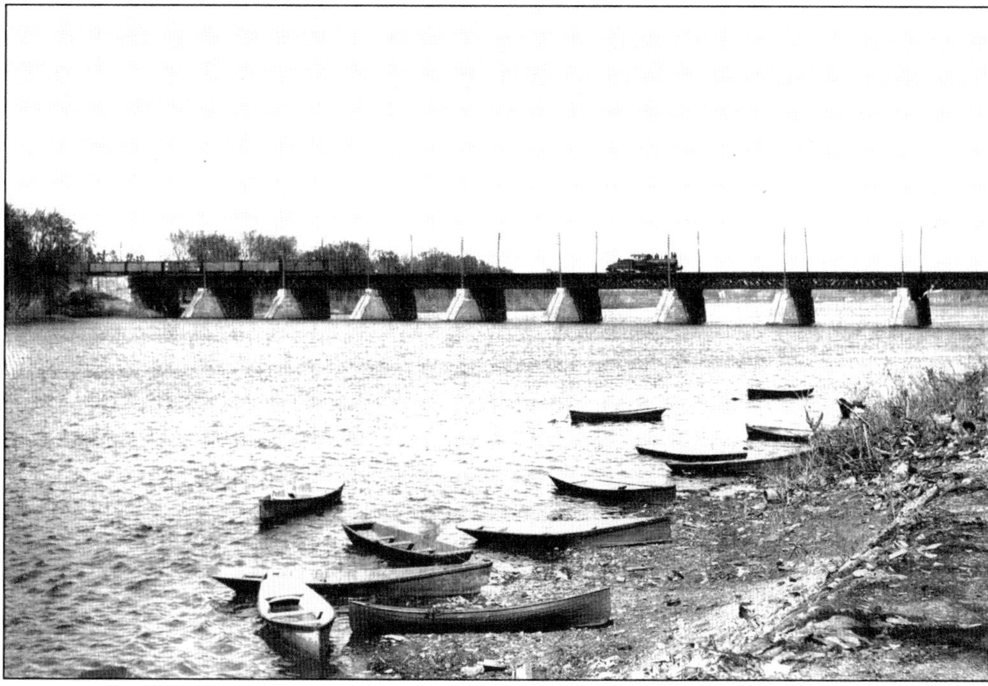

This view of the Mohawk River shoreline and the railroad bridge from the foot of North Street shows a solitary steam engine connecting to some train cars on the left in the spring of 1896. Notice all the canoes just sitting ashore.

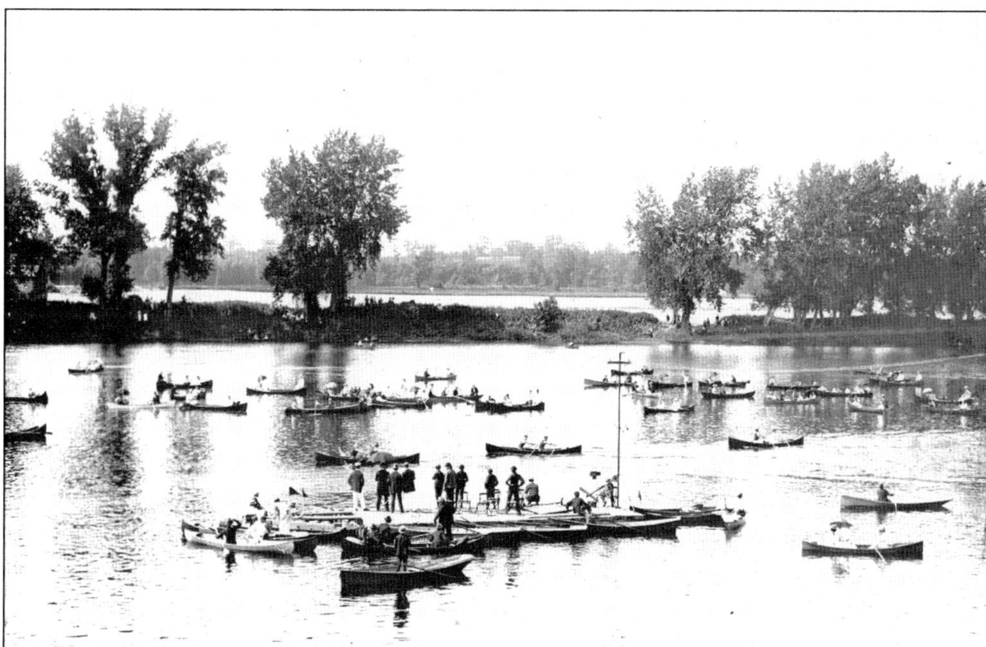

The Schenectady Regatta was sponsored by the Schenectady Boat Club (and still goes on). This race occurred on June 19, 1897.

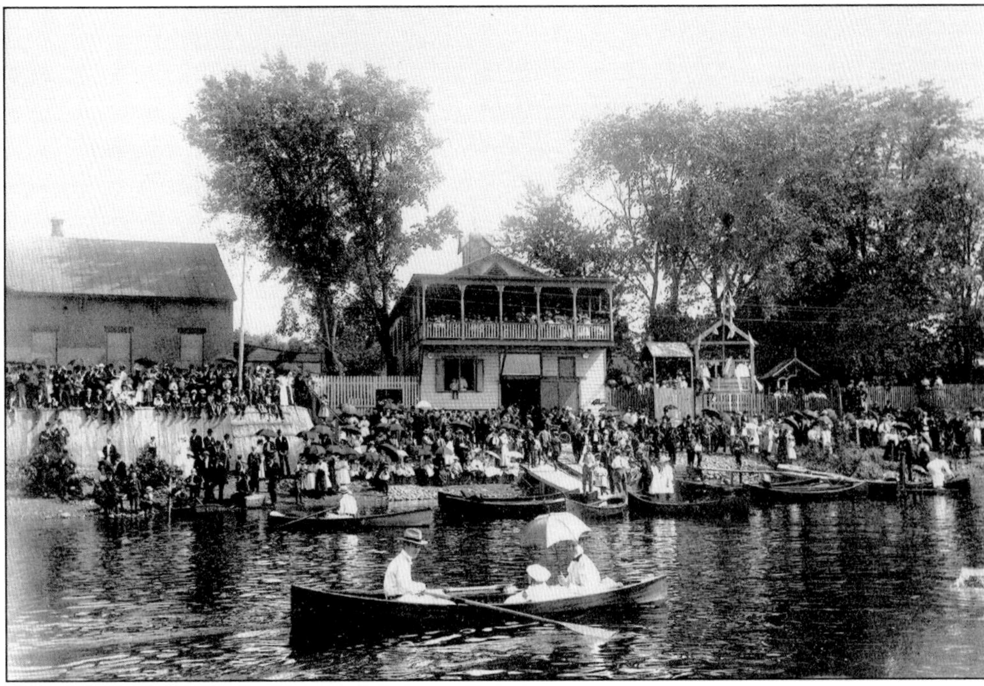

The Yates Boat House was a very popular place for local boaters. The upstairs had a ballroom where dances were held. The Yates Boat House was located just south of the Ferry Street pumping station, as seen here on the left.

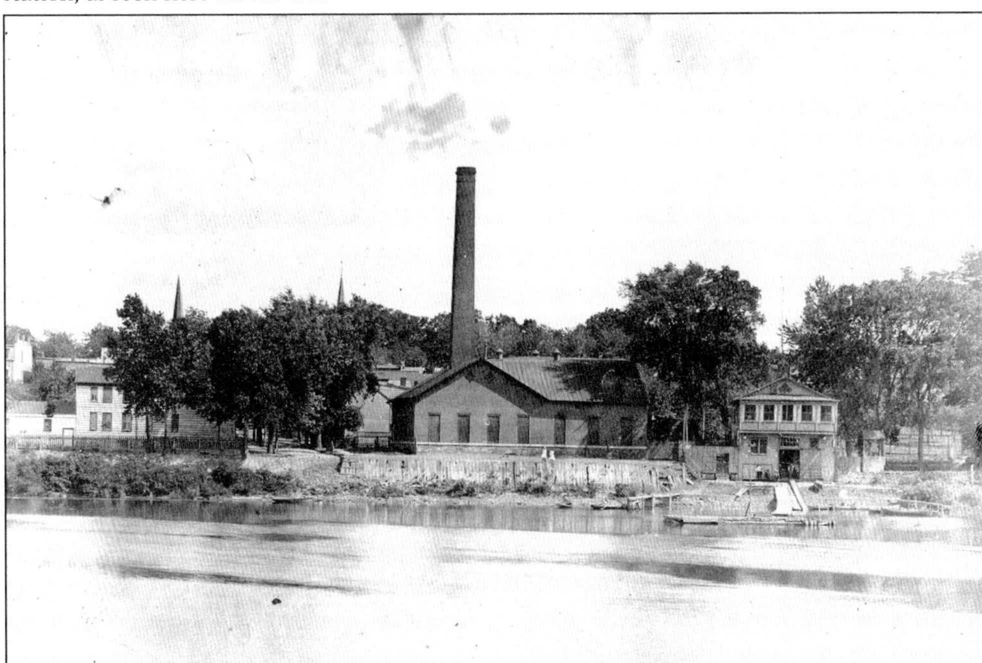

Here is a head-on view of the Ferry Street pumping station and the Yates Boat House. Schenectady's first water supply was stationed here until they began tapping into the aquifer in Rotterdam.

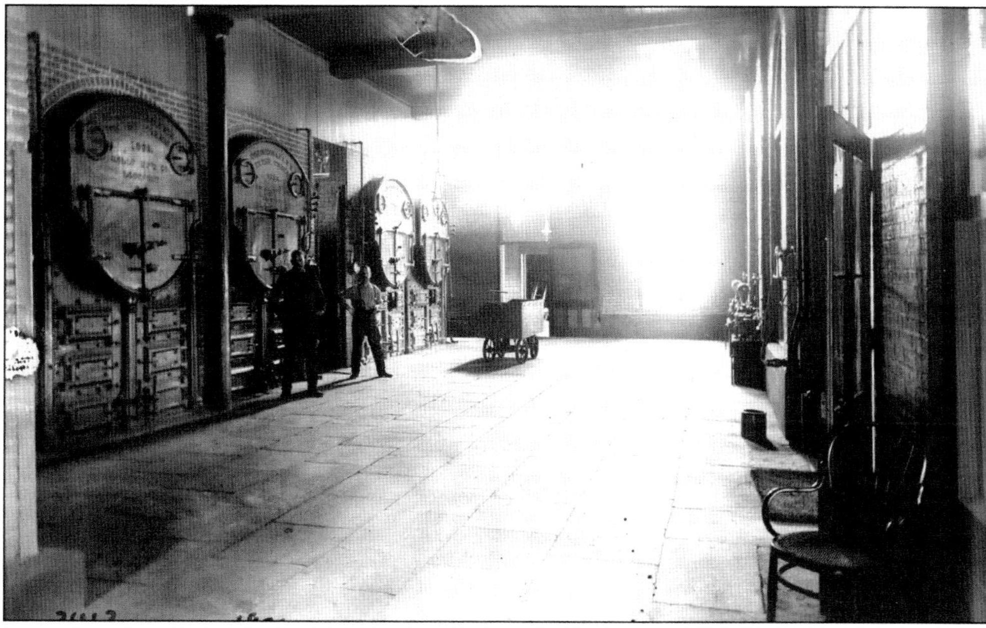

This is a rare view inside the Ferry Street Waterworks showing the boiler room on July 4, 1890, at 6:30 a.m.

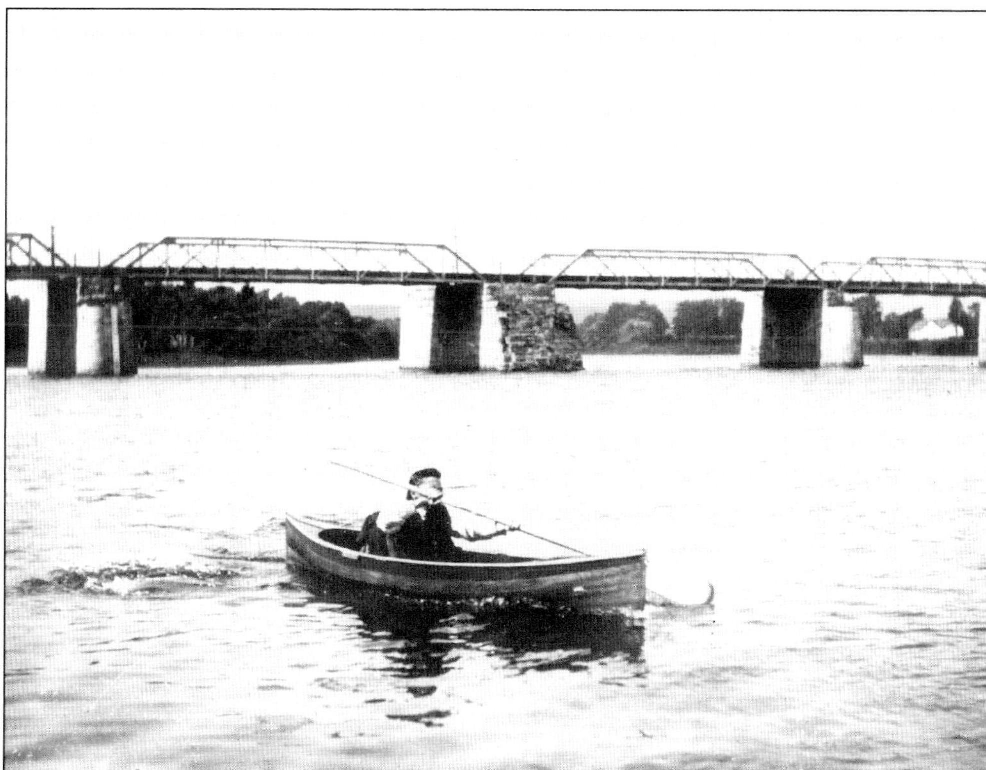

Here, world-famous electrical wizard Charles Steinmetz is paddling to shore just south of the steel Scotia Bridge around 1900.

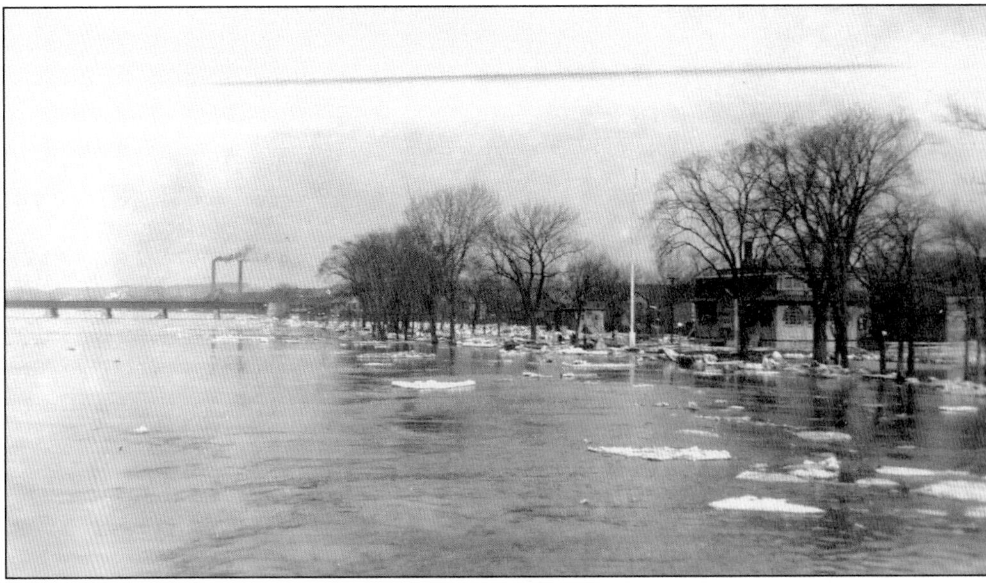

The Mohawk River constantly floods and has threatened the stockade for years. One of the first recorded events took place on February 24, 1772, and recorded in the *Albany Gazette*. The flood had destroyed the wharf and bateau house of John Visger Jr.

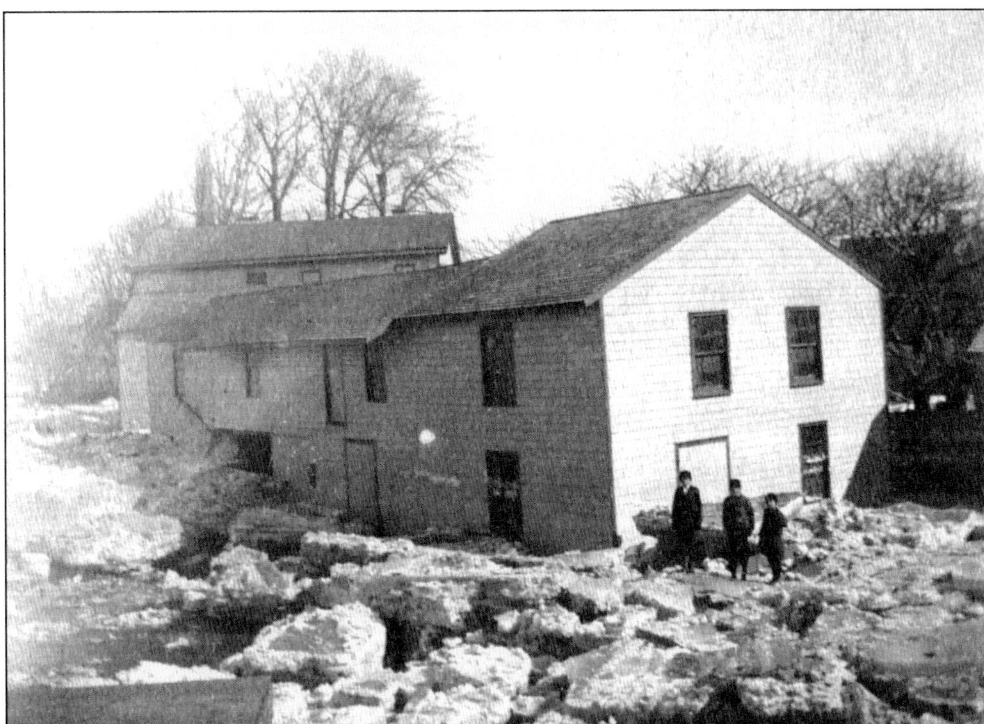

Here one can see the results of the massive ice pileups on businesses and homes along the river in the stockade in the late 19th century.

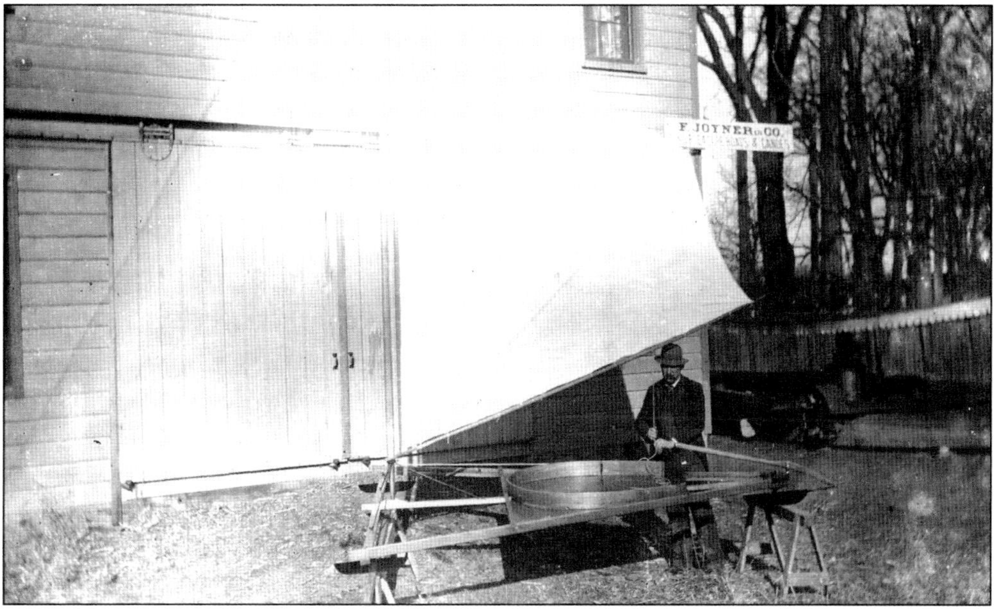

Fletcher (shown here) and Edgar Joyner made iceboats at their shop on the river in January 1890. In 1898, they were living and working at 19 Governors Lane. Schenectady became famous in the 18th century for building a type of large Durham boat called the "Schenectady Boat." Hundreds were built for the war effort.

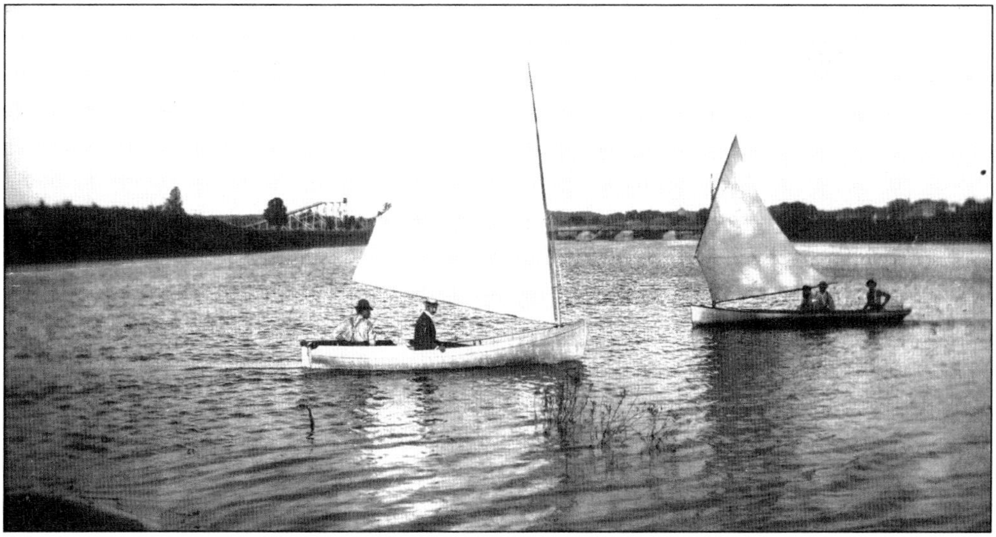

This is a great view of two sailing boats, the Scotia Bridge, and the toboggan slide (in the background).

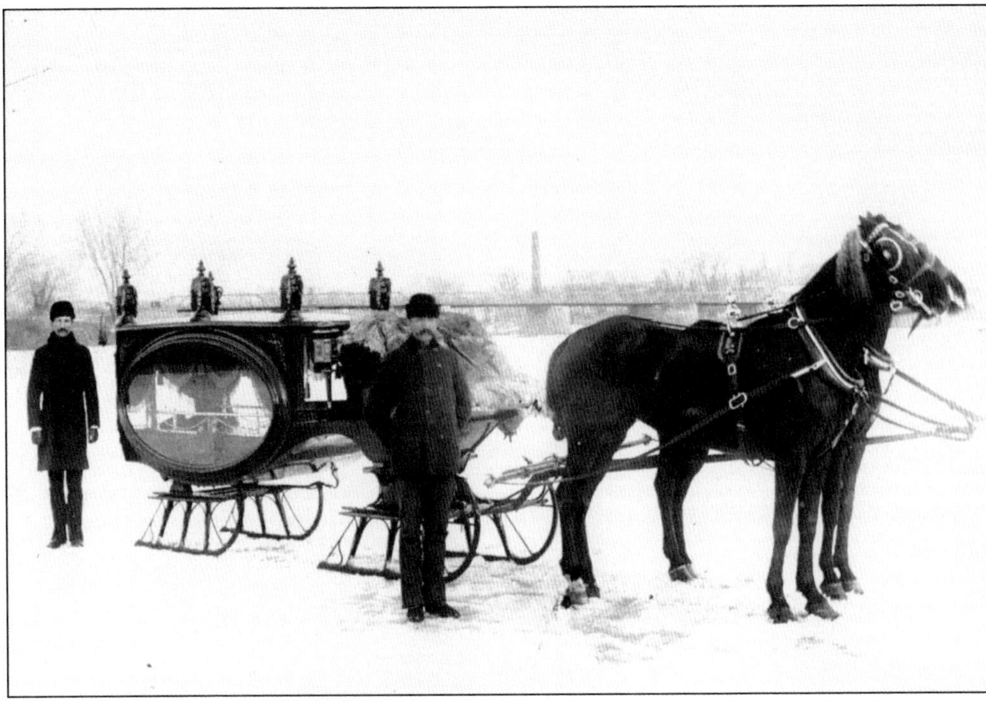

Yes, this is a hearse on a sleigh. Perhaps it was the only way to get a departed loved one across the river during those days, but why not take the bridge?

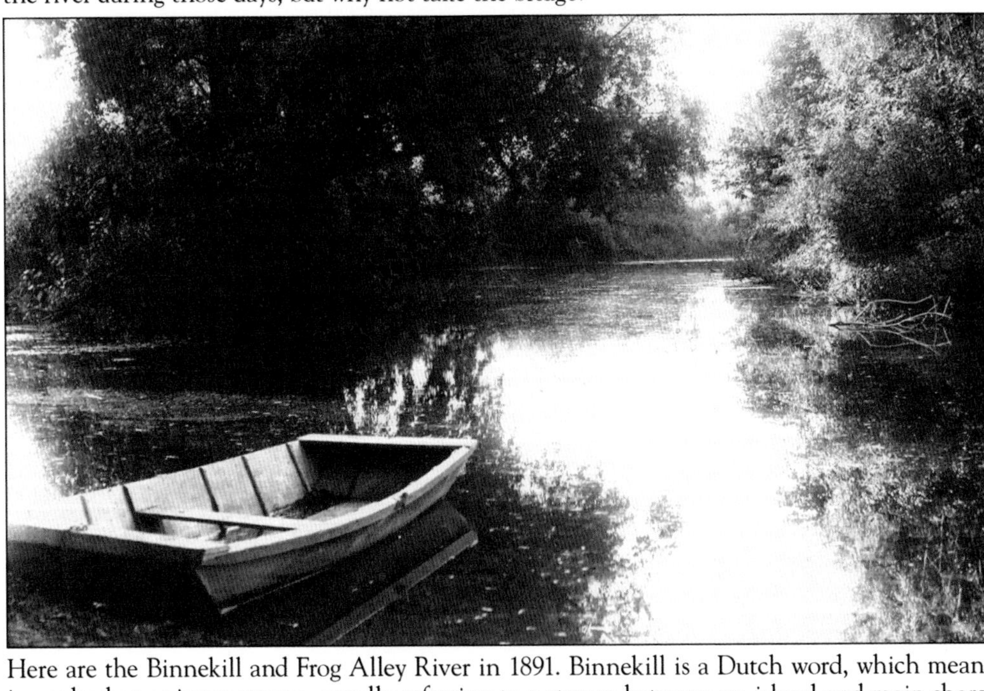

Here are the Binnekill and Frog Alley River in 1891. Binnekill is a Dutch word, which means inner harbor or inner stream, usually referring to a stream between an island and main shore. The Binnekill here extended through the east side of Van Slyck Island which has since been filled in and become part of Schenectady mainland. This part of the Binnekill was also known as Frog Alley River.

Nine

Lawrence the Indian

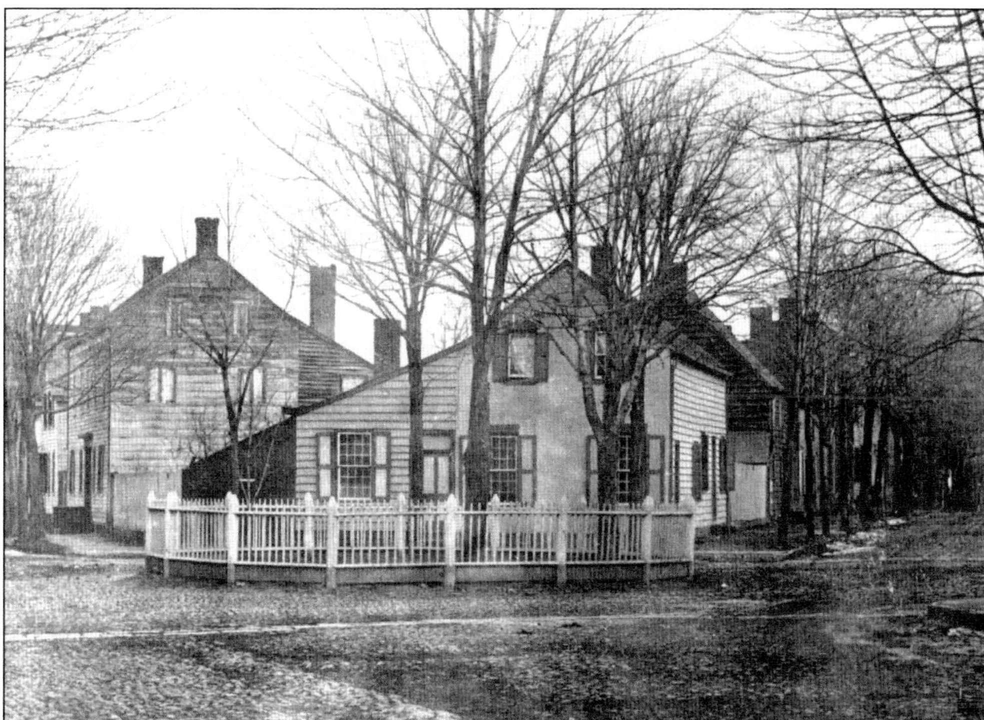

There is a section of the stockade that connects Ferry Street, Green Street, and Front Street to each other that in many ways is the center of the stockade. Here, three forts stood to protect the citizens, and there was also a grocery store. Arthur's Market has been in continuous business since 1795. This view of the area shows a small circular park with Front Street on the left and Green Street on the right. In the mid-19th century, this area would change.

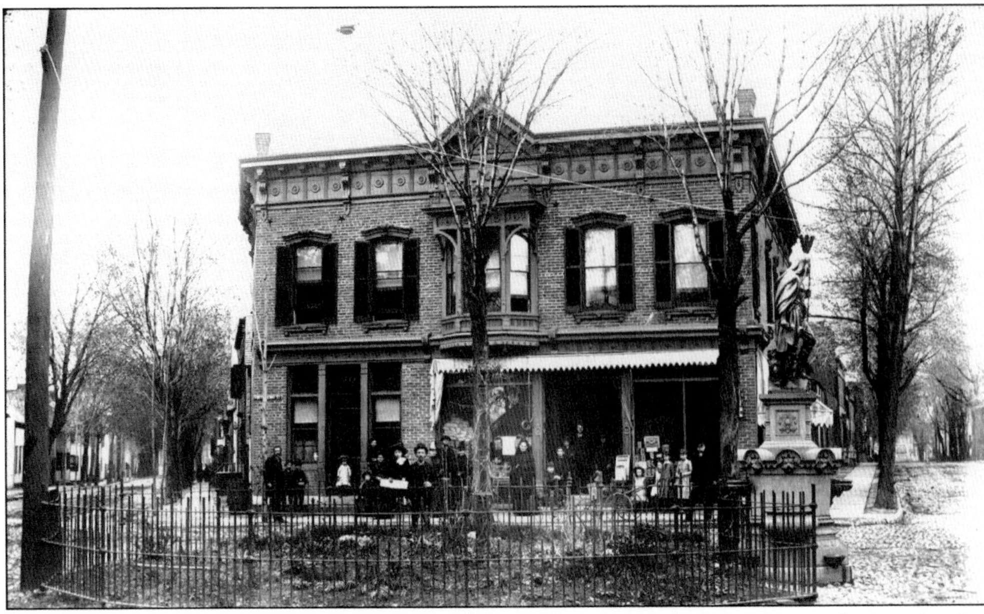

The Nicholas J. Swart grocery store provided supplies to stockade residents during the late 19th century. Swart lived around the corner at 201 Green Street. In 1886, he was a broom dealer, and the grocery store was known as Swart and Shankel. In 1887, a statue of an Native American, "No. 53 Indian Chief," was purchased for $500 from the J. L. Mott Iron Works and placed on the Ferry Street side of the small park, just outside the fence. This statue, *Lawrence the Indian*, was to honor Lawrence, a Mohawk who helped rescue a few of the Schenectady massacre victims up north with a party of his men.

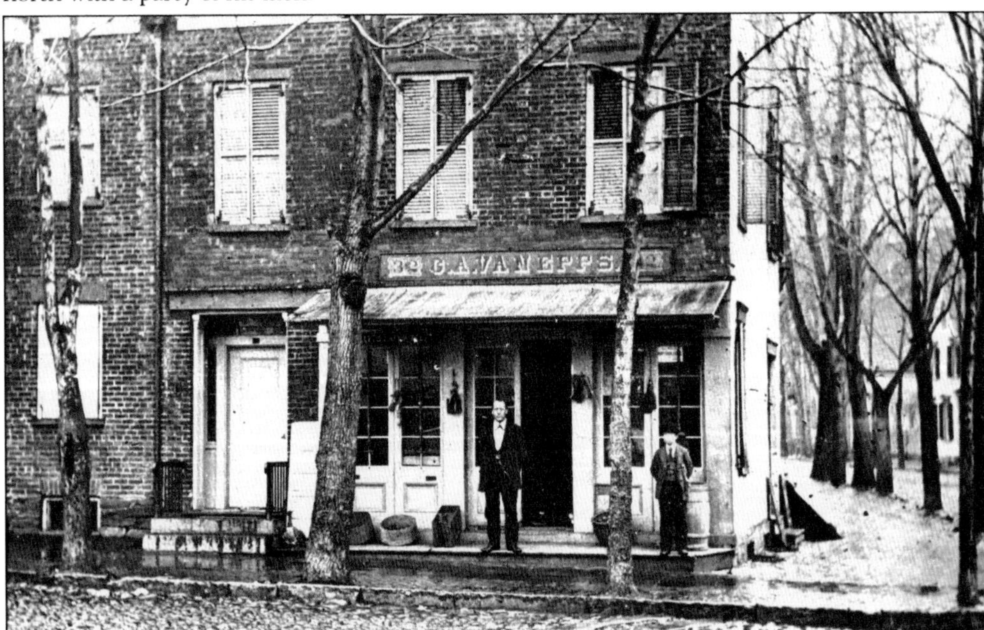

Arthur's Market at Ferry Street changed hands many times over the last 300 years. In 1906, Charles A. Van Epps, seen here, is listed as a janitor. He lived at 116 Front Street. This photograph is from the 1870s.

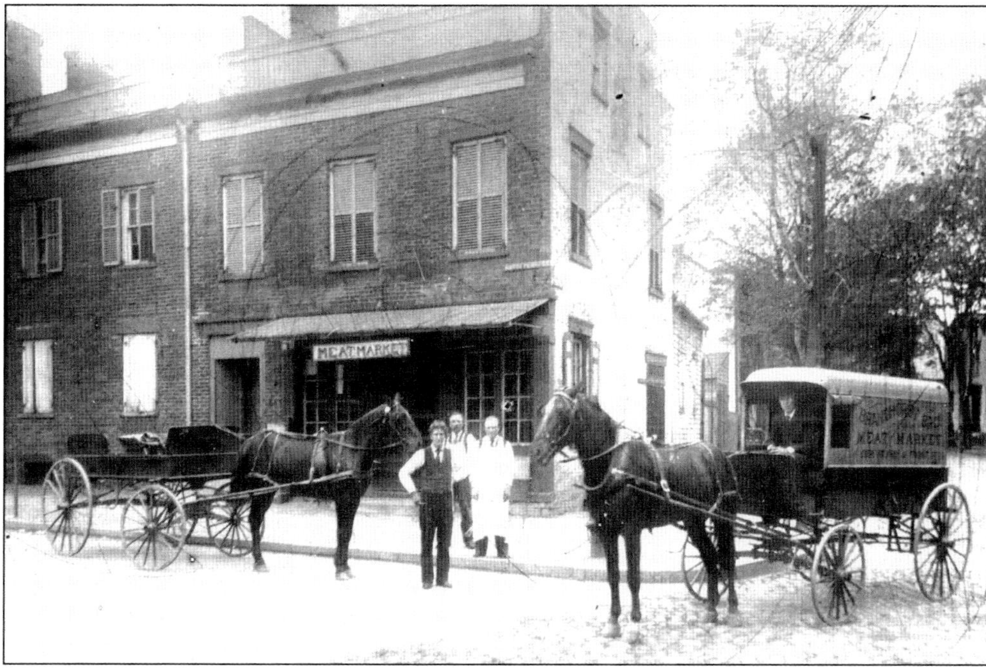

In 1899, 35–37 North Ferry Street was the home of the Brandhorst Brothers meat market. Charles A. and Christian F. lived at 319 Van Vranken Avenue and 215 Green Street, respectively. It appears that by 1903, Christian was running it himself as younger brother Charles opened a market at his new house at 102 Van Vranken Avenue.

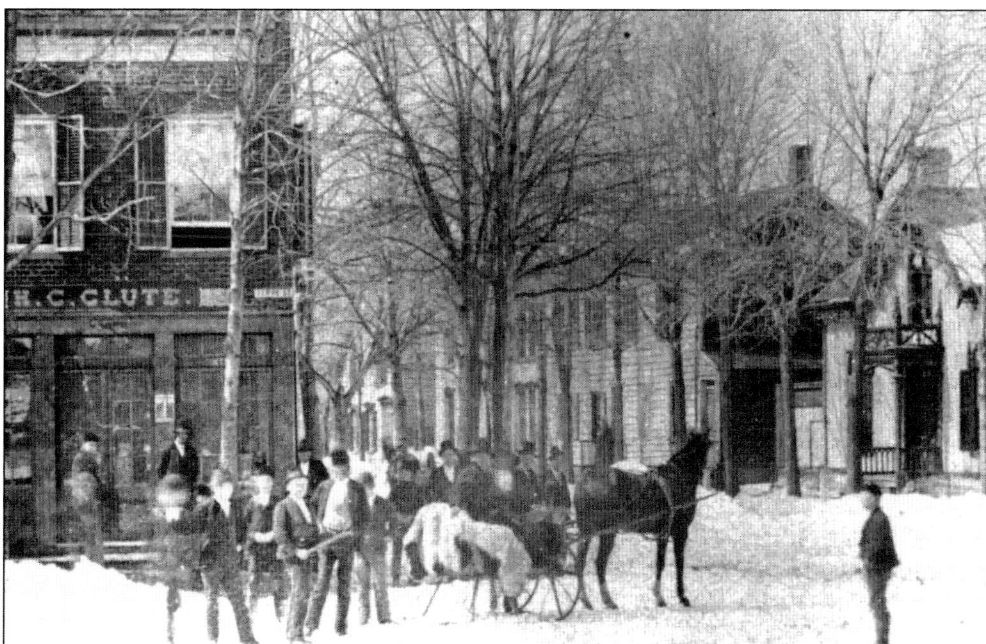

Here is another incarnation of the public market run by H. C. Clute. The Clute family was an early family name in the region. This could be Henry Clute, who lived at 54 Front Street in 1841.

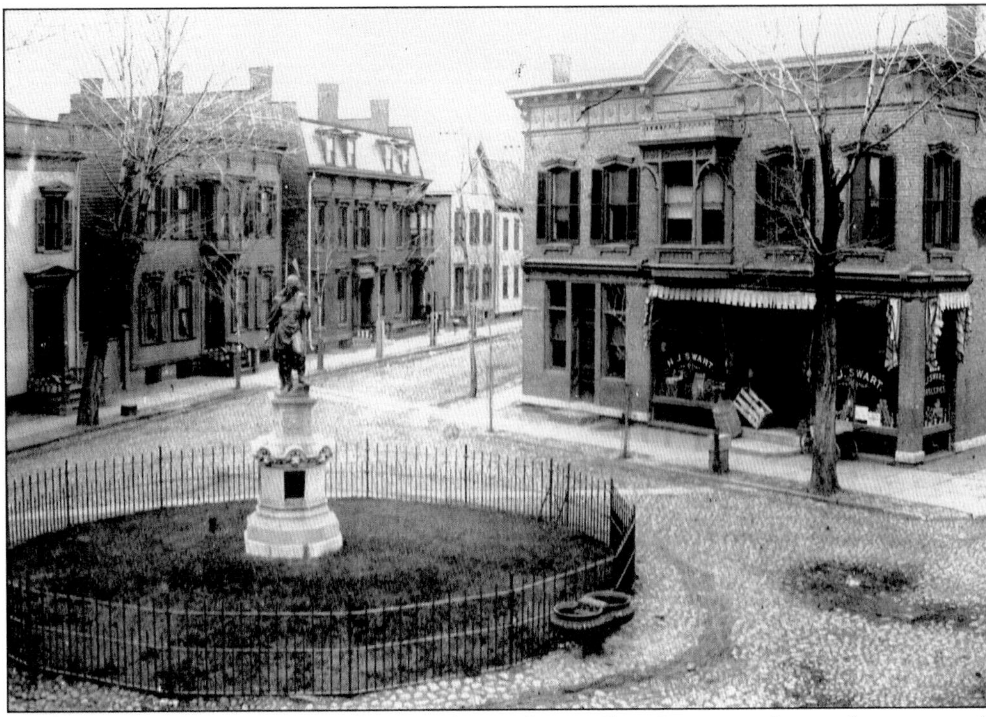

Lawrence the Indian was eventually moved into the small park, as seen here, where it stands today. Notice the cobblestone street and Swart's store (later known as the WGY Food Stores in the 1940s). The store is now a residence/office, but the two cast iron columns that held the glass windows are still there. Try to find them.

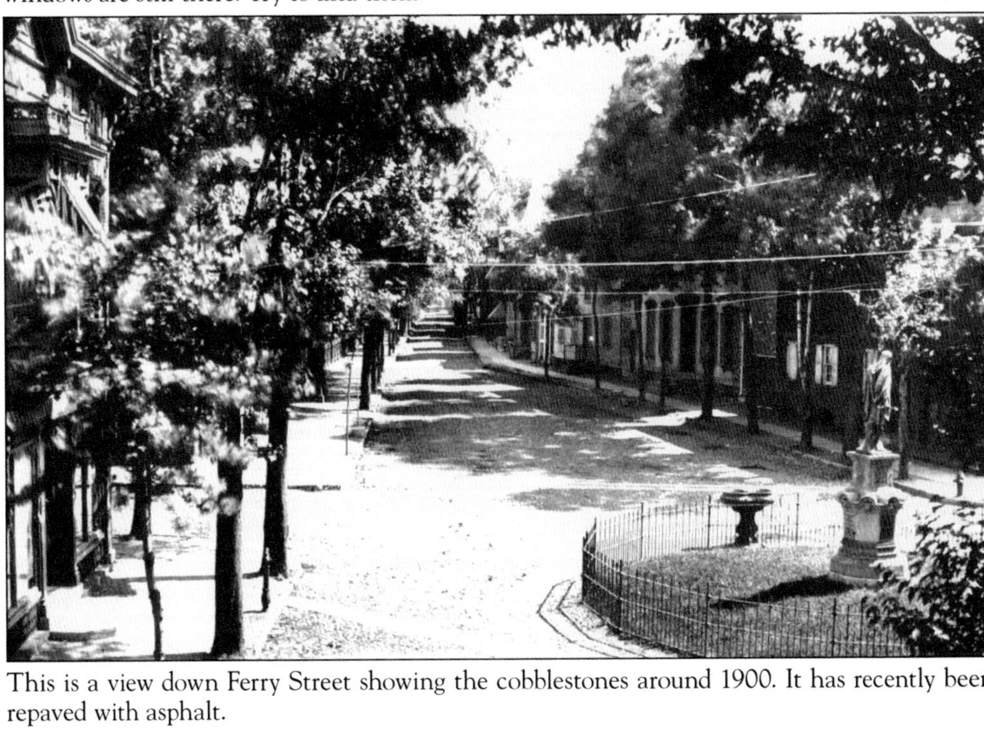

This is a view down Ferry Street showing the cobblestones around 1900. It has recently been repaved with asphalt.

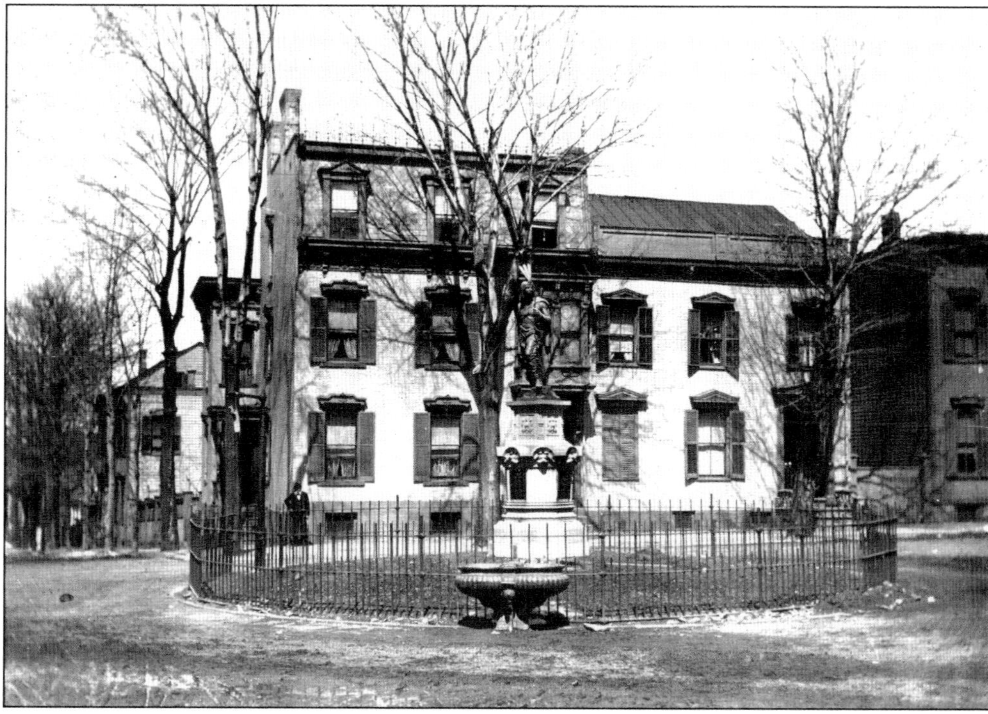

Here is a view of the park and statute looking towards Front Street; the northwest corner was known as Hall's Corner, which was the location of J. Swart's house.

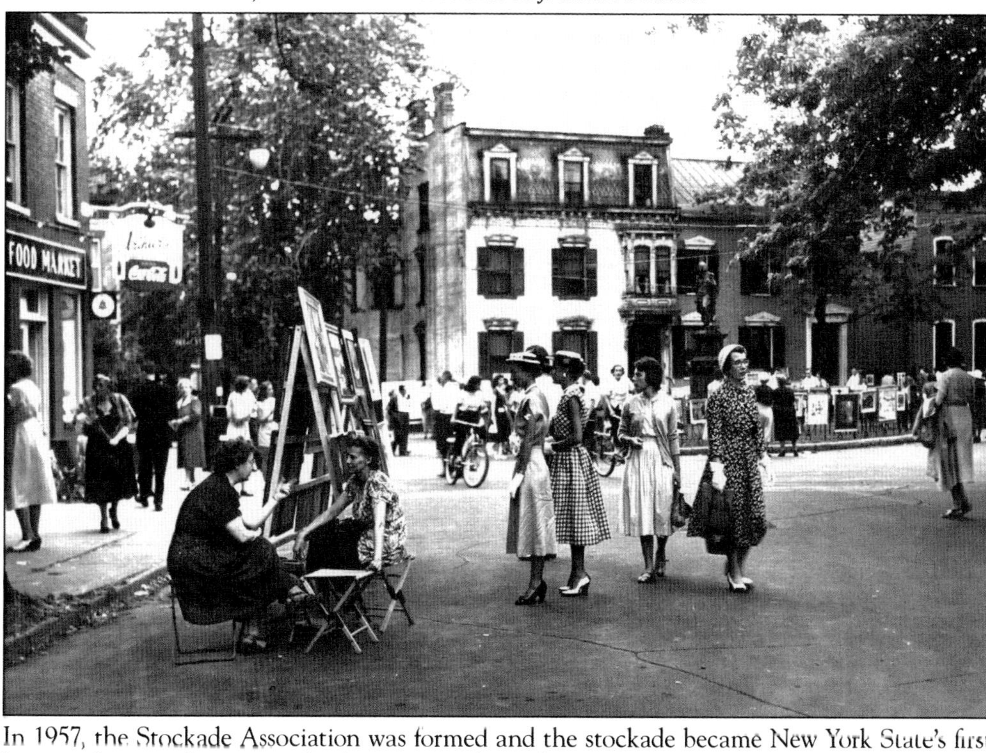

In 1957, the Stockade Association was formed and the stockade became New York State's first historic district when it was the first city to adopt a historic zoning ordinance in 1962.

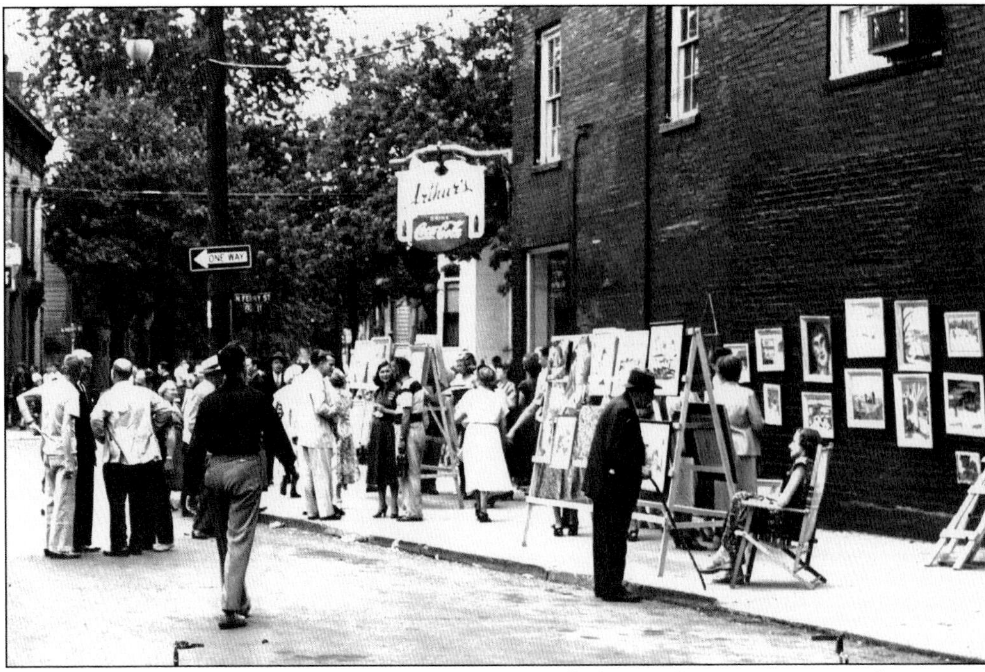

Since the 1950s, an annual artists fair and stockade walkabout, where one can view the interiors of historic homes, have been taking place. Thousands enjoy the stockade and hopefully this will continue for years to come. This photograph is from 1952.

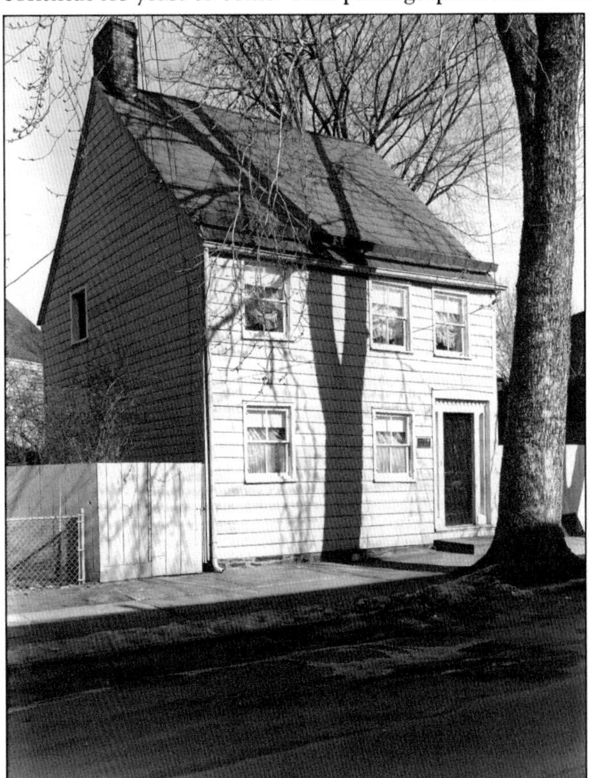

Green Street was cut at the intersection of Ferry Street and Arthur's Market in the 17th century. Here, Nicholas Veeder's slave house at 205 Green Street was built around 1789 and represents a time when slaves were owned by many Schenectady residents. Local newspapers constantly were advertising the sale of slaves or offered rewards for those that ran away.

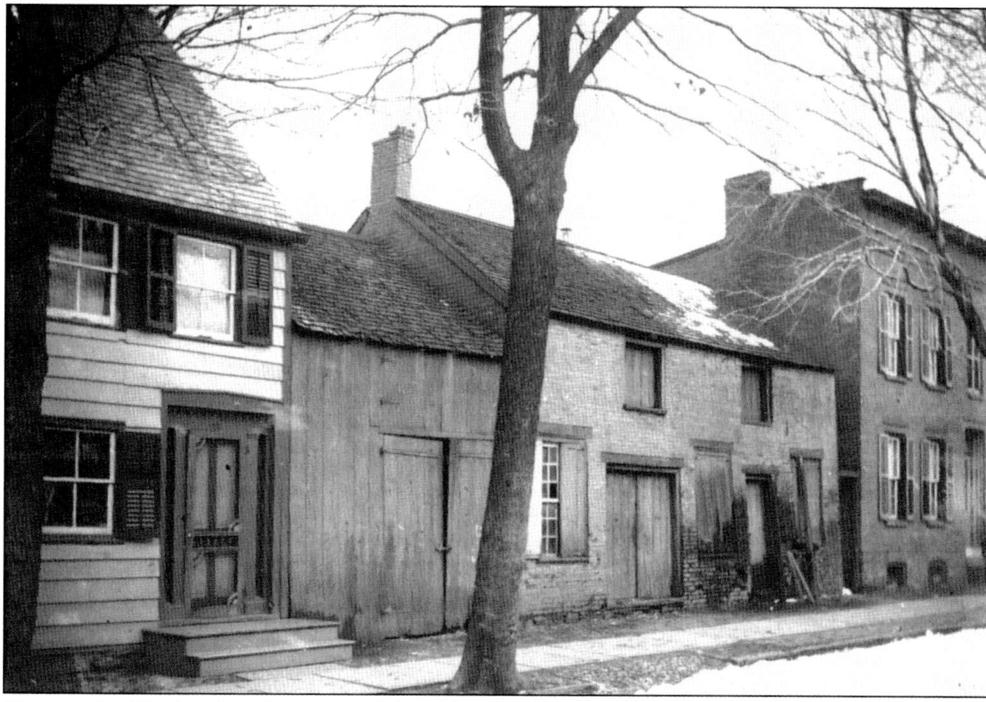
Next to the Veeder slave house was John Weait's carpenter shop, since demolished.

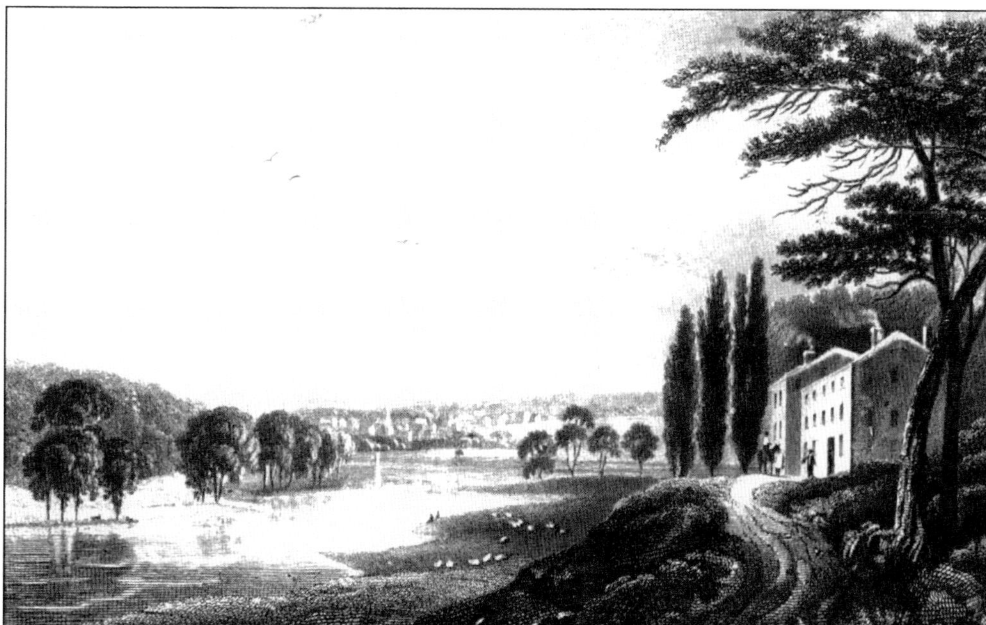
A bucolic painting of Schenectady was done as an engraving by James Archer and is titled *A Distant View of Schenectady on the Mohawk River*. It was published in 1826 in a memoir celebrating the completion of the New York State canal system in 1826.